STUDIES IN INTERNATIONAL ORDER

The International
REGULATION OF
CIVIL WARS

The International
REGULATION OF
CIVIL WARS

Edited by
EVAN LUARD

NEW YORK UNIVERSITY PRESS
NEW YORK 1972

© 1972 Thames and Hudson Limited, London

First published in the United States of America in 1972
by New York University Press

SBN: 8147-4953-4

Library of Congress Catalog Card Number: 79-185330

Printed and bound in Great Britain

CONTENTS

Contents

1   CIVIL CONFLICTS IN
MODERN INTERNATIONAL RELATIONS

Evan Luard

In the modern international system 'aggression' in the classical sense –
attacks across recognized frontiers – has become an increasingly rare
phenomenon. Since 1945 there are possibly seven cases that could be put
into this category: the Korean War, the attack on Guatemala in 1954,
Suez, the two Soviet attacks on Hungary and Czechoslovakia, the Indian
invasion of Goa, and the invasion of Honduras by El Salvador in 1969.
Even some of these cases were somewhat ambiguous: in Korea the frontier
was not strictly 'international'; in Guatemala the invasion was claimed
to have been organized by Guatemalans; Goa was a colony that was clearly
by history and geography a natural part of the Indian sub-continent; and
so on. Moreover, even in these cases the motivation was virtually never
territorial aggrandizement. Predominantly, the attacks were for coercive
reasons, to secure a government of particular political persuasion (Guatemala, Hungary, Czechoslovakia), to secure compliance with particular
political demands (Suez), or to secure redress for injuries (El Salvador). In
only one case, that of Goa, did any permanent territorial change result
from the attack.[1] Except in the first case casualties were light.

Against this, however, in the same period there has been a rapid increase
in the number of civil conflicts. There have been at least thirty significant
civil wars during this same period, without including sporadic disturbances
and unorganized guerrilla activity, or cases of *coup d'état*. A list of these
civil conflicts is contained in Table I. Even if frontier wars, and colonial
wars, were added to the list of external conflicts, civil wars would still
certainly represent well over half the total. Many were large in scale.

Both these trends represent a distinct change from earlier times. During
the late nineteenth century, most wars were external wars: either the local
wars of European nations with each other (such as the Crimean War, the
three Prussian wars, the Balkan wars) or the conquests made by European

7

powers in other continents, especially South-east Asia and Africa. Civil wars occurred: the American Civil War, civil wars in Italy and Spain, the nationalist risings in East Europe (though these really corresponded with colonial wars in recent times) and sporadic unrest elsewhere. But by modern standards they were a relatively small proportion of the total. The preponderance of civil conflicts in the modern period is perhaps unique in history.

After the First World War this balance first began to change. Between 1918 and 1939 there were thirteen major external conflicts: Poland-Soviet Union (1918–20); Afghanistan-Britain (1919); Romania-Hungary (1919–20); Greece-Turkey (1919–22); Poland-Lithuania (1920); Paraguay-Bolivia (1930–5); Japan-China (1931, 1933, 1935, 1937–45); Peru-Colombia (1932–4); Italy-Ethiopia (1935–7); Germany-Austria (1938); Germany-Czechoslovakia (1939); Italy-Albania (1939); Germany-Poland-Britain-France-Soviet Union, etc. (1939–45). But at the same time there were major civil conflicts in Russia, China, Spain and elsewhere, and revolutions and internal upheavals in over half the countries of Europe, and many of the countries of Latin America. In a considerable number of cases, there was external intervention in the civil conflicts: by Britain, France and Japan in the Russian civil war, by the Soviet Union in the Chinese civil war, by Germany and Italy in Spain, by the United States in Central America. Even some of the external attacks (by Romania on Hungary, by Germany on Austria in 1938 and on Czechoslovakia in March 1939) were associated with internal conflicts within the countries involved.

There were a number of reasons for the increasing prevalence of civil wars and external intervention in them in this period. The improvement in communications between countries, and the development of international political ideology, such as Communism, Nazism and Fascism, gave the government and population of one country an increasing interest in political developments elsewhere. The conditions left by the war, the proliferation of new and unstable states in Europe, unemployment, inflation, and the depression, all made revolution both easier and more desirable. Populations themselves, with the rise in education, became increasingly politically conscious, and were influenced by successful revolutions elsewhere, especially the Russian Revolution and Mussolini's *coup* in Italy. There was even an element of imitation involved in the establishment of militant political movements, the formation of private armies, the use of distinctive uniforms, salutes and catchwords: as in Italy, Austria, Germany and Hungary. Sociological changes encouraged internal dissent: the rise of an educated working class, including many ex-soldiers, the collapse of legitimacy, the economic misfortunes of the bourgeoisie, the spread of ideas of socialism and democracy among much wider sections of the population than ever before: all these made gross inequalities, or wholly autocratic régimes, less acceptable than ever before.

But some of the same factors that promoted internal dissent also encouraged external intervention. The shrinking of distance meant that the outcome of a civil conflict was not only of close political concern, but of direct strategic interest, to neighbouring governments. Conversely, such governments were much better able to undertake intervention. Direct military assistance could be given from considerable distances, as by Germany and Italy in Spain, at little cost and even without certainty of detection, something quite impossible before the invention of aircraft and the submarine. Radio and the mass media provided the means of influencing politically large populations in neighbouring countries and inciting them to revolution: as used by German radio in Austria, Czechoslovakia and Danzig. Assistance could be given in the organization of sympathetic political movements, as by the Nazis in Austria or by the Comintern in many parts of East Europe; even democratic socialist parties became linked in the Socialist International. This meant that large numbers of people and political organizations in many countries became internationally involved and concerned about the outcome of political conflicts in other countries. Europe, if not yet the world as a whole, became increasingly a single integrated political unit, in which inter-linked political movements undertook a continual struggle in many different capitals and cities. And the conflicts of nations (say between Germany and the Soviet Union) could be fought out to a considerable extent through client parties scattered throughout the continent.

After 1945 these trends became more pronounced and far more significant. Now, more than ever, the struggle between nations was undertaken through local political movements and rebellions. Furthermore, the strategic balance, and the development of nuclear weapons, meant that governments were less than ever prepared to risk the dangers of all-out conflict by open war, even with conventional weapons, when they could obtain similar ends by far less dangerous means. With hot war now so costly, cold war became the only alternative. The division of the world into ideological blocs engaged, so each thought, in a life and death struggle with the other, encouraged the belief that the outcome of every political struggle in every part of the world, however remote, was of vital concern to each. It promoted everywhere the effort to build up centres of local support, and the temptation to give covert support to these whenever a political dispute occurred. The CIA and the Cominform, rather than the respective armies and airforces, became the major protagonists in the contemporary world struggle.

But there was another reason why external wars became less common. They were less necessary. The frontiers of the world were now more clearly and definitively drawn than in any earlier age. In the inter-war period the settlement laid down at Versailles was widely questioned and challenged, not only by Germany and the other 'revisionist' powers but by many in other parts of the world who sympathized with them. Since Versailles itself had totally redrawn the map of Europe, there seemed little reason why the lines should not be redrawn yet again, to conform more closely with the principles which Versailles had purported to implement. In post-1945 Europe the settlement was almost everywhere regarded as final and unchallengeable. There were no frontiers that were seriously questioned: West Germany for a time hesitated to acknowledge the Oder-Neisse frontier as permanent, but only for bargaining purposes, and not because she seriously ever expected any change could be implemented. In Asia and Africa, illogical though many of the frontiers inherited from colonialism were, in practice they were accepted by the new governments as having a legally binding status: the OAU (Organization for African Unity) made this principle explicit in its charter. Even in Latin America, after a century or more of conflict, the borders, apart from one or two marginal exceptions (for example, between Ecuador and Peru, and between Argentina and Chile), had a growing degree of general acknowledgment. The effect of this change was that, since territory was not coveted, external attack became far less relevant to national aspirations. At the same time, with the greater firmness of frontiers, such attacks could far less easily find justification.

Conversely, with the further shrinking of the globe, the *internal* situation in other nations, especially those of strategic importance, became still more vital than before to their neighbours. With the development of modern military technology, it became yet more important for the United States that political control in Central America should be denied to her enemies, or to the Soviet Union that it should be denied in East Europe. Internal factors also made civil war more probable. The revolution of rising expectations had both political and economic implications. The knowledge of the type of political system that had been achieved in one country was a powerful inducement to comparable aspirations among its neighbours. Nasser's revolution in Egypt was an inspiration all over the Middle East; Castro's throughout Latin America; and China's in many parts of Asia. The increase in the number of politically educated, often at the same time unemployed or under-employed, increased the volume of political discontent within nations often still under autocratic rule. Growing consciousness of economic disparities and economic exploitation, whether from abroad or at home, also prompted movements for internal political change. Huge numbers of students in universities abroad acquired knowledge of socialist or democratic systems and principles, which raised their expectations and demands when they returned to their own countries.

Rising economic expectations had a similar effect. Here too, the development of communications had the result that those whose personal condition was abject often had clear knowledge, through cinema, the press, and television, of the opulent living standards of which they themselves were deprived, of those living abroad. The simple peasant, so beloved of Western writers, accepting destitution as a law of nature, became less common. Demands were raised here too. Though it is difficult to find examples of civil wars which have resulted solely from economic causes, it is an undoubted fact that in the modern world they have been more likely to occure in countries where standards of living were low. In Europe and North America they are today almost unknown. Among the developing continents of Africa, Latin America and Asia, they are common. Even among developing countries it is those with the highest standard of living which seem to have the most stable and democratic systems, and to be least subject to civil conflict: Chile, Venezuela and Mexico in Latin America, Malaysia and the Philippines in Asia, Zambia, Kenya and Ivory Coast in Africa. Those where civil wars have occurred, on the other hand, have often been those where economic conditions are harshest: Laos and Vietnam in Asia, Bolivia, Colombia and north-east Brazil in Latin America, Cameroon and Chad in Africa. Even though often the leadership in such conflicts is middle class, the final success of their efforts has usually depended on the existence of a peasantry or proletariat so desperate that they were ready to risk all on the remote hope of successful revolution. Whatever the other causes of such wars have been – political and ideological conflict, tribal divisions, agrarian conditions – they have frequently been aggravated and inflamed by economic backwardness.

What have been the *particular* causes of civil wars in this era? These wars can be grouped into a number of different categories. The categories are not clear-cut, and a number stand on the border between them. They may however be useful for the convenience of analysis.

In the first category are those where the political divisions in the conflict have corresponded fairly closely to those of the cold war: where one side has been inspired by Communist political sympathies, or had strong political support from the Communists; while the other has been inspired by commitment to the West and Western political ideals, and hostility to Communism, or has had strong support from Western sources. To this category in the inter-war period belong the civil wars in Hungary, the latter part of the civil war in China (1927–36), the civil war in Spain (though this was a complex variety of it) and some of the violence and disturbances in Germany, Austria and elsewhere. In the post-war period, perhaps the clearest examples are the civil wars in Greece and China, the post-independence phase of the Malayan emergency, the wars in South-east Asia, the post-Sukarno conflict in Indonesia, and the disturbances in the Dominican Republic; though in almost all of these, other factors were also at work. In most of these cases the Communist element belonged, to a considerable extent, to the main stream of Communism, and received the support, physical or moral, of the main Communist states, especially the Soviet Union. But there was also a considerable number of other post-war civil wars, in which the ideological beliefs of either side could not be so conveniently categorized; but in which two sides received, none the less, political sympathy and support, moral if not physical, from East and West respectively. To this category belong the wars in Cuba and the Congo, and possibly those in the Lebanon and Yemen.

Even among the former group, there has been a considerable variety in the nature of the beliefs upheld by each side, and the nature of the links with Communist countries or the West. There were those, such as the Greek civil war, where the Communist faction clearly received close support, both political and military, from neighbouring Communist countries. But there have also been others, such as the Chinese civil war, the Huk rebellion in the Philippines, the Malaysian emergency and the Indonesian conflict, in which, although the Communist side seems to have upheld relatively conventional Communist beliefs, they received little or no direct assistance from the Soviet Union or other Communist countries. There are those, such as the civil wars in Laos, Vietnam, Cambodia and Thailand, where one side was clearly supported and aided by Communist countries, but in which that support was divided between the Soviet Union and China, and in which the ideological beliefs of the Communist faction were similarly divided. Again there have been those such as the various guerrilla movements in Latin America, in which the inspiration has been primarily that of Castro's Cuba rather than either the European or the Chinese form of Communism. In the latter group, where external assistance from East and West was small, ideology has varied still more widely, and it is doubtful if such wars can be regarded properly as cold-war conflicts.

A second category of civil wars has been associated with other ideological struggles, emerging in other parts of the world since 1945. The civil wars in Lebanon and Yemen were products of the general struggle in the Arab world between radical Arab nationalist forces, mainly proclaiming allegiance to President Nasser, and the traditional, more conservative, and often monarchist, forces of the older Arab world. In Latin America, the civil war (if it can be called that) in Bolivia, and sporadic conflicts in Venezuela, Peru, Colombia, Guatemala and elsewhere, were more or less linked with the struggle between radical, anti-American and anti-capitalist forces often associated with Castro, and the political movement which he had deliberately sought to spread throughout Latin America, and their

TABLE 1: CIVIL WARS 1945–70

Ideological

(Wars in which a widely recognized government has been in conflict with elements declaring communist or anticommunist sympathies.)

Greece 1944–9
Philippines 1946–50
China (including offshore islands) 1946–50, 1954–8
Burma 1948–
India 1948–50
Malaya 1957–60

Laos 1959–
S. Vietnam 1959–
Indonesia 1965
Venezuela 1965–8
Bolivia 1967
Muscat and Oman 1969–
Cambodia 1970–

Political

Colombia 1946–58
Paraguay 1947
Cuba 1953–9, 1961
Muscat and Oman 1957–9
Lebanon 1958
Indonesia 1958–9

Cameroon 1958–62
Congo 1960–5
Yemen 1962
Dominican Republic 1965
Jordan 1970
Pakistan 1971

Minorities

Burma (Karens, Kachins, Shans and others) 1948–
China (Tibet) 1951
Iraq (Kurds) 1961–70
Sudan (Southern Sudanese) 1963–
Ruanda (Tutsis) 1963
Nigeria (Ibos) 1967–70
Chad (Arabs) 1968–
India (Nagas and Mizos), sporadic
Ethiopia (Eritrea), sporadic

[This list does not include a number of civil conflicts involving sporadic and disorganized engagements between government forces and hostile elements, not amounting to full-scale civil war, as in Peru, Guatemala, Thailand, Northern Ireland, India (Bengal) and other areas.]

conservative opponents. In Africa, the revolutionary guerrilla movements at work in the Portuguese colonies, Rhodesia and South Africa, can be regarded as engaged in another form of ideological warfare, in this case directed against white supremacy. Though these cases have in common that armed political movements in different countries have been inspired by common or similar political beliefs, it would obviously be false to say that ideology was the *cause* of civil conflict in any case. It would rather be true to say that the cause of such conflicts is the increasing contradiction, in all these three parts of the world, between new political and economic aspirations, often fed by the example of other countries, and the relatively conservative and unprogressive governments with which they sometimes find themselves confronted. This in turn leads to the spread of an ideology which, in all these cases, is specifically associated with the concept of revolution. So, in many different parts of the world, explicitly revolutionary and anti-revolutionary forces have found themselves in conflict.

Thirdly, there is a considerable category of civil wars which might be called 'post-colonial' in type. The end of colonialism has sometimes created a situation in which the newly established régimes were rapidly challenged by opposition forces. In some cases one faction, finding itself cheated of power in the newly independent state, sought to acquire it by violent means : as when Communist forces rose against newly independent governments in the late forties in parts of India, in Burma, Malaysia and the Philippines. Sometimes the party or coalition which had joined together in the independence struggle broke up soon after their objective had been achieved : as with the Indonesian nationalists who fought among each other in 1948, or when elements in the FLN challenged first President Benbella, then Boumedienne, in Algeria. In some cases, tribal or religious divisions quickly emerged within the fragile post-independence structure, as in the Congo, Cameroon, and in Chad. Sometimes the territorial settlement at independence leaves a minority dissatisfied and preferring union with another state : as with the Somalis in Kenya and Ethiopia. Finally there have been a considerable number where a large minority group within the new state has rebelled against the newly independent government : like the Kurds in Iraq, the Nagas in India, the Karens, Kachins and Shans in Burma, and the Ibos in Nigeria. A further variety of this last kind is where the two major groups are more equal in numbers in a bi-national state, as in Cyprus and Malaysia.

Fourthly, there has been the type of civil war that has arisen simply as a form of protest against dictatorial or oppressive government, but without strong ideological partisanship. To a considerable extent this was the case with the civil wars in Paraguay in 1947, in Cuba (1953–61), the abortive revolt in Indonesia in 1958, the revolt against the Sultan of Muscat in 1967–70, the attempted *coup* against the Emperor in Ethiopia in 1960 (almost a civil war in scale) and in other cases. This is perhaps the most common traditional cause of civil war and has clearly been one of the factors at work in a number of the other categories we have already examined.

There are one or two more general conclusions that can possibly be drawn about the civil wars of this period. First, contrary to the widespread belief, very few of the wars of this period, even in the first category described can reasonably be regarded as 'proxy wars', waged by the great powers themselves through obedient partisans in the countries concerned. If there is one clear conclusion about these wars it is that, except possibly in the case of the Greek Civil War, far from being invited or provoked by the great powers, they have broken out as a result of purely local factors. In the vast majority of cases, there were clearly understandable reasons why, in the context of the local political scene, intense dissatisfactions, leading to a state of civil war, could have emerged among important political groups without incitement from inside. Some of them may, at a later stage, have been intensified by cold-war rivalries. But in general the super-powers, far from provoking wars of this type to secure their political aims, seem normally to have found themselves dragged in against their own will by the local factions involved. The Vietnam War was not started by the Soviet Union or China, any more than that in the Dominican Republic was started by the United States, or the Cyprus conflict by Turkey or Greece, or the Congo wars by Belgium, or the Yemen war by the UAR and Saudi Arabia. Possibly the only cases in which it can be said that the aspirations of an external power served to *start* a civil war were the Bay of Pigs operation, which certainly could not have been undertaken without active American support, and the Che Guevara operation in Bolivia, which was wholly artificial and exported from start to finish. In general the problem of the super-powers on both sides in civil conflicts has been to avoid commitment, not to maintain it. The overwhelming majority of all the civil wars of this period has emerged fundamentally from the fragile political and economic structure of small, and often relatively new, nations.

Secondly, there seems considerable evidence to suggest that civil wars are not only more likely to occur in countries with a low standard of living (see p. 11 above), but where there is a genuine reason to doubt the representative character of the government concerned. In some of the countries where they have occurred, there had been no free elections at all : China, Paraguay, Indonesia, Muscat, Cuba, Yemen, Chad. In others there were grounds for doubting how far elections had been fairly conducted, or particular parties in them had been banned (Greece, Cameroon, Laos, Vietnam); in others they had been nullified by a subsequent *coup* (Congo, Nigeria, Dominican Republic). Even in Europe, though there were no civil wars, political disturbances were most likely to occur in areas such as East Germany, Poland, Czechoslovakia and Hungary, where there had been no opportunity for free political expression.

Thirdly, so far as external intervention is concerned, it seems to be the case that this is far more likely to occur on both sides, or not at all. There are a considerable number of these cases in which there has been no external intervention. But in those cases where it has occurred (Greece, Lebanon, Vietnam, Laos, Yemen, Muscat and Oman, and Cambodia), help has been given to both parties. Normally this is because intervention on one side will itself provoke intervention on the other, or at the least provide justification for it. There is perhaps also some evidence to suggest that (as one would expect) where intervention does occur the wars are both much more protracted and on a far larger scale : certainly by far the worst, judged by standards of loss of life, in the post-war world have been been the civil wars in South-east Asia, where external intervention on both sides has been most pronounced.

Finally, though the underlying reasons for many of these wars, as we have seen, have been basic political and other differences, the *specific* issues have often been clear and important constitutional questions: above all concerning the holding of elections. In a considerable number of these cases (Greece, Lebanon, Vietnam, Cyprus, Dominican Republic, for example) the principal issue at stake has been a demand that elections should be held at a certain time, or a challenge to elections recently held which were said to have been unfairly conducted. Other constitutional questions have often been at issue: in the Congo one of the main causes of dispute was whether the President had the right to dismiss the Prime Minister or vice versa; in Cyprus the constitutional arrangements to protect the Turkish minority and whether they can be changed by the majority unilaterally is the main underlying point at issue; in Nigeria the right of secession and the type of federal structure to be established, was a crucial point at issue. It is not, of course, surprising that civil wars often concern constitutional arrangements, since these in turn may determine the structure of power within the state. But it emphasizes the important part which a satisfactory constitutional system (and its subsequent fair observance) may play in providing a stable, political order, in which civil war may become less likely. It is the absence of legitimacy, of an established political order commanding general consent, which is often the ultimate cause of civil conflicts.

But it is not the fact of civil wars, but the prevalence of foreign intervention, which has so increased their significance in modern international relations. And it is worth considering the factors which mainly encouraged this.

There is an obvious difficulty of definition here. What represents 'intervention'? If what is meant is the active participation in fighting by the national forces of one state in the internal conflicts of another then external intervention has been rare in the civil wars of the post-1945 world:

far less so than in the inter-war period. Between 1918 and 1939, it happened in a considerable proportion of civil wars: the Western powers and Japan intervened in the Russian civil war, Romania in Hungary, Japan in the Chinese warlord conflicts, Germany and Italy in Spain. In all these cases it was the regular armed forces of external powers which were involved, overtly or covertly. Since 1945 this has been uncommon. It occurred on a large scale by North Vietnam and by the United States in the South-east Asian wars: but it became in this case so open and on such a scale that it is debatable whether those wars can be regarded as 'civil wars' at all. It occurred in the assistance given by United States naval forces in the Bay of Pigs operation. And intervention of a kind by regular forces has occurred i.. those cases where troops have been landed in a country engaged in civil conflict: as when United States troops landed in the Lebanon and British troops in Jordan in 1958, and when United States forces were sent to the Dominican Republic in 1965. But this has not involved active participation in open fighting. Egyptian and possibly Saudi forces took part in the Yemen civil war; but here too there was little attempt at concealment and some attempt at mutual restraint. Finally there have been cases of shows of force, such as those made by Turkey over Cyprus. Although none of these can be regarded as insignificant in their effect on the wars in question, they have been less than the all-out involvement of external powers in the inter-war period. In general, except in South-east Asia, the taboos against such intervention have remained in force.

Far more common has been the training and support of revolutionary forces on outside territory. The Greek Communists received support of this kind from Bulgaria, Albania and Yugoslavia, and probably from the Soviet Union. Cuban rebels were trained and armed in Guatemala and the United States in preparation for the Bay of Pigs operation (though since that time they have been held more strictly under control, especially in the United States). Cuba has at certain periods given general support for revolutionary forces in Brazil, Venezuela and elsewhere, though this too seems now to have ceased. South Yemen has given active assistance to the rebels in Muscat. China and the Soviet Union have given considerable assistance, though mainly on North Vietnamese territory, to the North Vietnamese and Vietcong. The active training and support of rebel forces can be regarded as a form of hidden intervention, little less serious in its effects than active involvement. And it of course occurs on behalf of government as well as anti-government forces (as in the provision of United States 'advisers' to the forces of South Vietnam and Laos).

A third, and still more limited form of 'intervention' is the sale of arms to the forces of either side in a civil war. This has occurred widely, and almost universally, in the civil wars of the post-1945 period. Here one should distinguish between the supply to rebel forces and to government forces. The latter is today widely regarded as justifiable. Indeed to cut off supplies to government forces could be regarded as an act of open hostility and be deeply resented by that government: the British government frequently justified its supply of arms to Nigeria by the argument that if they were to cut off that supply, not only would Nigeria be permanently alienated, but the arms themselves would certainly continue to be obtained from other sources, including the Soviet Union. The Nigerian war is, in any case, almost the only example of such civil conflicts in which there has been even a demand for the cessation of the supply of arms to government forces: none of those who demanded it in the case of Nigeria ever made similar demands, for example, in the case of the sale of arms to Malaya against rebel forces there, to India when she was fighting the Nagas, to Burma when she has been involved in several civil conflicts, or to the Congo when she fought secessionist forces, or indeed in any of the other civil wars since 1945.

The supply of arms to rebels is more widely condemned. But here there is the difficulty of obtaining accurate evidence. The Soviet Union probably made available some captured arms to the Communist forces in China, and was reported to have sent arms to Lumumba in the Congo (but at that time regarded Lumumba as the rightful Prime Minister). China has probably made arms available to rebel forces in Burma, Thailand and India, as well as to the rebel factions in Indo-China. The CIA is widely credited with having sent arms to right wing forces in Laos, Guatemala, Iran and other countries. Cuba is known to have sent arms for a time to rebel forces in Latin America. France, Portugal and South Africa sent them to the Ibos in Nigeria. Iran was said to have armed the Kurds in Iraq. In none of these cases, except the first, have the sales been openly admitted. In some cases such arms are said to have been obtained from private sources, but there is a clear obligation on governments to control all sales from private as well as public sources so this justification carries little weight.

Can one make any further generalizations about the circumstances that encourage external intervention? The clearest conclusion that can be drawn is that such intervention is far more likely to occur in states, especially small states, that closely adjoin powerful neighbours. The Soviet Union was closely involved in Greece and still more so in Hungary and Czechoslovakia, all of which it thought important to its own safety and interests, while in such countries as Vietnam, assistance has been probably the minimum it could reasonably get away with. The United States intervened in an active and forceful way in Guatemala, Cuba and the Dominican Republic, all of which it regarded as vital to its strategic interests but with less decisiveness elsewhere. China intervened in more or less extreme forms in Korea and Vietnam, but not in any effective way in Africa, Latin America or the Middle East.

As we saw earlier, intervention of one external power is more likely to occur if there has already been intervention on the other side. United States support for South Vietnam stimulated further North Vietnamese and Soviet support for the Vietcong, and vice versa. Soviet support for Lumumba stimulated United States support for Kasavubu and Mobutu. Egyptian support for Republicans in the Yemen stimulated Saudi support for the Royalists. Where there has been no external support on one side there has usually been none on the other: in Colombia, in Cyprus, in Lebanon, in Indonesia, and so on. Often the main factor therefore in stimulating intervention is not so much the desire to win a particular area over to one side, but the desire to deny it to the other. In general where there is confidence that a country will in any case remain neutral, all external powers prefer not to become embroiled.

If external intervention in civil wars is becoming more common and civil wars themselves more frequent, how far does international law proscribe such outside interference? The role of international law in such conflicts is considered at greater length by Dr Higgins in her chapter below. Here, a few general comments may be offered.

Internal conflicts in themselves have been regarded as, to a considerable extent, beyond the realm of international law. International law was held to govern the relations between states. What states did within their own frontiers, how they responded to threats to their authority within such areas, was regarded as a question within the domestic jurisdiction of each country. It was not always held even that the rules of war, as laid down in international law, need be observed in conflicts of this kind.

This distinction has, however, increasingly broken down. The concept of fundamental human rights, which are to be acknowledged and respected by all governments, even within their own territory, has come to influence legal concepts on civil wars. Here again the development of communications, having the effect that knowledge of internal wars and of the sufferings involved has become widespread elsewhere, has meant that it became increasingly difficult for governments to withdraw themselves from the provisions of generally recognized legal norms even when dealing with their own nationals in their own territories. In particular the UN has increasingly come to accept internal disturbances as potential 'threats to international peace and security', and so subjects of international concern: for example in relation to South Africa and the Portuguese territories. And the UN has explicitly demanded the observance of the Geneva Conventions concerning prisoners of war in relation to freedom fighters in Southern Africa.

External intervention in civil war has more clearly been recognized as of concern to international law. But international lawyers themselves have not always been at one in their views on the subject. According to traditional doctrine, the attitude of external powers must depend on the scale of the civil conflict or the stage which it has attained. A kind of gradation from 'revolution' (where all rights were on the side of the government) through 'insurgency', to 'belligerency' (where both sides must be accorded roughly equal rights) was recognized.

It was always accepted that a government might from time to time be obliged to deal with internal disorders on a small scale. In this case the situation was one of revolution, and an outside government might continue to recognize and give assistance to the legal government, as at any other time. At the other extreme, if the conflict had reached a pitch of sufficient intensity, and especially if the rebel forces had attained control of a sufficient area of territory, external governments were under an obligation to adopt a position of strict neutrality. This they did by recognizing the 'belligerency' of the insurgent forces. Their duties then became the same as those of 'neutrals' in any international conflict, so that they were bound to give no assistance to either side in the conflict, whether legal government or rebel forces. Some legal writers recognized an intermediate stage between these two, in which external governments recognized the 'insurgency' but not the 'belligerency' of the rebel forces; in this case assistance to the recognized government, but not to the rebels, was usually regarded as legitimate (though again views varied).

Even under traditional international law, a considerable amount of discretion was given to outside governments concerning the recognition they gave. For example, though the recognition of the belligerency of rebel forces was said to be a 'duty' in certain circumstances, this was only so if they occupied a 'substantial part' of national territories, if they had adhered to the rules of war, and if recognition of this kind had become a 'practical necessity'. All of these terms are so imprecise that in practice governments tended to give rebel régimes recognition according to political convenience rather than any clear or objective criteria. Naturally the formal recognition of the 'belligerency' of a rebel force was in practice an act of calculated hostility to the ruling government. Most outside governments preferred to avoid any such provocative move: when Britain, even at a time when the rules were stricter than today, gave such recognition to the Confederate forces in the American Civil War, this caused considerable resentment to the United States government. Since the First World War the recognition of 'belligerency' has scarcely ever been accorded; and not at all since the Second World War. Recognition of rebel forces as a legal 'government' is more likely to occur : in Laos for a time the United States and the Soviet Union were each supplying arms to different factions which each regarded as the legal government. But many lesser ways of showing sympathy for rebel forces could be found, which fell short of overt recognition : in the Spanish Civil War, the British government accorded the Franco forces the right of insurgency, which itself was a minor form of acknowledgment.

The rights and duties of outside states in cases where the insurgency, but not the belligerency, of rebel forces has been recognized, and the conditions which make such recognition necessary, have not been clearly agreed among international lawyers. It is generally thought to permit the external power to undertake contacts for certain purposes and to acknowledge the authority of the insurgent forces in particular respects, as a matter of convenience. But in general, once again, in modern times few governments have made any attempt to define their attitude to rebel forces in such explicit terms. 'Insurgency' has not in practice been recognized any more than 'belligerency'.

The provisions of international law on the duties of states in civil war have in this, as in so much else, thus remained theoretical only. In practice its provisions have been disregarded or forgotten by governments which have framed their own policies according to their own national interests.

This is, indeed, scarcely surprising given the very wide differences that continue to exist among international lawyers on these points. In general in recent times some have sought to maintain the old concept that all external powers had a duty to remain neutral in civil wars whatever legal status had been accorded. Others have affirmed a big distinction between aid to a legally recognized government and aid to rebels. The international lawyers of the United States, for example, were totally divided in their judgment of the legitimacy of United States action in the Vietnam war because of differences on these points.

There have, however, been various attempts to lay down laws of a kind. In 1900, the Institute of International Law laid down a set of rules concerning the rights and duties of states in cases of insurgency. In 1928, a number of Latin American states, increasingly concerned at the frequent intervention of the United States in civil conflicts in the sub-continent, agreed on a Convention on the Duties and Rights of States in the Event of Civil Strife, strictly limiting the right of intervention. In 1949, the UN General Assembly passed a resolution, subsequently entitled The Essentials of Peace Resolution, calling on all nations to 'refrain from any threats or acts, direct or indirect, aimed at impairing the freedom, independence or integrity of any state, and fomenting civil strife and subverting the will of the people in any state'. In 1950, a further resolution condemned intervention or assistance in civil conflict aimed at 'overthrowing' the legitimate government by threat or use of force. Yet another resolution in 1965 declared that no state should 'interfere in the civil strife of another state'. Perhaps more important, certainly more detailed, than any of these, the Principles Concerning Friendly Relations Among States, passed during the Twenty-fifth Anniversary of the UN in 1970, declares: 'Every State has the duty to refrain from organizing, instigating, assisting or participating in acts of civil strife or terrorist acts in another state or acquiescing in organized activity within its territory directed towards the commission of such acts, when the acts referred to in this paragraph involve a threat or use of force.' A subsequent 'principle' in the same document, concerning the duty not to intervene in matters within the domestic jurisdiction of any state, contains a similar provision: 'No state shall . . . interfere in civil strife in another state.'

Principles laid down in this way are not necessarily strictly observed by states in practice. But it is probably true to say that there is a progressively greater readiness in modern times, as shown in the failure to recognize 'insurgency' or 'belligerency', to give *a priori* presumption of legitimacy to the rights of existing governments, and of illegitimacy to all rebel forces. This can scarcely be regarded as surprising, given the fact that the rules are themselves laid down by a club of governments.

Finally, it is worth considering, as a prelude to the studies of individual cases that follow, the principles applied by international organizations in confronting civil conflicts.

The drafters of the UN Charter do not seem to have envisaged that the UN would have any role at all to play in relation to the civil wars. The provisions of Article 2 (7) reaffirm the traditional rights of national sovereignty in so categorical a way that they provide at first sight a clear bar to international discussion of such disputes. The Article lays down that: 'Nothing contained in the present Charter shall authorize the United Nations to intervene in matters which are essentially within the domestic jurisdiction of any state . . .; but this principle shall not prejudice the application of enforcement measures under Chapter VII.' The Article has been quoted many times to resist attempts by the Organization or any of its members to discuss internal conflicts. Such arguments were used by almost all the colonial powers to prevent discussion of colonial disputes, and by South Africa to prevent discussion of apartheid and the conflicts resulting from it. They have also been used by the governments of nations where civil wars were taking place: for example the Nigerian government used every effort to prevent discussion of the Nigerian civil war in the UN when this was proposed.

But there are other provisions of the Charter which can be quoted, and

TABLE 2: UN ACTION AGAINST MAJOR CIVIL WARS 1946–67

Civil War	UN action
Greece 1945–9	Establishment of UN Special Committee on the Balkans and inspection of northern frontier
Philippines 1946–50	None
Colombia 1946–	None
China 1946–9	None
Burma 1948–	None
Cuba 1953–9, 1961	None
Malaya 1957–60	None
Muscat 1957–60, 69–70	Special Representative of UN Secretary-General sent to investigate and report
Lebanon 1958	Dispatch of observation group to prevent infiltration and supervise withdrawal of foreign troops
Indonesia 1958–9, 1965	None
Laos 1959–	Dispatch of Secretary-General's Representative and investigating committee
S. Vietnam 1959–	Discussed at one meeting of Security Council
Congo 1960–5	Use of UN troops, already dispatched, to restore law and order and unitary government
Iraq 1961–70	None
Yemen 1962–	Dispatch of observers to prevent outside intervention
Cyprus 1964–	Dispatch of UN peace force to prevent civil war and restore order
Dominican Republic 1965	Dispatch of Secretary-General's Representative to observe and report
Nigeria 1967–	None
Cambodia 1970–	None
Jordan 1970	None
Pakistan 1971	Relief activity only

equally often have been quoted, to *justify* discussion of such issues. It can, for example, be convincingly claimed that internal conflicts can sometimes represent 'threats to the peace', and so be subject to discussion under Article 39, which provides that 'the Security Council shall determine the existence of any threat to the peace ... and shall make recommendations, or decide what measures shall be taken ... to maintain or restore international peace and security'. This is obviously so by definition if the word 'peace' in such a context embraces peace *within* states as well as between them. But even if the word is construed to mean *international* peace, it can plausibly be argued that, in a world as small as today's, civil conflict, if not rapidly contained and pacified, may become a threat to the peace of neighbouring countries. This is what the UN has already ruled in the case of conflicts in Southern Africa – over South Africa, Angola and Rhodesia – which are essentially civil conflicts and not different in kind from other civil wars. Still more clearly the Security Council's right to 'investigate any dispute or any situation which might lead to international friction' (Article 34), and to recommend terms of a settlement under Article 36, give it authority to examine internal disputes if it so wishes.

Certainly in practice the UN has not hesitated to discuss internal conflicts in certain cases, whether or not on such grounds (the UN today does not always specify under which article of the Charter it discusses a particular dispute). Of the civil wars of the post-war period (excluding colonial wars and those concerning minorities), over half have been confronted by the UN in some form or other : and this has been increasingly true as time went on. At first, UN action was only attempted if some clear evidence of external intervention could be found : such as the allegations of assistance for rebel forces from Communist neighbours in the case of the Greek civil war, from Syria and the UAR in the case of Lebanon (1958), from Britain in the case of Muscat (1958–60), from North Vietnam in the case of Laos (1959) and from the UAR and Saudi Arabia in the case of Yemen (1962–5). All of these questions were discussed, mainly on the grounds of external interference. But in latter years, the UN has been increasingly ready to take action in such cases irrespective of the charges of external intervention. The most intensive and prolonged action of its history took place in the Congo, when only in the first month or two could external intervention on any scale (the presence of Belgian troops) be regarded as the main problem being confronted. In Cyprus, though outside intervention was always a possibility, the main role of UN forces has been rather to pacify internal conflicts than to restrain external contenders. And in the Dominican Republic, though the presence of United States troops can be quoted as a form of external threat, the main task of the UN Secretary-General's representative in that dispute was to mediate between local factions.

In its increasing readiness to take some form of cognizance of these disputes, the UN has merely been recognizing a reality of the modern world. Political conflict, even within frontiers, today cannot be totally insulated, and becomes a matter of concern, not only to its neighbours but to the international community as a whole. As frontiers, with shrinking distance, come closer together, it matters less and less whether conflict occurs across or within them. And since, as we have seen, a large proportion of all conflicts are today civil wars, and since in a considerable number of them some external involvement takes place, the UN would clearly be failing in its main task if it were not to seek to pacify these, as much as external wars.

So far, however, the UN has shown little consistency in its approach to such questions. It for long made no effort to consider the Vietnam War, though this was clearly for many years the principal threat to the peace of the world. The same is true of the civil wars in Laos and Cambodia, where intervention on both sides was never in doubt. Most members consistently refused to discuss the Nigerian civil war, though in this case there is no doubt that there was external assistance for the rebel forces and on a lavish scale. The various guerrilla movements in Latin America were not discussed, though there were many accusations of external involvement. Yet, as we have seen, in very many other cases, not essentially different, the UN did discuss them. This inconsistency has fatally weakened the UN in its approach to the problem. The fact that it was ready and willing to discuss some civil-war situations but not others, even when external intervention clearly had occurred, only served to create a state of uncertainty and confusion. It also significantly reduced the inhibitions against intervention which the probability of discussion, and public denunciation, might otherwise have exerted.

Where UN action has been taken, the techniques used, as the studies that follow show, have varied very considerably: from the passage of resolutions, through fact-finding and observation, to full-scale involvement in restoring law and order, as in the Congo and Cyprus. The success of these operations has varied equally widely. And we shall consider at the end of this volume how far any conclusions can be drawn about the relative effectiveness of these various options. It is the purpose of the chapters that follow to describe in some detail the steps which have been taken in specific cases and to analyse their success. Since the first attempt to organize international action in a civil-war situation goes back before the UN began to the Spanish Civil War, the first chapter looks at the attempts made by the international community during that conflict.

TEXT REFERENCES

1. In the Korean case, since the country remains divided, the small territorial change can be regarded as provisional. The list of cases does not include limited conflicts concerning the delimitation of a frontier (as between Algeria and Morocco, China and India, or China and the Soviet Union); nor does it include conflicts arising directly from the creation of new states, such as the India-Pakistan and Middle East conflicts. Neither of these can properly be termed 'aggression'. The Vietnam War is regarded as being originally a civil war.

2 THE SPANISH CIVIL WAR

Hugh Thomas

The Spanish Civil War has been regarded as a 'rehearsal for the Second World War' and as an object lesson in how international rivalries are played out on foreign soil. But as an incident in international relations its importance is without doubt that it provided for two and a half years a major source of dispute between the then great powers. It constituted, that is, between mid-1936 and early 1939, a chronic international crisis, occasionally erupting – as occurred over the shelling of the Spanish port of Almería by the German navy in 1937 – into a possible direct cause of world war, a direct cause which some have argued would have been more appropriate as a *casus belli* than Poland.[1] Somewhat surprisingly the late Sir Ivone Kirkpatrick (at the time a counsellor to the British embassy in Berlin) seems in retrospect to have thought the same: 'Once again,' he remarked in his memoirs (*Inner Circle*) 'our failure to appreciate the reality and the urgency of the German peril caused us to throw away an excellent opportunity of pulling Hitler up.'[2] Certainly, whatever moral judgment one may now make about the issues involved in what Anthony Eden referred to, in a famous speech, as the 'war of the Spanish obsession', it is impossible to get a clear picture of the general European diplomatic history of the late 1930s without reckoning the Spanish Civil War as a determining factor. It is on the one hand arguable that, had it not been for the Spanish war, the left in the democracies would never have seen the unwisdom of pacifism; and, on the other, that the Spanish war really forged the alliance between Germany and Italy which became known as the Axis.

Nevertheless, despite its importance as an international event (quite apart from its obvious traumatic importance in the history of Spain), certain myths about the Spanish war still persist in the popular mind. The first of these is that the Spaniards were in some way the victims of the rest of Europe; that the other powers intervened in the conflict in order to further some aspect or other of their own foreign policies, with the Spaniards themselves left to make the best of a generally declining inter-

26

national situation. There is undoubtedly something in the popular conception. Thus it can certainly be argued that it would have been much better
for Spain if the civil war had broken out, in, say, 1931 (at the time of the
fall of the Monarchy) than in 1936. In 1931, the issues though less sharply
defined than in 1936 were much the same as those at the time of the civil
war – the regional problem, the role of the Church in the State, the place
of organized labour in society and so on; the general European situation
was far less excited. Leaving aside, however, the question whether a war
could in fact have occurred at any stage earlier than 1936 (that is, when all
possible alternatives to war had been exhausted for a solution to Spanish
problems) the fact remains that in July 1936 it was not Europe, and not any
European power, which insisted on intervening in the Spanish conflict, but
the two Spanish parties which insisted themselves that outside powers
should help them.

Furthermore, the course of events at the beginning of the civil war
proves that neither side in the conflict can be said to be more at fault than
the other in these respects. Both the Republican, or legitimate, government
and the rebels made what use they could of past promises and understand-
ings to get what they could, regardless of what the other was doing. Thus
in July 1936, on the one hand, the Republican Prime Minister, Giral, made
an urgent appeal for military help from Léon Blum, the Prime Minister of
France; while on the other hand a representative of General Franco, the
insurrectionary commander in Morocco, was dispatched to Rome to make
the same request of Mussolini. Three days later, while the issue was still
extremely unclear in Spain itself, France sent other emissaries to Hitler in
Germany, while another rebel general, General Mola, with whom at that
moment General Franco was not perfectly in accord, sent similar missions to
both Rome and Berlin.

In the meantime, on 20 July, Blum had decided, after discussion with his
Foreign Minister and War Minister (Delbos and Daladier), to help the
Republic. The Spanish Ambassador in Paris, the Marqués de Cárdenas, specified exactly what his government wanted, though he himself quickly
resigned his post because of sympathy with the rebel cause. An atmosphere
of intrigue and rumour grew in Paris, partly as a result and that in its turn
had profound consequences. Thus Cárdenas, after resigning, told the British
what his late employers had wanted from the French, so that the British,
with full knowledge of the facts, were able to try and bring pressure on
France to restrain them from this assistance to Spain. At the same time,
French ministers who were hostile to assistance to Spain apparently (and
the information would be unbelievable if it did not clearly occur in the
German doplomatic archives) told the German Ambassador that Blum had
decided to supply Spain, in particular with Potez bomber aircraft.

The Spanish Minister in Paris, Castillo, and the Military Attaché, Barroso, next followed their chief, Cárdenas, into retirement, refusing as they did so to sign the necessary papers for the purchase of war material. They immediately told the French right-wing press what they knew, causing a considerable uproar. In the afternoon of that day, 25 July, the French cabinet met to discuss Spain. A communiqué was issued stating that France would not assist the Republic. But in fact they planned to do so, through private arms-dealing channels, and for the next week or so the Spanish embassy in Paris, now temporarily run by a loyal old Socialist politician, Fernando de los Ríos, was the centre of an elaborate network of arms dealing.

On 25 July Mussolini also made a decision, in his case, to help the rebels and it is clear that the impending French assistance to the Republic seems to have been a factor, at least, in his decision. Mussolini had refused Franco's emissaries twice and only agreed when on this third occasion they were even more pressing, with the spectre of French help for the other side being a main talking point.[3] The chain reaction had thus begun. It was taken a step further when, on the night of 25 to 26 July, Hitler saw Franco's other envoys, after the opera at Bayreuth. He too agreed to help, for a variety of reasons.[4]

The German and the Italian assistance to Franco proved most reliable and continued until the end of the civil war. Without doubt the size and the regularity of this assistance was one of the reasons why Franco won the war. It was supplemented by the geographically valuable assistance of Portugal almost from as early on in the course of the conflict; thus General Ponte, an emissary of General Mola, transmitted a request for help to Salazar in person on 26 July and received an unqualified assurance of aid.[5] But, thanks partly to British interference, or divisions within the French cabinet itself, French assistance to the Republic, which had started off so encouragingly – at least for their customers – and which had clearly been an element in what in the 1960s would have been called the 'escalation' of the situation, was nothing like so assured. Indeed, though some aircraft were dispatched to Spain, along with some other weapons, the French frontier with Spain was closed from early August 1936, and remained closed, except for short intervals, until the end of the war. Some help was undoubtedly got through from France to the Republic, in some instances because of the sympathy for the Republican cause of individual French officials or ministers within the government. But France was never anything like such a reliable ally for the Republic as Germany, Portugal and Italy were for the rebels.

This role of provider, after French inadequacy had become clear, was in practice fulfilled by Russia. But here again the initiative came from Spaniards, even though the details of what precisely transpired are obscure. In September 1936, Largo Caballero, the Socialist leader, formed a government in which he included two Communist members. A prominent old revolutionary, Antonov-Ovseenko, had already come to Barcelona as Consul-General and M. Rosenberg had reached Madrid as Ambassador in late August. Both Spanish and foreign Communists were known to be pressing Stalin to help the 'Spanish revolution'. Sometime in September – we do not yet quite know when – Stalin made the decision and appointed a unit of the NKVD to organize military aid in Russia and to receive it in Spain. By the middle of October, Russian military assistance was beginning to arrive in Spain by sea, and, at the same time, the International Brigades, the famous international legionaries, organized by the world Communist movement but not entirely Communist in composition, were established in Spain as a branch of the Republican army. This was apparently agreed by treaty between Largo Caballero on the one hand and three prominent international Communists (Luigi Longo, Stephan Wisniewski and Pierre Rebière).

Nevertheless, even with respect to this assistance by the only prominent 'revolutionary' state, it is quite clear that it was the Spanish side which took the initiative and sought to persuade the Russians to help them. During the difficult months ahead, too, it was the Spaniards who at all times were found complaining that the Russians were not sending enough or were sending the wrong sort of material or were trying to favour the Communist units as opposed to the anarchist ones.

Admittedly, during the course of the conflict, both sides were to be heard arguing that they were fighting against a foreign invader, the Germans and Italians on the one hand and the Russians on the other; and both sides used nationalism to shore up their propaganda. But nevertheless there can be no doubt that it was the Spaniards who drew the great powers into their affairs and not the great powers who insisted on intervention. Once other states had become involved, of course, it was difficult for them to withdraw since they found protégés to whom they had loyalties and commitments, and since they had to consider their international prestige; while both Spanish parties clearly had, as might be expected, difficulties with their respective allies – Franco disputing with Germany over matters of payment (particularly over the mining rights that the Germans wanted in return for their help), the Republic encountering difficulties over Russia's insatiable desires to discipline the Communist or non-Communist affiliated parties in Spain itself. The biggest scandal in Republican Spain was thus the great row which followed the mysterious murder of Andrés Nin, the leader of the Marxist, but anti-Communist, group with special following in Catalonia, the POUM (*Partido Obrero de Unificación Marxista*). But the existence of these inter-allied wrangles does not alter the fact that the initiatives for foreign intervention were taken and sustained by the Spaniards, as indeed is suggested by the fact that on most of these wrangles the Spaniards gave way.

The second main myth attaching to the Spanish war relates to what was often referred to at the time and since as the 'farce of non-intervention'. A case can in fact be made for this. When the Spanish war broke out in July 1936, Britain and France, shaken by Hitler's remilitarization of the Rhineland, were interested in trying to achieve some kind of general stabilization in Europe by means of what they termed 'a new Locarno'. The outbreak of a civil war in Spain, as well as being a disagreeable surprise, was an unwelcome interruption to these hopes and schemes. As suggested earlier, the outbreak of a civil war presented the most disagreeable challenge to the French government whose pacifism was only matched by their, at least verbal, internationalism. They therefore proposed to their British friends an international instrument whereby the war in Spain should so far as possible be insulated.

All European countries would refrain from sending either arms or men to Spain and this undertaking would be supplemented by a list of prohibited military equipment of all sorts. This was a compromise scheme much disliked by most French ministers, including even Léon Blum, but which he and others supported with the expectation that it would assist in the preservation of European peace. It was put forward at a time when it was by no means clear when, or even whether or not, countries such as Germany or Italy would intervene in the conflict, and long before there seemed any chance that Russia would.

The British government responded enthusiastically to the French idea. Indeed they almost made it their own. Within a short time, their ambassadors abroad had secured not only verbal undertakings from the European countries that they would assist neither party in Spain but acceptance of the idea that the ambassadors of the countries signatory to this agreement should attend a series of meetings in London. This so-called Non-Intervention Committee would superintend the Non-Intervention Agreement, and thereby preserve the peace of Europe, rather on the model of the Ambassadors' Conference in London during the Balkan wars before 1914.

This scheme was put into effect by the British as from early September 1936. The plan was criticized by the Republican government in Spain on the grounds that it limited what they regarded as their legitimate right, as a properly constituted government, to buy arms where they wished. It placed the government of Spain and the rebels virtually on the same footing. For this reason the Non-Intervention Agreement was from the beginning attacked by the more violent partisans of the Republican cause. However, it was supported not only by the Socialists in the French government and by the vast majority of the English Labour Party but also by the Democratic party in the United States and indeed by most social democratic causes throughout the world. The assumption behind this attitude was that it would be far better for the Spaniards to fight each other to the death than for anyone else to become involved. No mediation plan was in any way related to these plans. No one therefore can know whether the civil war would really have been over sooner had this international plan been fairly fulfilled by its signatories. Spaniards might perhaps have been hitting each other with sticks and stones after three years if Heinkel and Chato fighters had not been available.

At all events this simple and 'realistic' attitude was not possible. The reason for this was that both Germany and Italy, in the month following the Non-Intervention Agreement, made absolutely no real concessions to it. Assistance to Franco from both countries was not merely stepped up but, so far as Germany was concerned, put on a regular basis. Portugal was fully brought into the multinational deception. The consequence was that Russia announced in mid-October that she would hold herself in no way obliged not to help any party which she chose to back in Spain any more than certain other countries. In many ways, therefore, by October 1936 the whole programme of non-intervention seemed to have broken down. At that time, too, the English Labour Party, in its way an important and typical pressure group, announced its refusal to regard the Non-Intervention Agreement as having any further validity. It therefore seemed that Europe could only be in for a free for all in Spain, during the course of which the slightest incident might make world war inevitable.

It was this possibility that caused the British to put forward what should no doubt be called the 'leaky dam theory', from the remark of the British Foreign Secretary, in a speech the next year, that a 'leaky dam was better than no dam at all'. This view admitted that non-intervention was not working very well. But it assumed that both sides in Spain were being helped by one or other of the powers sympathetic to it and that, while it would no doubt be very much better if everyone had indeed left poor Spain to itself in the circumstances which had in fact arisen, it was better to be realistic and try to salvage something, if, by doing so, war could still be avoided.

The consequence was the development, largely as a result of the arguments of the British, of a so-called control scheme whereby the international agreement would be guaranteed. Henceforth it would not be left to individual countries to ensure that neither their men nor their arms went to Spain. On the contrary, naval and land forces supplied by the major international powers would attempt to prevent arms-shipping through the presence, off Spanish shores, of fleets, and by the establishment of patrol officers on the frontiers. This scheme with some modifications was finally agreed and put into effect by international agreement on 20 April 1937.

This plan was full of oddities. Thus it allocated to Germany a stretch of the Spanish coast to supervise and guarantee against 'illegal' international assistance, while Germany was, as everyone knew very well, one of the main breakers of the agreement. (Admittedly, Germany was not assigned the stretch in northern Spain along which it regularly replenished the Spanish Nationalist forces.) The scheme of international control, though an ambitious one, was not yet set up under the aegis of the world peace-keeping authority, the League of Nations, since all parties (except the Spanish Republicans) had attempted to prevent the League from interfering in the internal affairs of Spain. It excluded any effort at aerial control, on the grounds that it was technically impossible to organize. The methods of international control were limited to naval supervision on the sea and control at frontiers.

Finally, though the intentions of Britain and France were clearly always for the best, it remains curiously difficult to be certain what German and Italian intentions were. Even with the abundance of documentation now available on at least the German position, this has merely served to show that at that time the German government spoke with many voices. It is clear from the German foreign policy archives that in February 1937, the German Ambassador in Nationalist Spain, von Faupel, had been assured by his foreign ministry that Germany really wanted as 'effective a control as possible'. Both Germany and Italy hurried up with their massive assistance to Franco in the weeks before the day the control plan was due to be put in operation, on the assumption that hereafter they would not be sending any more material or men. Meantime, Russia was quite plainly interested in whether or not the control plan could be made to work, being by this time aware of the immense difficulties there were lying in the way of any continuous aid to the Republic, at least by the Soviet Union. Finally, Portugal, who had jibbed at the idea of international observers on her side of the Spanish-Portuguese frontier, for reasons of 'sovereignty', was brought to accept a number of British observers, officially ranked as members of the British embassy in Lisbon, as 'international controllers'. The annual cost of the scheme, about £900,000 according to estimates, was to be divided between the non-intervention countries.

Had this scheme worked, it would no doubt have been regarded as a prototype for the international management and insulation of a potential civil war. It did not, however, do so though the reason lay not with the inadequacy of the control system itself. On 20 April the scheme came into operation, German and Italian naval vessels establishing themselves in the Balearics, British vessels lying off the northern Basque and Asturian shore. But on 26 April Guernica, the sacred city of the Basques, was destroyed by, it was immediately rumoured, German aircraft, so causing a major crisis. On 24 May the Italian cruiser *Barletta* was bombed by Republican aircraft while lying in the harbour of Palma de Mallorca and on 26 May Republican bombs fell on the German patrol vessel *Albatross* in Palma. Palma harbour was a known centre for Nationalist arms shipping, especially from Italy, and was fair game, as both Italy and Germany must have known. However, on 29 May a far worse incident occurred, when Republican aircraft bombed the German battleship *Deutschland* in Ibiza harbour. In consequence Germany bombarded the Republican port of Almería and withdrew from the naval patrol.

The British then set about trying to badger the Germans to return to the control system. While they tried to do so, the flow of arms to Nationalist ports from Germany and Italy (which had never quite dried up in April), was resumed and continued, with some interruptions in no way connected with international control, until the end of the war. Russian shipments also continued, though the increasing audacity of Italian submarines in sinking these supply vessels caused frequent delays and stoppages.

The rest of the history of non-intervention in Spain is quickly described. In July, Britain proposed a scheme whereby naval patrol was to be replaced by observers at Spanish ports. There were also to be observers on merchant vessels. Both Spanish parties would be granted 'belligerent rights' at sea after a substantial number of foreigners in Spain on both sides had been withdrawn. Endless discussion continued over these points during the course of the summer of 1937. This British plan was ultimately accepted by the non-intervention powers as a 'basis for discussion' in November. The two Spanish parties were asked to accept commissions which would number the foreigners who were in Spain and arrange for their withdrawal. (These foreigners were all regarded as 'volunteers', for either revolution or counter-revolution, though this description scarcely applied to the Italian contingents and not entirely to the Germans.) Both Franco and the Republic accepted the plan, with qualifications: Franco thought that belligerent rights should be granted to him once 3,000 volunteers had been withdrawn, but the British replied that 75 per cent of the volunteers should go first. The delegations in London haggled over these percentages for another six months, and it was not until June 1938 that agreement was finally reached there. In Spain itself during these months new points of view were persistently put forward: Franco wanted the immediate grant of belligerent rights, followed by withdrawal, while the Republic was insisting that the Foreign Legion should be included in the withdrawal plans for Franco's forces. By this time, probably, no one except the British was very serious about these schemes. The Spanish Nationalist Foreign Minister, Jordana, explained in June 1938 that 'a way must be sought of strengthening Neville Chamberlain's position ... in principle but by skilful reservations and counter-proposals to win as much time as possible to prosecute the war in the meantime.'[6] This had of course been very much the German attitude throughout, except possibly for a few weeks in the winter of 1936/7. In the end, a number of Italians were withdrawn from Spain on Franco's side, and the International Brigades on the other: the withdrawal of the, by then, much reduced International Brigades coincided, as everyone appreciated, with the abandonment of Russian and Communist commitments both to the Spanish and the international collectivist cause.

This account of the attempt to contain foreign intervention undoubtedly makes a melancholy story. But the complaint against the British government (and the French, who after the German remilitarization of the Rhineland followed British policy all the time for fear of finding themselves fighting Germany on their own) was that, out of a kind of wish-fulfilment, they continued to maintain the façade of non-intervention until long after it had become plain that the Germans and Italians were regarding the whole scheme with complete cynicism. The Russians were also devious, though it is fair to recall that, with a great show of self-righteousness, they had formally announced, in October 1936, that they were not going to keep to non-intervention any more than anyone else – a formula which to their satisfaction at least gave them a blank cheque for every type of intervention they judged appropriate.

Much play throughout these negotiations was made of the question of belligerent rights. These rights allowed states at war to obstruct war material from reaching the harbours of their enemies by action against merchant vessels on the high seas. The Nationalists were always anxious to be accorded the rights, and the Republic as anxious that this should not happen, not only for obvious commercial reasons but also because the granting of these rights would confer an international status on the rebels. The Republic continued to regard themselves as the legitimate government of Spain right until the end of the war. During the course of the conflict there was much discussion of the matter in the British cabinet, Britain being the most interested party since it would have been British ships which were the next nearly affected. As it was, however, British merchant vessels continued to carry supplies, and sometimes (as in the famous case of the trader known at 'Potato' Jones) arms hidden beneath other supplies, until the end of the war, and with belligerent rights never being granted to the Nationalists, these ships were always able to call on the navy to assist them while they were outside the three-mile limit.

The denial of belligerent rights gave rise during the course of the conflict to a series of crises whose resolution was unrelated to the Non-Intervention Agreement but affected the supply of arms and other equipment, some military some not, to Republican Spain. As earlier described, the only major country to assist the Republic was Russia and the only way whereby substantial quantities of goods of any sort could be got from Russia to Spain was via the Mediterranean. (It is true that some equipment did go, following the volunteers of the International Brigades, through France but this was unreliable since the French governments mostly kept to the rules of the Non-Intervention Agreement and kept their frontier closed.) From the early summer of 1937 the Russian ships in the Mediterranean began to be followed and in some cases attacked and sunk by 'unknown submarines' – suspected at the time of being Italian and since confirmed as such. This 'piracy on the high seas' was quite against the rules of international law and practice, but there was no means whereby Republican Spain or Russia could enforce that law and practice. However, the submarines shortly became bolder and began, either by accident or design, to attack other than Russian merchant vessels, including British ones, and finally even, by accident, attacked the British destroyer *Havoc*. This finally forced the British into action. A conference against piracy was held, in September 1937, at Nyon, on the lake of Geneva. Neither Germany nor Italy attended, and this enabled the British and the French to work out a scheme for the patrol of the Mediterranean by naval vessels of all riparian states. The British and French fleets were to patrol the Mediterranean west of Malta and to attack suspicious submarines if they could. The effect of this agreement was, however, as so often during the 1930s, somewhat spoiled by the ultimate admission of Italy as one of the policing states. It was quite true that for some months the torpedoings in the Mediterranean did come to an end. But by February they had begun again, though now Mussolini was specially careful to avoid British naval ships. Russian vessels were regularly attacked and sunk so frequently that for months the supplies of the Republic from this source were almost brought to a halt. The wits of Geneva – familiar ghosts at the feasts of the 1930s – were heard suggesting that the 'unknown statesman' should erect a monument to the 'unknown submarine'.

There remains for consideration only the question of the League of Nations and the Spanish war. Regularly at meetings of the League Assembly and Council, the Spanish representatives would raise the question of foreign intervention in the conflict; and regularly Britain and France would seek to prevent the inclusion of this item on the agenda. This, due to their enormous influence with the smaller states who looked to them for protection, they were always able to do. The Republicans were continually fobbed off with requests for patience and usually they were unable to do more than accept these procrastinatory manoeuvres with a heavy heart.

Finally, Anglo-French policy towards the Spanish Civil War was virtually never formulated with any specific concern for Spain alone. The politicians of the democracies were concerned with their general European policies which, until the end of the Spanish Civil War, meant in fact the appeasement of Germany and the attempt to divide Italy from Germany. This was unfortunate for the Spanish Republic as it was for Czechoslovakia. Even fewer Anglo-Saxons were ready to go to war for Spain than they were for Prague.

TEXT REFERENCES

1. Thomas, Hugh, *The Spanish Civil War*, Pelican edition 1968, p.769.
2. Kirkpatrick, Sir Ivone, *Inner Circle*, London 1959, p.85.
3. Tamaro, Attilio, *Venti Anni de Storia*, vol. III, Rome 1952–3, p.200 and Cantalupo, *Fu La Spagna*, Milan 1948, p.62.
4. They are discussed at length in Thomas, p. 299. Since writing the above, I have had an opportunity to discuss this meeting with Johannes Bernhardt, the German businessman who really led Franco's delegation to Hitler. The main point to emerge from this was that it was Hitler who suggested the dispatch of troop transport aircraft to Spain and not Franco who requested it.
5. Iribarren, José María, *El General Mola*, Madrid 1945, p.123.
6. German Foreign Policy in Documents, Series D. vol. III, London 1951, p.725.

3 THE GREEK CIVIL WAR

John Campbell

In examining international efforts to insulate the Greek Civil War we must first look at the origins of the struggle and of foreign intervention in its troubled course.

Greece fell to the Germans in April 1941. The remaining months of the year were passed in painful adjustment to life under enemy occupation and the indignity of a local régime which collaborated with its forces. Since all political parties had been proscribed under the dictatorship of Metaxas in August 1936 and the remnants of this government had gone into exile with King George, Greece was politically a void. The political groups which Metaxas had principally oppressed by exile and imprisonment, in particular the Communists and the republican Liberals, were among the first to seize the opportunity to rebuild their organizations and think of patriotic resistance to the enemy. Bourgeois political parties in Greece suffer from the weakness of an organization based on personal circles of friends and clients. Although there were examples of individual daring and enterprise, the Republicans' early efforts to build resistance groups were largely dissipated in the manoeuvres and discussions of political figures paradoxically enjoying a new-found freedom. The Greek Communist Party (KKE), however, had a corporate structure and discipline, and an organization adapted to conspiratorial underground existence. The subtle techniques of Metaxas's security police, it is true, had reduced the party to long inactivity, but many of the rank and file had remained undetected, waiting to be regrouped when eventually the German occupation released the party's leaders.[1]

At first the Communists fixed their attention on restoring the party's organization in urban areas where traditionally it had been strong, for instance among the refugees and tobacco workers. The disastrous shortage of food during the first winter of the occupation and the threat of deportation to Germany for forced labour were stark problems in the face of which it was relatively easy to draw men into clandestine groups. In the late summer of 1942, however, the activities of guerrilla bands in the Pindus Mountains, led by a lapsed Communist, Aris Velouchiotis,[2] began to affect the party's thinking and strategy. It had become apparent that the occupation forces lacked the resources to hold in strength more than the principal towns and lines of communication. In effect, two-thirds of the country, covered by formidable mountain ranges and holding half the population, was unoccupied by the enemy. The prospect of a native resistance movement sharing control of the country was now evident, and since already small but growing Republican bands were also appearing in the countryside it was necessary to act promptly.

The evidence of the KKE's own literature [3] makes it clear that from the beginning its aim was to win exclusive control of resistance in Greece as a preliminary to seizing the state after liberation, whether by force or by carefully influenced elections. It is also clear that the party hoped to conceal this intention behind a popular and patriotic front known in its political aspect by the initials EAM (National Liberation Front) and in its military organization as ELAS (The People's National Liberation Army). In these organizations the substantial, as opposed to the merely titular, positions of authority were invariably held by Communists. And although it is true that Communists were in a minority on EAM's council, the more significant fact was that they selected their radical or socialist allies and that the latter were either dominated by KKE or of no independent importance whatsoever. Building on Aris Velouchiotis's original enterprise, and drawing on the disciplined resources of Communist cadres, ELAS rapidly expanded its influence in the mountains of southern and central continental Greece during 1943.

Guerrilla resistance in the mountains was not spontaneous. Villagers joined ELAS generally from considerations of fear or prudence. Nevertheless, they were impressed by the administrative energy of EAM,[4] for instance in providing schools and repairing roads, an attitude of local concern which contrasted with the indifference of distant public servants in the past. In this sense it would be wrong to suggest that EAM nowhere had a popular base. But the expansion of its influence also required a ruthless process [5] of destroying non-Communist bands within reach of its own forces. After the killing, capture or dispersion of their members they were accused of collaboration with the enemy. Since some survivors of these attacks later joined the anti-Communist security battalions of the Greek collaboration government, such accusations gathered a certain retrospective force. By the early summer of 1944 only Zervas's EDES (National Republican Greek League) could offer serious competition to ELAS. Its continued existence was dependent on British supplies and money and British interventions with ELAS through the Allied Military Mission, a policy explicitly intended to prevent EAM claiming the right to form a provisional government of Greece at the moment of liberation.

Yet, paradoxically, a major impediment to Greek Communist ambitions was the attitude of the Soviet Union. Throughout the war in Europe, and for almost a year after it had ended, the Russians avoided unnecessary frictions with their allies. During the war they needed military supplies from the Western allies, and immediately after it an agreement over a Soviet security zone in Eastern Europe. They could not know that the strength of the Western armies in Europe would be so rapidly reduced, but they did understand the sensitivity of some Western leaders to the possibility of Communist expansion. It was for this reason that Stalin advised Tito to remain on terms with King Peter and chided him for allowing his partisans to wear provocative red stars. In the spring of 1944, when Tito was unchallenged in Yugoslavia and ELAS was with difficulty restrained from exercising a full hegemony over the Greek resistance, Churchill sought an agreement with Stalin based on their differing concerns and apprehensions. In May 1944, the Russians agreed to consider a British suggestion that the two countries should respectively 'take the lead', the one in Romania's affairs, the other in Greece's. Partly due to American distrust of a division of the Balkans into spheres of influence this agreement was not finally accepted by the Russians until Churchill's visit to Moscow in October 1944 where it emerged in the curious form of the so-called 'percentages agreement'. Russia and Great Britain would respectively have 90 per cent dominance in Romania and Greece; Russia would predominate by 75 per cent in Bulgaria; in Yugoslavia and Hungary the influence of the two powers would be balanced, each claiming 50 per cent.[6]

In Greece the Russians had already honoured this agreement before it was actually concluded. Early in July 1944 EAM was intransigent. As the Germans withdrew and before the British arrived it planned to seize Athens and announce its provisional government. On 25 July, a Russian military mission led by Colonel Popov arrived in the Greek mountains. No documentary evidence exists to reveal the advice which Popov gave to the KKE.[7] The fact remains that barely two weeks after his arrival EAM was suddenly convinced of the merits of cooperation, accepted five unimportant portfolios in the Papandreou government which was due to return with the British forces from the Middle East, and in the Caserta Agreement[8] placed the guerrilla army of ELAS under its command. It is true that after EAM had peacefully welcomed the return of its British allies to Greek soil in October, it attempted in December, under infinitely less favourable conditions, to drive them out by force. The ELAS uprising was the product of the Greek Communists' impatience with the methods of political infiltration while ELAS, under the threat of demobilization, remained in physical control of the greater part of the country. There is little doubt that Tito encouraged this attempt,[9] and it is possible that the Russians secretly tolerated it. Nevertheless, in its public diplomacy the Soviet Union remained correct. No material or propaganda support was given to ELAS. Colonel Popov remained with the British HQ in its hours of crisis and the Bulgarians were kept within their borders. Churchill later commended the Russians for their restraint and at Yalta in February 1945, after the rising had been crushed, Stalin cynically approved[10] of British policy in Greece on the assumption that his own actions in Bulgaria and Romania must similarly remain unquestioned.

The December rising cost the British and the Greeks a month of bitter street fighting, vast material damage, and 11,000 casualties including the slaughter of civilian hostages taken by ELAS. Some supporters of EAM were permanently alienated by these brutalities; many others were deeply disillusioned by the discovery that their assumption that the Soviet Union was morally bound to intervene was false, and therefore the prudential consideration (never far beneath the surface of Greek politics) that ELAS would emerge as the victors was inaccurate.

Now little middle ground was left for moderate men. The British could not fully restrain the force of right-wing reaction, particularly in the countryside. On the other hand, their limited military strength and anxieties about the position of democratic parties in the Balkan countries under Soviet influence led them to impose lenient terms on EAM in the Varkiza Agreement.[11] Only certain quantities of mainly obsolete arms were handed over. The KKE remained a legitimate political party. Those Greeks who feared Communist influence, disliked EAM's form of radicalism or now simply believed it would not win, declared loudly their support of the monarchy and the Right (which included, as well as monarchist Populists, many liberals or Republicans who in the circumstances abandoned their hostility to the King). But men of the Centre with reformist ideals who associated King George with the Metaxas dictatorship and a policy of authoritarian repression, felt compelled to remain with EAM, or even at this late hour to join it, whatever its recent record. Many without deep political commitments, but with a known record in the ELAS resistance movement, could no longer escape from it. Soon resistance fighters charged with 'common crimes' outnumbered collaborators in the prisons. Thus the nation was divided. Each incident of terror defined more clearly the lines of schism in a country already crippled by food shortages, unemployment, and galloping inflation.

As the general situation in Greece deteriorated Stalin's attitude to its problems changed. At Potsdam when the Western allies and the Russians made reciprocal complaints about conditions in Bulgaria and Greece the 'percent-ages agreement' was already abandoned. Western indignation about the treatment of non-Communists in Romania and Bulgaria was unceasing during the autumn and winter of 1945. Russian indignation over Greece was no less. More generally, Stalin's sharper and more aggressive attitude towards his allies dates from this period. The need at home to reverse the liberal domestic policies of wartime required that the neighbouring countries on Russia's western borders should accept her guidance and adopt a form of government known as 'people's democracy'[12] in which key positions were held by Communists supported by insubstantial colleagues from peasant or socialist parties whose future only led towards their own elimination.

At this early and insecure stage of their development the countries of the Eastern bloc proved their solidarity with the Soviet Union by the uniformity of their opposition to régimes of any other kind. Albania, Yugoslavia, and Bulgaria shared not only an ideological opposition to the makeshift government in Athens but national antipathies towards the Greeks[13] and ancient territorial ambitions, so that the temptation or the duty to support the cause of KKE was indeed acute. The Party had decided, in February 1946, not to participate in the elections due at the end of March, but instead to turn to a campaign of guerrilla terror.[14] It is probable that this course was neither advocated nor forbidden by Stalin. In February, however, the Americans had given diplomatic recognition to the govern-ments in Sofia and Bucharest: and already the limits of British resources for a continental role were becoming evident. A policy of limited aggression, indirectly and cautiously effected, probably appeared at this time as a course relatively without risk.

For this business Tito was a local agent ambitious on his own account to integrate a bloc of Balkan Communist states under his leadership. Yugo-slav and Bulgarian officers held preliminary staff talks with the KKE in February 1946.[15] In March the Yugoslavs promised Zachariades, the General Secretary of the Greek party, supplies and a base camp at Bulkes near Belgrade. At Rubig in Albania, and Berkovitsa in Bulgaria similar facilities, but on a smaller scale, were offered by the Albanians and Bul-garians. However, the safe refuge of the long northern frontiers, across which guerrillas could advance and withdraw at will, was the essential service which the Communist governments gave to KKE. In these arrange-ments Tito was cautious in the limited quantities of war material he sup-plied at first, but probably quite explicit about the price of his support.[16] A Macedonian people's republic including areas of Greek Macedonia, and possibly the Pirin district of south-western Bulgaria, would become part of Federal Yugoslavia or a wider Balkan union. And Bulgaria would absorb

41

Greek Thrace. These ambitions were easily visible during the summer of 1946 in the articles of Yugoslav newspapers pressing for self-determination in 'Aegean Macedonia' and claiming that 250,000 Slav Macedonians lived in Greece.[17]

Not only Tito's aims but the course of the struggle in Greece gave increasing emphasis to the Macedonian question. Initially the KKE had hoped to paralyse the state by using the core of 5,000 hardened ELAS guerrillas still at large (immediately available and easily armed) to spread terror in the villages of continental Greece, in conjunction with widespread political strikes in the towns where overnight the pace of inflation decimated the real value of wage adjustments. But, despite the success of these tactics, the logic of the contest and the pressure of its own militants forced the party continually to raise the scale of conflict. In October, Markos Vaphiades was appointed to coordinate the guerrilla forces newly designated as the Democratic Army of Greece. He could increase the strength of his army to 30,000 effectives and replace its casualties only by resorting to methods of forced conscription among a Greek peasantry now intensely weary of war and uncertain of the outcome.

More seriously, at least a quarter of the soldiers in the Democratic Army were drawn from the Slavophone communities. Many of them had fought during the occupation in the Slavo-Macedonian National Liberation Front (SNOF), an organization which had pressed for Macedonian unity and had owed its primary allegiance to Tempo, Tito's agent in Macedonia. Indeed, its uneasy relations with EAM over demands for 'self-determination' had on occasions resulted in armed clashes. Thus Markos, in his efforts to increase the pressure on the Athens government, could not avoid the impression that the civil war was, at least for some participants, not merely a defence of democratic rights but an aggressive enterprise to seize territory from the Greek state. Despite the wide range of his raiding activities, even into the Peloponnese, the tactical use of the frontier and his supply routes forced him to base his strength precisely in those areas which, it might be expected, would be ceded by Greek Communists to their allies. Moreover, his army received supplies and moral support from the very states with declared ambitions for Greek territory; and on Christmas Eve 1947 a Provisional Democratic Government of Greece was established in the strip of territory adjoining their frontiers.[18] These were all circumstances which could complete a convincing case that the civil war had developed into an external threat against the sovereignty of Greece.

Already in March 1947, when economic weakness forced Great Britain to withdraw her support from Greece, America had accepted this interpretation and through the Truman Doctrine declared her intention to resist Communist insurgency. By the end of the year, Stalin had decided that his opponents were in earnest. He refused to recognize, or allow his Balkan satellites to recognize, the provisional government which Markos had speculatively announced. In February 1948, Stalin sarcastically reprimanded the Yugoslavs for their initiatives in policy; the dispatch of Yugoslav forces to Albania, diplomatic meetings not authorized by Moscow, negotiations with the Bulgarian leader Dimitrov for forms of Balkan federation of which Stalin disapproved. He reverted to his earlier disapproval of the Greek revolt which could not be prolonged, he said, in the face of resistance from America, 'the strongest nation in the world'.[19] Stalin's caution had returned and with it his always barely suppressed suspicion of Tito whose independent strength was based on an authority established before the Red Army had arrived. The expulsion of Yugoslavia from the Cominform followed in June 1948 and, soon afterwards, the gradual disengagement of Yugoslavia from the Greek affair, ending in the closing of the frontier in July 1949, denied the Democratic Army the minimum conditions under which it could fight its unequal war. By the end of August 1949 the Democratic Army had been finally defeated.

In the international debate about the fundamental causes of the war, one side stressed the popular origins of the EAM movement under the occupation, its genuine resistance to the Germans, and its democratic ideals. The imperialist obsession of the British to return a fascist King to Greece had precipitated the rising of December 1944. The civil war from 1946 to 1949 was simply the result of the moral anomalies in which collaborators went unpunished and democrats were persecuted for honest resistance. The other side claimed that EAM was a Communist front, its recruits were enrolled by force, and it fought more Greeks than Germans. In December 1944, it had attempted to seize the state and establish a people's democracy. Abandoning legitimate parliamentary opposition by boycotting the elections in March 1946, it renewed its attempt to take the state by force in an unconcealed alliance with Communist régimes to the north and at the cost of promised cessions of national territory in Macedonia and Thrace. Unremarkably, as we have seen, each of these stereotypes held an element of truth.

The attempts of the United Nations to solve the disputes between Greece and her neighbours, and by implication to end the civil war which created them, have to be considered in the light of the circumstances we have described. The civil war was, of course, in part a domestic crisis, but even in its origins in the Resistance under the German occupation it was inextricably involved with international Communism; and in the period after the Varkiza Agreement the factor of foreign involvement grew continually in significance. Without the support of the three Communist states on the northern frontier, especially Yugoslavia, the civil war could not have developed as it did. Similarly, it is improbable that the Greek state would have survived without the support first of the British and later, and more decisively, of the Americans. And although other causes played their part the event which principally precipitated the Greek Communist collapse was the withdrawal of aid and the closing of the frontier by the Yugoslavs. This, and not the efficacy of the resolutions of the General Assembly, debates in the Security Council and the reports of special commissions, brought the fighting to a halt.

ιAfter the Second World War the United States did not feel immediately threatened by Soviet ambition. Her monopoly of the atomic weapon and her overwhelming industrial strength seemed to promise a period of security. The problem was rather how to retain her international dominance in a manner not incompatible with her traditional dislike of foreign commitments and territorial imperialism. The American government believed that the UN would develop as an organization[20] in which it could use its moral and political authority to compose the pattern of post-war commercial and international relations which it wanted and to provide the necessary institutions to resolve disputes between nations. Spheres of interest and exclusive alliances both limited the effectiveness of such an organization. This explains in part Cordell Hull's distaste for the 'percentages agreement'; and at Yalta Roosevelt's attempt to disarm Stalin's suspicion about Anglo-American relations. Yet it was clearly impractical to imagine that the Soviet government which itself believed that the stability of its domestic régime required its careful segregation from the West and a security zone of sympathetic governments in the states on its western frontier, could allow itself to submit the interests of its country to the jurisdiction of an organization in which it was bound to be in a minority in both the General Assembly and the Security Council. The Russians believed that the role of the UN would be determined at any time simply by the state of relations between the two major powers. Since the Americans were distressed at the way the Russians used their procedural veto to prevent the formal expression of majority opinions and angry at their shrewd use of debates for making propaganda, and the Russians for their part were resentful and suspicious that the Americans should expect them to submit to the accident of numbers, the effect of these contrary expectations of the international organization was only to increase the tension in their gradually worsening relations during the first years of the Peace.[21]

This view is justified by the history of international interventions in the Greek Civil War. The ninth Article of the Varkiza Agreement foreshadowed the first instance of these when it provided that the Allied Powers should send observers to verify the fairness of elections.[22] As early as 4 May 1945, Stalin had informed Churchill that the Soviet Union would consider such control to be a gross interference in the internal affairs of an allied country. He declined to participate. The need to resist Western pressure for any form of joint supervision of elections in Romania and Bulgaria, which directly concerned the security of the Soviet Union, was one ground for refusing to take part. This prudence seemed amply justified at Potsdam when Truman demanded that the Yalta declaration on liberated Europe should be applied to Romania and Bulgaria, where he suggested the three powers ought immediately to reform the governments to include proper representation of all democratic elements. In private, Stalin complained to Churchill in a retrospective reference to the 'percentages agreement', that he was not meddling in Greece.[23] And at the same time he accused the Greeks of aggression against their neighbours.

This indicates a second reason for the Soviet reluctance to co-operate with the Western powers. The Left would not win the Greek election but Soviet supervision of the poll would legitimize the position of the victors. It suited Stalin better to claim that the Greek government was a monarcho-fascist conspiracy, that any election under its administration, however closely observed, would be grossly biased, that the Greek territorial claims on Northern Epirus (Albania) and Bulgaria, as well as frontier incidents provoked by the government's forces, proved beyond debate its aggressive intention, that the British by the presence of their forces and training missions for the Greek army and police, and their control over daily adminis-tration, were responsible for the aggressive policy of the Greek government and its persecution of anyone who had been associated politically with the Left or patriotically with the Resistance. By simultaneously claiming that his Balkan clients were threatened, yet allowing them to think of forming a free Macedonia within a Yugoslav or a Balkan Federation, Stalin instilled both the ambition and the sense of insecurity to draw them into un-questioning dependence.

It was in keeping with these tactics and in retaliation for Iran's complaint against Soviet conduct in northern Persia that, on 21 January 1946, the Soviet government addressed a letter on the Greek question to the newborn Security Council.[24] It complained that the stationing of British troops in Greece had become a threat to international peace. On the same day the KKE in Athens demanded the withdrawal of British troops and the forma-tion of a volunteer corps of trained resistance fighters to prepare for an armed struggle. The apparent occasion for this declaration was an out-break of right-wing terrorism in the Peloponnese. In the debate which followed in the first week of February at the Security Council, the Soviet representative assiduously discussed the effect on domestic politics of the presence of British troops. And in case any false inference should be drawn from the Greek to the Romanian and Bulgarian cases he pointed out that

British troops in Greece were not there to protect the communications of forces stationed in defeated countries.[25]

Bevin's reply was based principally on the fact that British forces were in Greece only because its government had invited them to remain in the belief that they were a necessary guarantee of security. Although this explanation was acceptable to the majority of the Council's members, the Russian accusations were nevertheless embarrassing for the British, served the general policy of consolidating Soviet control over the Balkan satellites in the manner that has been suggested, and prepared the ground for hostile criticism of the elections due at the end of March 1946. The victory of the right-wing Populists at these elections, from which the Communists and their sympathizers had withdrawn in protest at the conditions of the contest, and the report of the Allied Mission on their administration (AMFOGE),[26] offered material for further attacks. The registers were admittedly incomplete, it was open to question whether the observers were impartial, and more certainly they were unfamiliar with Greek electoral habits. Of those entitled to vote only 49 per cent did so and, although the report claimed that on the whole the elections were fairly fought, their estimate that only 9 of the absent 51 per cent represented political abstentions was a wishful speculation. For those who were still uncommitted such arguments were not easily dismissed.

Before the Greek problem again came before the Security Council at the end of August 1946 the situation inside the country had grown worse. In the week before the election, to mark the Communist withdrawal from the electoral contest, guerrilla bands had already raided isolated villages in the area of Mount Olympus. During the summer the frequency of violence increased. It both provoked and was encouraged by new legislation of considerable severity which permitted the arrest of suspect persons without a warrant. Leading non-Communist supporters of EAM (Svolos, Bakirdzis, and Sarafis) were exiled. The fact that leaders of the extreme right 'X' organization were also arrested hardly protected the new Populist government from accusations of persecution. The prospect for the economy was dark. A demonstrably unrealistic budget, unemployment in the towns, and the hardships caused by the unceasing inflation, seemed to be bringing the Greek state close to collapse. In search of props for internal stability, the Populists persuaded the British to agree to bring forward the plebiscite on the monarchy from 1948 to 1 September 1946. And throughout August the government presented its case before the Peace Conference asking, among other demands, for territorial adjustments with Yugoslavia and Bulgaria, and entering the more considerable claim for the cession of Northern Epirus (southern Albania) to Greece.[27]

On 29 August the Security Council sat to debate the complaint of the

Ukraine against Greece's aggressive behaviour and the country's internal disputes which made it a threat to peace in the Balkans.[28] Both the plebiscite and the territorial claims appeared prominently in these representations. And it is unlikely that the submission of the complaint on 24 August, exactly a week before the Greek plebiscite, was in any way accidental. In supporting his Ukrainian colleague, Gromyko repeatedly drew attention to the seriousness of border incidents with Albania. The provocative sallies of the Greek militarists on the eve of the Paris peace conference were a strange coincidence, he believed. They confirmed the aggressive intentions that underlay the Greek claims. Yet these were only possible because of the presence of British forces which were cynically employed to crush democracy. It was in these conditions that the plebiscite had been arranged. A free and fair expression of the will of the Greek people was, therefore, out of the question. This, he concluded, was a flagrant intervention by foreign troops in which the sovereign rights of Greece were completely disregarded.[29]

The Greek defence was in part a rebuttal of the Ukrainian allegations, in part a catalogue of counter-charges. The resort to the Security Council was a move calculated to support the Greek rebels. When the Bulgarian and Yugoslav armies totalled almost half a million men the suggestion of Greek aggressive intentions was absurd. Rather one should deplore the Yugoslav press campaign suggesting that Greek Macedonia should become part of a Macedonian state. The British delegate in his turn admitted that the electoral conditions of the plebiscite were not satisfactory by British democratic standards but they were eminently better than those in certain other Eastern European countries .[30] This was a thinly disguised reference to the plebiscite on the monarchy in Bulgaria which in three days' time was to give an overwhelming majority in favour of a republic. When the representative of the United States spoke on the day following the Bulgarian plebiscite he pointed out that the thirty-one per cent of votes cast against the Greek King seemed to him to represent a significant number of unafraid voters in a plebiscite said not to be free. As to the Greek claims in Northern Epirus it was extraordinary that the statement of a legal position could become evidence of aggressive intent. The American position was unambiguous, including unqualified approval of the presence of British troops.

This indicated a distinct shift in American policy at the UN. When the Soviet Union had made its complaint in January, American support for her British ally was unemphatic. Although, by then, the State Department was no longer prepared to make concessions to the Russians in direct diplomatic relations, its representatives at the UN had not finally abandoned their original view of the organization as an international institution for conciliation in which prejudged positions and established alliances were inappropriate, at least in public debate. But by September 1946 there was little hope that any argument in the Security Council could alter Soviet policy. Nevertheless it was a forum for propaganda, important for the Russians in satellite countries where the institutions of a people's democracy had not been fully imposed, important for Western governments which had to carry with them less easily regimented electorates, while in areas under dispute, such as Greece, each side struggled to increase the number of its local suporters. In these conditions debates at the Security Council became elaborations of opposed positions which the veto safeguarded against the consequences of collective decisions.

The concluding phase of the Ukrainian complaint illustrates these relations. The American delegate proposed, and Gromyko rejected, a resolution calling for the dispatch of an investigating commission of three impartial observers to examine border disturbances (and the situation of ethnic minorities which complicated them) on Greece's frontier with Albania, Yugoslavia and Bulgaria. In the American view the cause of these disturbances lay in the aggressive infiltration of guerrilla bands from the north, in the Russian view it could be attributed to the aggressive intentions of the Greek monarcho-fascist government which persecuted the Slav Macedonians and their own electorate, and survived in power only by reason of the British presence. With the operations of Communist bands gathering impetus in the Pindus Mountains, and since 'impartial' observers would very probably prove to be anti-Communist – at least by Soviet judgments – Gromyko applied the eighth Soviet veto of the year after seven votes had been given in favour of the resolution, one against, with one abstention.[31]

In Greece the situation grew steadily worse. Attacks on vulnerable villages increased. On 14 November, for instance, Skra was assaulted by a band of 700 guerrillas from across the Yugoslav border; 150 houses were burned down and 19 soldiers were killed.[32] Communist commentaries on the violence became more emphatic. Duclos, the French Communist leader, claimed that the fate of European independence would be decided in Greece. A long resolution of the Politbureau of the Greek party informed its followers on 20 November that the people would smash the government of national enslavement if the anti-popular and reactionary Anglo-American support were to cease.[33] It called for the formation of a coalition government of all parties including EAM. The day after its publication this resolution was given a wider circulation in the broadcasts of Radio Moscow. Extracts from the unpublished report of a British parliamentary delegation to Greece which had been leaked to the press shared some common ground.[34] It also recommended a coalition government, although without the participation of the extreme left, as well as a general amnesty and the repeal of special security measures. The rebel Democratic Army of Greece, which in the previous month had replaced ELAS, added further detail, both by its change of title and its denial that it used foreign territory or supplies, to the picture of a genuinely domestic civil war provoked by a right-wing régime kept in power by foreign intervention.

In these circumstances both the Americans and British approved of a Greek complaint to the Security Council in protest against the systematic violation of her northern frontier. For the Americans, feeling their way uncertainly towards a firmer opposition to Communist encroachments, it was very necessary to persuade popular opinion in the United States that, in Greece, America was resisting external aggression and not suppressing native democracy. It was, after all, less than two years ago that she had righteously questioned British actions during the December troubles in 1944. For their part the British hoped that a Greek initiative at the UN would give her an opportunity to justify her position in Greece but, more importantly, to draw her American ally into a final realization that she must share the burden.

The Greek complaint was discussed at the Security Council for nine days beginning on 10 December.[35] Tsaldaris, the Prime Minister, spoke with bitterness about the situation in Macedonia. The purpose of guerrilla attacks launched from a privileged base beyond the borders of Greece was nothing less than an attempt to separate 'Aegean Macedonia' from Greece and to set up a régime in the rest of the country contrary to the wishes of the overwhelming majority of the people as expressed in free elections observed and approved by foreign representatives. The propaganda in the Communist press for the inclusion of Greek Macedonia in the Yugoslav Federal Republic proclaimed the purpose of their provocative actions. Tsaldaris had prefaced his remarks by demanding that the true situation on Greece's borders should be immediately investigated.[36] The Yugoslav representative who followed him denied the charges, referred to Greek claims on the territory of her northern neighbours and added that what the situation required was rather an investigation of conditions inside Greece.

The American delegate was less anxious to debate the allegations in the Greek complaint than to argue that whatever view one might take about the causes of border incidents there was no disagreement that a dispute existed between Greece on the one side and Albania, Yugoslavia and Bulgaria on the other. Therefore it was the duty of the Security Council to investigate the facts without immediately attempting to prejudge the issues. For this purpose a commission of investigation should be set up. While the British delegate supported this proposal Gromyko showed no inclination to avoid contention. He reiterated the argument that fundamentally the question was a problem of internal politics. It was generally agreed that the

Tsaldaris government was unpopular. It was indisputable that the represent-atives of the democratic parties and organizations in Greece were taking no part whatsoever in its government. Indeed, there was a savage terror in progress against democratic parties. These causes had no relation to the actions of neighbouring countries. Yet the speech ended with a small sensa-tion. Russia would support an amended version of the American proposal for an investigation to study in Greece, Yugoslavia, Albania and Bulgaria the causes of the present tensions.[37]

Any explanation of the Russian volte-face is admittedly speculative. They probably did not wish to be seen yet again in the role of the obstructing power. Moreover, with the general situation in Greece deteriorating the security measures of the Greek government, and the cases of hardship and injustice which their implementation inevitably raised, would give the Communist members of the commission some lively opportunities to affect world opinion. In this respect the constitution of the Commission from representatives of the countries on the Security Council was an important advantage. There was to be no attempt to find allegedly impartial observers as had been suggested when the United States advocated a similar investiga-tion at the time of the Ukrainian complaint. After the withdrawal of their ambassador from Athens in August the Russians almost certainly welcomed this opportunity to return to the Greek scene through a procedure which would make it more difficult for the British or Americans to act unilaterally. Also the terms of reference of the investigation were broad, not limited to discovering the facts of border disturbances but extended to uncovering their 'causes and nature'. Such terms accommodated the Soviet case very conveniently and made it probable that the work of the Commission would be protracted over a considerable period of time, during which not only would the Greek government have to suffer the embarrassing testimony of hostile witnesses but its own efforts against the rebels would be somewhat inhibited. Indeed, these terms represented a considerable modification of the original American resolution.

That proposal had restricted the investigation to the border incidents and to the immediate areas in northern Greece and the three adjoining Communist states where they had occurred. But the speeches of the Yugo-slav and Soviet delegates made it soon apparent that no resolution would pass the latter's scrutiny (and the sanction of his veto) which did not offer the Russians the opportunity of proving that incidents on the border were merely one symptom of a civil war whose fundamental cause was internal, not external, to Greece. In effect the Commission was acceptable to the two sides only because it allowed each to pursue its own particular prejudgment. Inevitably the Commission became, above all else, a forum for conflicting propaganda which effectively embittered the struggle it was intended to resolve.

Particular national aims, naturally, were varied. The Greek National Government and their British allies had to convince the Americans that the country was in fact in danger of collapsing before an external Communist attack. This was urgent since it was known that the British could not continue unaided to carry the burden of supporting Greece. In its turn the American government required the support of international non-Communist opinion to justify to its own public the action it might decide to take. One can infer a number of related Soviet aims: through aggressive propaganda to help preserve the solidarity of its developing bloc; through concentration on the growing chaos inside Greece to divert international attention from the true dependence of the revived guerrilla bands on external aid; and by the same means to persuade Western public opinion, particularly in the United States, that the actions and cause of the Greek government were undemocratic and unjust. The last was no doubt its principal intention. The free Western press might be the very means to prevent or at least hinder the Americans from rescuing the shipwrecked régime in Athens. Although they had faced admittedly graver handicaps in resisting the Communist persecution of opposition parties in Bulgaria and Romania, the Americans had shown little resolution to stand fast over those issues. On the one hand, by the end of 1946, there was insufficient evidence to indicate which, if any, of Great Britain's failing imperial positions America would be willing to take over. On the other, the serious embarrassment which, even in wartime, the British had suffered from criticism in England and America over their handling of Greek problems during the troubles of December 1944, had deeply impressed the Russians. The picture of events in Greece which the evidence of the Commission could be arranged to present might prevent Great Britain or America from effectively intervening in Greece.

In manipulating the affairs of the Commission, the Communists showed a single-minded tenacity and technique which the Western delegates could seldom match. The representatives of the plaintiff and defendant countries (Greece, Albania, Yugoslavia and Bulgaria), accredited to the Commission simply as liason officers, were soon permitted, as the result of Soviet persistence, to attend all meetings except the restricted sessions, and to interrogate any witness in exactly the same manner as members of the Commission.[38] This at once reinforced the position of the Soviet Union and Poland among the other members of the Commission and indeed, more critically, placed the Greek liaison representative at a grave disadvantage, since any question, assertion, or deposition, put forward by him was generally countered by five contrary statements of the Communist allies. Indeed, by the time all four liaison countries had introduced their cases, Yugoslavia, Albania and Bulgaria had been explaining their views with copious quotations from the Western press for seven days while the Greek representative had spoken only for one hour and fifteen minutes.[39] By unremitting persistence and interminable repetition the Communists exhausted the time at the Commission's disposal and the patience of other delegates. Seventy-five per cent of the time spent on questioning witnesses was used up by Communist interrogators who turned away from the circumstances of border incidents, from any debate of the public statements of Yugoslav ambitions in Macedonia[40] which could hardly have been denied, and continually forced the discussion back to the familiar themes: the undemocratic monarcho-fascist origins of the Greek government, the presence of the British troops which kept it in power, the persecution of democratic parties, the imprisonment and execution of former resistance fighters, and the territorial claims of Greece on her northern neighbours tabled at the Peace Conference which proved the government's imperialistic designs and were indeed the true cause of border incidents.

In keeping with their attempt to monopolize the debate, the Communists pressed the Commission to hear the views of any organization which would endorse and repeat their interpretation of events. Of seven Greek organizations which brought their testimony to the Commission no fewer than five had Communist affiliations[41] or sympathies, including EAM itself and the General Confederation of Labour. The latter organization, although re-formed since 1945, remained morally within the orbit of EAM. Circumstances could hardly allow it an independent position. Before the Commission its spokesman dwelt on the oppression of organized labour. Fear, insecurity and revenge which governed the behaviour of many supporters of the Right, as well as the security measures which became more stringent as breaches of law and order increased, provided genuine material for those who wished to make a case against the government. And to give emphasis to the formal evidence of favourable witnesses the Greek Communist Party was present to stage demonstrations outside the buildings where the Commission held its deliberations. These, then, were the scenes played out before the representatives of the international press, whose rights to be present during the work of the Commission were consistently defended by the delegate of the Soviet Union.

There was, of course, little prospect that the non-Communist members of the Commission would be persuaded by the Soviet Union's case or the evidence of its allies. Apart from the political prejudgments which some of these delegates brought with them the Communists' procedural tactics soon alienated whatever sympathy might originally have existed. As the Communist delegates worked ponderously through their repetitious statements and interrogations other members took to writing letters and reading newspapers. Although the Commission sat in Athens from 30 January to 18 February and in Salonika from 25 February to 22 March and subsequently spent only three days in Sofia and four days in Belgrade, brief field-trips, made from Salonika to and beyond the Yugoslav and Bulgarian borders with Greece, and a visit to the camp at Bulkes from Belgrade, were enough to convince the majority of the Commission that the traffic across Greece's northern borders was not restricted to political refugees but included in the opposite direction numbers of armed men and quantities of supplies.

The *mise en scène* of a public conflict in words which had characterized the Commission from the beginning continued at the report stage. The Soviet Union refused at any point to be bound by a majority decision or to be satisfied with simply indicating its disagreement. Since numbers were irrelevant, it insisted on the tabling of a second parallel report for which it claimed in principle an equivalent validity. The contents of the two reports were unsurprising.[42] Eight of the eleven members accepted the majority report. The Soviet Union and Poland opposed it, France abstained.

The report concluded that Yugoslavia, and to a lesser degree Albania and Bulgaria, had supported guerrilla warfare in Greece. It found that in Yugoslavia most of the activity had centred upon the camp at Bulkes where the Yugoslavs indoctrinated, trained and equipped Greek refugees for guerrilla war in Greece.[43] The report also found that the Yugoslav and Bulgarian governments had promoted a separatist movement among Slav minorities in Greek Macedonia. It agreed that the domestic situation in Greece had contributed to civil war in northern Greece and in other parts of the country. This was partly attributable to the activities of the Greek Communist Party; but also to the fact that the Slavophone and Muslim minorities in Macedonia and Epirus 'had been victims of retaliatory excesses'. This, in the view of the Commission, had encouraged the formation of groups hostile to the government. Yet this did not relieve Greece's northern neighbours of the duty not to assist subversive attempts against another government. The argument of the minority report followed closely the themes elaborated in the statement of the liaison representatives of Yugoslavia, Bulgaria and Albania. We need not repeat them here.[44] The Commission's report included its recommendations; that the four countries should resume normal relations; that the refusal of any government to cease aiding guerrillas should be considered by the Security Council as a threat to peace within the meaning of the Charter of the UN; that a small commission of representatives of states, not permanent members of the Security Council, should be established to investigate future violations of the frontier.

The Yugoslavs were immediately hostile to this last suggestion. The existence of such a commission implied a presumption of guilt directed at Greece's neighbours. It could not travel and interview witnesses in Yugoslavia without that country's consent. To do otherwise, it was argued, would be a violation of Yugoslavia's sovereignty. On 29 July 1947, at the Security Council, an American resolution which adopted in substance the Commission's proposals was supported by nine of the eleven members but inevitably failed to pass the Soviet veto.

On the Commission itself one non-Communist, M. Daux, the representative of France, had declined to associate himself with the conclusions of the majority. He doubted whether one could consider particular events in abstraction from the history of the Balkans since 1940. Moreover, formal conclusions implied attributing responsibility to one party or another. This could only prejudice the true work of the Commission which was pacification and conciliation.[45] In fact, one must conclude that conciliation of the kind which M. Daux had in mind was never the purpose of either of the principal parties. The Americans were already investigating the needs of the Greek economy when Greece tabled her complaint at the Security Council. On 3 February, a few days after the Commission began its work in Athens, the American Ambassador in Greece, McVeagh, was reporting rumours that the British would soon be forced to withdraw their aid. Only a fortnight later, on 18 February, Mark Ethridge (the American delegate on the Commission) required no further evidence to report that all the signs pointed to an impending move by the Communists to seize the country.[46] By 24 February, the British had served notice that they must withdraw from Greece on the first of April. Ethridge's view confirmed other reports which Truman had received about the character of the Greek insurgency. Once the decision had been taken to resist the establishment of Communist régimes in countries not originally occupied by the Soviet army and the message, promising aid to Greece and Turkey, which came to be known as the Truman Doctrine,[47] had been delivered to a joint session of Congress on 12 March 1947, American policy at the UN became principally concerned with justifying this policy of material as well as moral opposition to any extension of Communist jurisdiction.

The view that the Russians were fundamentally reasonable people if properly treated, was still held by many Americans. Traditional isolationism supported the natural wish to bring the 'boys' back home, to stop wasting good American money abroad, and to avoid the charge of imperialism which the Americans had so often levelled at the British. There was, too, that deeply rooted suspicion that Americans were being asked again 'to pull British chestnuts out of the fire'. If it was true that by the end of 1946 a majority in the nation understood that America must play a leading international role it was generally assumed that this leadership would be exercised economically and virtuously through the agency of the UN. Thus the Truman Doctrine was a confusing and disturbing development for many Americans, not only because it seemed to raise the real possibility of war with Russia, but also because it indicated an early disillusionment with the role of the UN on which Americans, more than sceptical Europeans, had set their hopes. Critics in America objected to the President announcing his plans as a national policy rather than as suggestions to be laid before the UN. For them it would have been preferable if aid to Greece had been offered and administered indirectly through the institutions of the UN. Not surprisingly the Russians made the same suggestion when the relation of American Aid to the work of the UN investigating Commission was debated in the Security Council in April. In a belated defence of his position, the President argued in the Jefferson Day Speech on 5 April 1947 that the new Doctrine was intended to support, not to disregard, the work of the UN.

The truth, in fact, was the reverse. The President had to rally whatever support he could muster at the UN to justify to the American public his uncompromising stand. In this context, numbers were important. The presumption was that the majority at the UN represented those countries which truly lived in the spirit of the Charter. Some of the sting of domestic criticism was drawn by relating foreign aid to this principle. When the Bill came before the Senate Foreign Relations Committee, Senator Vandenberg introduced an amendment which required the abandonment of the programme if at any time a majority in either the Security Council or the General Assembly disapproved of its aims or progress.[48] By this concession and helped by the gradual hardening of public opinion as the methods used in Stalin's arrangement of his eastern security zone became more clear and less acceptable (for instance, in January 1947 at the Polish elections and in February in the purging of the Hungarian Smallholders' Party, events which only gradually and cumulatively altered established views), Truman was able to move beyond the Bill for aid to Greece and Turkey, signed on 22 May, to a more general defensive economic recovery programme for Europe, the Marshall Plan, which was unveiled by the Secretary of State at Harvard on 5 June. Already by the end of that month Soviet Russia had declined to participate in it and the definition of the division in Europe had become uncomfortably precise.

It was against this background that the Security Council had debated the report of its Commission on border incidents. As we have seen its recommendations were vetoed by Soviet Russia on 29 July. The next step was to bring the Greek problem before the General Assembly in the autumn in the form of an American resolution embodying the Commission's proposals which, on 21 October, after bitter debate, was carried by 40 votes to 6 with 11 abstentions.[49] To this the Communist response was a Russian resolution proposing 'measures to be taken against propaganda and the inciters of a new war'. It condemned, in particular, the criminal war propaganda of the United States, Greece and Turkey. It called for action against its circulation, a reduction in armaments, and the control of atomic weapons. In this form the resolution was predictably lost. For the Russians, however, numbers were not important. Only the riposte and its political content, as an act of international presence, mattered.

The conflict in debate was faithfully reflected in the membership of the new United Nations Special Committee on the Balkans (UNSCOB) established through the American resolution on 21 October 1947. Russia and Poland were elected to membership but both declined to take part. There were tactical reasons which also influenced this withdrawal. Despite their mastery of procedural techniques the Russians had not overcome their Western opponents on the earlier Commission. The benefit in propaganda had perhaps been disappointing. And they had found the experience of an international commission making critical investigations on Communist territory acutely uncomfortable. Stalin, moreover, was cautiously assessing the American stand in Greece, and also possibly, with some suspicion, the exuberant negotiations of Tito with other Balkan leaders. In these circumstances the Russians avoided the possible embarrassments of formal membership of a UN committee concerned with an area where policies might have to be reversed or at last severely revised. It is apparent that the Russians valued membership on the earlier Commission on Greek border incidents when in fact their concealed intentions were the opposite of conciliatory; and declined membership in UNSCOB when, as a result of American resistance and suspicions of Yugoslav indiscipline, their policy had become more temperate. It was precisely the realities of this policy which had to be disguised. The refusal of Poland and Russia to serve on the Committee, the accusations of Greek violations of the frontier by that country's three Communist neighbours, and their general hostility towards UNSCOB's efforts at conciliation on the frontier partly served this purpose.

Without Russia and Poland, UNSCOB consisted of Australia, Brazil, China, France, Mexico, the Netherlands, Pakistan, the United Kingdom and the United States. It became a Commission hardly remarkable for its sympathy with the Communist case. Through its reports [50] it made public the gradual accumulation of evidence which, in its view, revealed the scale of external support for the Greek guerrillas. War supplies and other materials were received from Albania, Yugoslavia and Bulgaria. The frontier itself was used as a haven by wounded rebels and hard-pressed guerrilla units. And the rebellion was given moral and propaganda backing by a radio transmitter near Belgrade. The report published on 2 August 1949 [51] dealing with the period after the Soviet-Yugoslav dispute, indicated a variation in the pattern. As Yugoslav aid gradually diminished, Romania had become host to the radio station and cared for the wounded. Similarly, in a special report[52] published on 21 May 1948 UNSCOB provided evidence for the charge that the Greek Democratic Army had sent large numbers of Greek children across the northern frontier for care and indoctrination. Some, it was claimed later, returned as trained boy-soldiers to fight in the war. The traffic in children was peculiarly damaging to the rebels' reputation, for although some were the children of willing supporters of the guerrillas, a greater number were involuntary hostages. In Greece itself, the parallel with the conscription of Christian children for service in the Janissary corps under Ottoman rule was a propaganda theme with subtle psychological effects. And since the Communists claimed that the children were refugees escaping from the alternative fate of hostages in the hands of monarcho-fascists, their return was embarrassingly difficult after the effects on world opinion of their removal had become evident. At the end of the civil war only a few of the 25,000 children had returned.

Did UNSCOB serve to deter intervention? Its effectiveness in making plain the interference of Greece's Communist neighbours in her internal affairs is not in doubt. The ability to check these activities is less clear. The Committee itself claimed that its existence had this result. It is probable that while it did not prevent the passage of armed men and materials across the frontier it made it desirable to conceal this traffic from view as far as was possible. It probably suggested, also, limits to the number of advisers and volunteers from north of the frontier. In these respects it may have restricted the numbers of men and the volume of supplies that might otherwise have passed.

It has to be remembered that throughout the war Albania, Yugoslavia and Bulgaria doggedly persisted in claiming that they had given no support to General Markos's men beyond the offer of political asylum to persecuted democrats. In the presence of UNSCOB's observers some caution was needed if these statements were to appear even formally credible. Russian policy, no doubt, required that they remained so. There was one occasion shortly after the formation of UNSCOB when it used a more threatening tone. On Christmas Eve 1947, Markos announced the establishment of the Greek Provisional Government. On 29 December, UNSCOB adopted a resolution declaring that even *de facto* recognition of this government, followed by aid to the insurrectionary movement, would constitute a grave threat to international peace and security. If there was evidence of association between the provisional régime and the Balkan governments UNSCOB would call a special session of the General Assembly. The following day the American State Department issued an almost similar declaration.[53] To the chagrin of the Greek Communists these warnings were heeded.[54]

The agreeable consistency between American policy and UNSCOB's find-ings did not go unremarked. Although the Committee gave some attention to the problems of refugees and the treatment of ethnic minorities it is true that it used most of its time and resources in watching the frontier for assumed illegal traffic from the north. Unlike its forerunner, the Security Council's Investigating Commission, it was not forced to consider in detail the behaviour of the legitimate Greek government as a cause of its own threatened collapse. In the General Assembly debate in October 1948 Com-munist delegates argued that Greece had become an American colony,[55] that the establishment of UNSCOB was contrary to the Charter, that its reports were based on insubstantial rumour (since it had been denied access to the countries north of Greece), and that its personnel, particularly in the observer groups, was so largely American that the character of UNSCOB as an agency of imperialism could not be doubted.

Although no non-Communist countries were willing to make accusations of comparable severity, three members of UNSCOB (Australia, Pakistan and Brazil) expressed disquiet about the emphasis in the Committee's work on the defence of Greece and the absence of any real effort towards conciliation. The Australian delegate in the Assembly debate of October 1948 said that UNSCOB had gone beyond its powers in investigating, instead of merely observing, incidents, particularly since the observers had no access to three of the four countries concerned and had to rely on witnesses from only one of them.[56] Underlying this argument was the belief that the attribution of responsibility to particular countries only made conciliation more difficult. An Australian resolution was carried in the Political and Security Com-mittee on 10 November 1948, providing for a meeting in Paris[57] of the four Balkan countries with the Australian President of the Assembly (Dr Evatt), the Secretary-General, the chairman of the Political Committee (Mr Spaak) and its rapporteur (Mr Sarper).

The perhaps naïve hope that the more private atmosphere of the negotiat-ing table with the mediation of UN officers, uninfluenced by the great powers, would provide a reasonable solution was soon removed. On 14 December 1948, Dr Evatt revealed that the first attempts had failed. Part of the Communist terms for a settlement leading to a renewal of diplomatic relations with Greece had been the recognition of the existing Greek-Albanian frontier as definitive. It was well understoood that this was a concession which nationalist Greeks could not easily or willingly offer. The predictable refusal threw the onus of the breakdown on the Greeks and renewed the charge of Greece's potentially aggressive intentions.

Almost a year later, on 28 September 1949, when the fighting in Greece had virtually ended, the Australian delegate again proposed in the First Committee that a new conciliation group should be established.[58] As before, the four UN officers met with the representatives of the four Balkan countries, and on this occasion also with the representatives of the United States, the Soviet Union and Great Britain. On 18 October, the committee admitted its failure in circumstances almost similar to those of the previous year. The Russians had insisted on Greek acceptance of the existing frontier with Albania and once again the Greeks refused. Military victory did not encourage them to reconsider a fundamental concession they had already declined to give when their affairs had been at a lower ebb; yet the defeat of the Greek Communists put the Russians and their allies in a position where, for reasons of prestige, they did not wish to ask for anything less. Their clients had been defeated in the field, there was no need for them to suffer a further reverse in negotiations. Even as the exhausted contestants laid down their arms the UN could achieve nothing towards conciliation.

There is a sense in which the efforts of the UN to end the civil war in Greece were almost irrelevant to the outcome. Tito's decision to close the frontier between Greece and Yugoslavia in 1949 had made it impossible for the Greek Communists to stave off a defeat which had already been prepared by the military supplies and economic aid for the government introduced in massive quantities by the Americans. American aid provided for victory and, by persuading the Greeks that the United States would not allow the National Government to be defeated, drew to its support those who merely waited to discover which side would win. Meanwhile, by the end of 1947, Stalin had decided to avoid a critical confrontation with America over Greece. The American monopoly of atomic weapons at this time and his country's industrial inferiority hardly permitted such a folly. It was, nevertheless, a period of Soviet expansion, encouraged at least in the beginning by uncertain evidence of American resolution, and marked by Stalin's speech in February 1946 in which he proclaimed that the Soviet system would never be secure until the capitalist encirclement of the Communist countries had been reversed.[59] There were reasons, then, for continuing to support the rebellion. Soviet prestige and authority within the Russian security bloc of East European countries would have been greatly damaged if the Greek comrades had been immediately abandoned. Moreover, the solidarity and discipline of the countries under Russian protection, the tightening of political controls in Russia itself, and the relative segregation of the populations of these countries from too easy contact with the West, required a condition of tension, a state at least of balanced opposition, along the newly defined frontier between the Communist world and the rest of Europe.

In Greece this could be achieved by limited and indirect hostilities. Fighting was restricted almost entirely to the local contestants in a civil war in which the United States materially supported the legitimate government but did not commit her soldiers in a combatant role; and Russia gave only moral support to the insurgents but allowed her satellite allies to provide camps on their territory and limited quantities of war supplies. The crucial advantage which the Communist governments conferred on the rebels by allowing them to use their frontiers as a tactical refuge could be conveniently confused in debate with the offer of political asylum to refugees. The Yugoslavs probably permitted a limited number of Macedonian volunteers, who were not easily distinguishable from Slavophone Greeks, to fight in the ranks of the Democratic Army. No formations of foreign troops, however, took part in the war on either side. In Greece itself the inactive but symbolic presence of British troops marked the choice between civil and international war.

These conditions in themselves did not necessarily constitute a stable system of safe and balanced opposition. The very caution of Stalin and Tito in not provoking the Americans by admitting that Communist governments were giving the insurgents practical aid made it difficult for the American Administration to justify to its own public an uncompromising intervention in Greek affairs. Meanwhile, General Markos had unexpected success. At the end of January 1947, by using classic hit-and-run tactics, he already controlled a hundred villages. The impotence of the Greek government was so grave that delay in replacing and increasing the aid which the British could no longer maintain was leading rapidly to a crisis. In this dilemma the Americans might be forced to intervene with armed force in circumstances where a Russian response that could preserve Soviet prestige and avoid the threat of war might be hard to compose. Thus the importance of the Truman Doctrine was not only that it gave the Greek government the physical and financial means to survive the insurgent attack, but that it was proclaimed in time to set a limit to the extent of foreign Communist intervention before this had been already overstepped.

It was a significant although unintended consequence of UN action that the early reports of the American delegate on the Security Council Investigating Commission confirmed Truman's growing conviction that Greece was in peril, and provided the assurance that an offer of American aid would be internationally justified by the report of the Commission. It was, consequently, important that the Russians agreed to the American proposal to establish the Commission. And that subsequently, when the Truman Doctrine was announced, they did not deny that Greece needed aid but criticized the programme essentially on the grounds that it ought to be administered by officials of the UN and not manipulated to consolidate a political position in Greece. It is probable, of course, that the Russians agreed to the establishment of the Commission because they wanted to expose

Greece's domestic persecutions and embarrass the government in its measures against the guerrillas. But in this we can see that the Russians had discovered that the institutions of the UN offered certain advantages in carrying into practice their delicately balanced policy of limited aggression. This sometimes required an awkward withdrawal which in the international setting of the Security Council, or the Assembly, could be virtuously offered in the spirit of peace, and could be completed without indignity. The veto itself was a bargaining counter for a power whose resolutions were normally outvoted at the Security Council.

Principally, however, Russia valued the UN because through the Security Council she was permanently in touch with her chief adversary in a multilateral context where serious disputes between the two powers could be publicly debated with less inflexibility and risk than in a direct negotiation, and in terms of a competitive concern for the peace of the world which neither wished to deny. It is arguable that the Russians would have found it difficult to agree in direct negotiations with the Americans to accept a commission on Greek border incidents which, whatever advantages it might offer for propaganda, was empowered to investigate on Communist territories. Similarly, without their involvement in the UN it is doubtful if the Russians could have publicly regarded the Truman Doctrine as other than a direct attack on themselves. Particularly in the context of UN affairs, the Russians claimed to appear as the true champions of peace against the warmongers of the West. Indeed, in making effective use of the world organization as a platform for this kind of accusation, they had some success in attacking official policy in America and in building up opposition to it in the electorates of America's allies. But the assumption of this role meant the acceptance of some restraints. Since the Communist countries would not admit they were actively assisting the insurgents the presence of UNSCOB observers probably inhibited in some degree the flow of men and supplies across the frontier. Nor would the Russians recognize, or allow their satellite allies to recognize, the establishment of a provisional government, on Christmas Eve 1947, by General Markos, although he may have been encouraged to take this step by Tito and Dimitrov as a response to the American Aid Bill. In themselves such constraints were unwelcome. Yet they checked and, in a manner, institutionalized Communist participation in the civil war; and in that sense contributed to the safe expression of the Russian policy of limited hostility.

The Russians needed an enemy (for reasons which have been suggested), but they had no need to invent one. Nevertheless, the immediacy and credibility of the threat depended on hostile exchanges and, as we have seen, these in any form of direct military or even political action were restricted in their possible severity. In their place the lengthy, repetitious and often abusive debates at the Security Council and the General Assembly, and, on the issue which concerns us here, the Commission for investigating Greek border incidents, served as a setting for reciprocal accusation and insult, the significance of which may be too easily discounted.

The UN became a form of international political theatre in which ritual gestures of opposition could be safely exchanged between the protagonists in a situation of some abstraction from the conditions of conventional diplomatic relations. Because of the assumed bonds of international community between its members and the indirect multilateral form of discussions, degrees of hostility could be shown in debate at the UN which, if they had been expressed in direct diplomatic notes, might have been interpreted as severing relations. These, one must remember, were the early years of the UN in which many governments and ordinary people had invested their hopes for peace. Meetings of the Assembly, the Security Council, and the different committees, still held a dramatic moral quality. Debates over the issues of the Greek Civil War were often reported in the non-Communist press, particularly in radical and socialist newspapers, in editorial comment unflattering to the American case. These were important and plausible sources which Communist propaganda used to convince the public in Russia and the satellite states that the threat along the frontier of their eastern bloc was indeed real.

It cannot be claimed that if the UN had not existed, or had not taken the actions which it did, that it would not have been possible for the Americans and the Russians with their attendant allies to support the two sides to the civil war without themselves directly entering the fighting. A fact of crucial importance was that neither side wanted to go to war over Greece. Nevertheless, it is reasonable to suggest that the UN created a safer environment for this limited struggle. Partly this was so because the United States, Russia and Great Britain as the principal powers at the UN had roles and obligations in the Organization which, for subtly different reasons in each case, none of them was willing to abandon. They were forced to maintain close relations over the issue even if these were hostile relations. It is true, as some have said, that this hostile co-existence within the UN where each side attributed the misdeameanours of the other 'to the very nature of the opponent's social and political system' gravely increased the tension; at the same time, however, it also contained it and offered a form of release.

The UN was not able to prevent the civil war breaking out, a war whose domestic origin was almost immediately and inextricably bound to the aims of conflicting foreign states. It could not materially stem its course, nor fundamentally alter the outcome. Yet the war ended without the fighting passing beyond the borders of Greece or involving the troops of other nations. For this not inconsiderable blessing the UN shares a measure of the credit.[60]

TEXT REFERENCES

1. For the situation during the early months of the occupation see, C. M. Woodhouse, *Apple of Discord*, London 1948, Chapter 2, *passim*; and D. George Kousoulas, *Revolution and Defeat*, London 1965, Chapter 11. For Greece under Metaxas see, John Campbell and Philip Sherrard, *Modern Greece*, London 1968, pp.157–163.
2. During the dictatorship of Metaxas Velouchiotis had signed a declaration of 'repentance'.
3. Kousoulas, op. cit., p.147.
4. Woodhouse, op. cit., pp.146–7.
5. Ibid., pp.137–8.
6. Robert Lee Wolff, *The Balkans in Our Time*, Cambridge Mass. 1956, pp.259–64.
7. Woodhouse, op. cit., p.144.
8. Ibid., p.306.
9. Kousoulas, op. cit., p.201.
10. Wolff, op. cit., p.266.
11. The agreement signed on 12 February 1946 between the Greek Government and EAM delegates. For the text see, Woodhouse, op. cit., p.308.
12. Brzezinski, Zbigniew K., *The Soviet Bloc* (rev. ed.), Cambridge Mass. 1967, pp.25–32.
13. This was less marked in relations between Serbs and Greeks.
14. Kousoulas, op. cit., p.233.
15. O'Ballance, Edgar, *The Greek Civil War 1944–1949*, London 1966, p.121.
16. Shoup, Paul, *Communism and the Yugoslav National Question*, New York and London 1968, p.153, pp.157–8.
17. At this time the Slavophone population in Greece was probably about 120,000. Cf. R. V. Burks, *The Dynamics of Communism in Eastern Europe*, Princeton 1961, p.104.
18. *Documents on International Affairs 1947–48*, RIIA, London 1952, p.322.
19. Djilas, Milovan, *Conversations with Stalin*, London 1962, p.164.
20. Ulam, Adam B., *Expansion and Coexistence*, London 1968, p.408.
21. Ibid., p.412.
22. Xydis, Stephen G., *Greece and The Great Powers 1944–1947*, Salonika 1963, p.65.
23. Ibid., p.109.
24. UN Security Council, *Official Records*, 1st Year, 1st Series, no.1, p.15.
25. Ibid., pp.73–4.
26. Cmd. 6812, HMSO, London 1946.
27. Xydis, op. cit., pp.270–84.
28. UN Security Council, *Official Records*, 1st year, 2nd series, no.4, pp.33–39; no.5, pp.145–9; no.6, pp.153–71; no.7, pp. 173–97; no.8, pp.200–12; no.9, pp.214–56; no.10, pp.260–81; no.11, pp.284–97; no.12, pp.300–21; no.13, pp.324–41; no.14, pp.344–64; no.15, pp.365–92; no.16, pp.393–422.
29. Ibid., no.7, pp.180–9.
30. Ibid., no.9, pp.241–9.
31. Ibid., no.16, pp.410–12.
32. O'Ballance, Edgar, op. cit., p.128.
33. Rizospastis, 21 November 1946

34. Foreign Office, *Report of the British Parliamentary Delegation to Greece*, London August 1946, HMSO, 1947.

35. UN Security Council, *Official Records*, 1st year, 2nd series, no.24, pp.529-59; no.25, pp.563-83; no.26, pp.588-613; no.27, pp.615-36; no.28, pp.639-46.

36. Ibid., no.25, pp.564-80.

37. Ibid., no.28, pp.639-46.

38. Edgar F. Puryear, Jr., 'Communist Negotiating Techniques: A Case Study of the United Nations Security Council Commission of Investigation Concerning the Greek Frontier Incidents', unpublished Ph.D. thesis, Princeton University 1959, p.161.

39. Ibid., p.216.

40. Ibid., pp.325-6.

41. Ibid., p.192.

42. Report by the Commission of Investigation Concerning Greek Frontier Incidents to the Security Council, Document S/360, 23 May 1947.

43. Ibid., Vol.I, pp.167-82.

44. Ibid., Vol.I, pp.183-238.

45. Ibid., Vol.I, p.245.

46. Harry S. Truman, *Years of Trial and Hope 1946-53*, London 1956, p.105.

47. Documents on International Affairs 1947-48, RIIA, London 1952, pp.2-7.

48. Millis, Walter (ed.), *The Forrestal Diaries*, London 1952, pp.252-3, 256-7.

49. UN *Official Records*, Second Session, General Assembly, Resolutions, pp.12-14, 109 (11).

50. UN *Official Records*, Third Session, General Assembly, Supplement no.8, 'Report of the United Nations Special Committee on the Balkans', New York 1948. (Period to 16 June 1948.)

Ibid., Supplementary Report no.8a, Paris 1948. (Covering the period 17 June to 10 September 1948.)

Ibid., annexes, Paris 1948. (Covering the period 11 September to 22 October 1948.)

51. UN *Official Records*, Fourth Session, General Assembly, Supplement no.8, Report of UNSCOB, New York 1949.

52. Published in the first UNSCOB report noted above.

53. *Documents on International Affairs 1947-1948*, RIIA, London, 1952, p.323.

54. Kousoulas, op. cit., 1965, p.249.

55. UN Doc. A/C.1./S.R.177.

56. UN Doc. A/574, Annex IV.

57. UN Doc. A/728; A/C.1./380. For an extended account of these attempts at conciliation see, Harry N. Howard, 'Greece and Its Balkan Neighbours (1948-49)', in *Balkan Studies*, 7, Salonika 1966.

58. UN Doc. A/C.1./481.

59. Brzezinski, op. cit., p.44.

60. I wish to thank Dr. R. K. Kindersley for reading and criticizing the manuscript of this chapter.

4 THE LEBANESE CIVIL WAR

Malcolm Kerr

Lebanese politics in some ways resemble those of many American cities. The population of about two million is roughly comparable to that, say, of Philadelphia; its religious and ethnic divisions (seven major religious sects, and a large number of Armenians in the city of Beirut) might be compared to an American urban mixture of Italians, Irish, Negroes, and Jews; the various communities tend to compete, not always on equal terms, for public works, patronage, and educational benefits. There is also the fine art of machine politics practised by district bosses, conducted on the basis of personal prestige, distribution of favours, minority grievances, and a good bit of skulduggery.

Lebanon is a country and not just a city, even if a third of the population does live in Beirut. Machine politics in the city operate differently from machine politics in rural areas; the city is the natural arena of demagogues, the country of semi-feudal landowners. There are not one or two machines competing for power, but ten or fifteen, none of which extends beyond a handful of parliamentary constituencies. A national election in Lebanon is composed of a scattered series of local contests in the various districts, each of which produces its own conflict of issues and organizations as well as personalities.

Furthermore, as an independent country rather than as a mere city, Lebanon lacks the broader political and social framework afforded to cities elsewhere by the existence of a national government and hinterland. This means that, on the one hand, all types of issues – national as well as municipal – are eligible to be raised in Lebanon, including the most funda-mental constitutional questions; while, on the other hand, lacking the safety-valve of a wider national political scene, political life goes on in a parochial atmosphere, and the full attention of politically-minded persons is necessarily devoted to local issues. The ambitious politician and the dis-satisfied minority cannot look beyond the confines of the local scene to find

65

an appropriate outlet – not, at least, without internationalizing Lebanon's problems. In this sense, Lebanon is a Brooklyn or a Baltimore cut off from the United States, a hothouse of local issues without the ventilating currents even of New York City, let alone Washington. The parliamentary democracy and rule of law that the country has enjoyed cannot rest on the support of anyone but the tiny and refracted population of Lebanon itself. Conversely, however, this situation offers a standing invitation for outsiders to become involved, usually disruptively.

These institutions have been subjected to severe strains on several occasions since the constitution was first introduced in 1926, and more particularly since Lebanon achieved her independence from France in 1943. Much the most dramatic and serious of these occasions was the crisis of 1958, when the parochial quarrels of Lebanese factions became closely entangled with international conflicts in the Near Eastern hinterland over which Lebanon had no control.

The political system rests on two somewhat contradictory principles: liberal democracy on the one hand, and a predetermined division of roles among the religious communities on the other. The constitution of 1926 reflects the general provisions of that of France under the Third Republic: a President of the Republic, a Council of Ministers responsible to an elected Chamber of Deputies, freedom of political organization, and the basic personal liberties of speech, worship, assembly, press, and so forth. But once independence was achieved, the Lebanese President became a much more powerful personage than the President of France, as he inherited the extensive authority of the French High Commissioner of the colonial period.

There is no reference in the constitution itself to the political status of any religious group, but only a loosely worded provision that government posts should be spread on a reasonable basis among the communities. This provision, taken at face value, would not necessarily detract from the liberal and secular character of political life, nor require any institutionalization of the position of confessional groups. But it has been implemented, through customary practice as well as through the electoral laws enacted by the parliament, in such an elaborate and precise manner as to become the second great principle of political organization, pointing in a very different direction from the first.

By rigid custom, the President of the Republic must be a Maronite Catholic (an adherent of a peculiarly Lebanese rite loosely tied to Rome), the Prime Minister a Sunni Moslem, and the Speaker of the Chamber of Deputies a Shi'ite Moslem. The Commander-in-Chief of the army and the director of the internal security service are invariably Maronites. Somewhat more flexibly, the cabinet seats are distributed among all major sects

66

in rough proportion to their size: a typical cabinet would include three Maronites, three Sunnis, and two from each of the Shi'ite, Druse, Greek Orthodox, and Greek Catholic sects. Civil service, police, army, and diplomatic positions are also supposed to be equitably apportioned; but in practice the Christian groups, and especially the Maronites, tend to hold an advantage, as a legacy of their traditional predominance and their higher educational level; while the Shi'ite Moslems, who populate the most backward rural areas, have been considerably underrepresented.

The most detailed application of sectarianism is found in the electoral system. The number of Deputies has fluctuated from one election to the next as the law was amended, but since 1943 always in multiples of eleven: 44, 66, 99, etc. This has enabled a permanent proportion of six Christians to five Moslems (the Druses being considered as Moslems for this purpose) to be elected. Each seat is reserved for candidates of a particular sect. Since 1960, for example, the 99 seats have been apportioned to include 54 Christians and 45 Moslems, broken down among 30 Maronites, 11 Greek Orthodox, 6 Greek Catholic, 4 Armenian Orthodox, one Armenian Catholic, one Protestant, one miscellaneous Christian minorities, 20 Sunnis, 19 Shi'ites, and 6 Druses. These blocs are supposed to reflect the proportional size of each community; as no census has been taken since 1932, however, no one can be sure how equitable the numbers really are. If, as is widely believed, the Moslem groups have, for some time, constituted a slight majority in the country, the preponderance assigned to the Christians rests only on an agreed fiction.

Be that as it may, the division of offices as described above has long been essential to the survival of the fragile consensus upon which the survival of the Lebanese state depends, for it provides each group with a minimum assurance not only that its leaders will enjoy office but also that its interests will be respected. The formula was negotiated between the leading politicians on the eve of independence in 1943, and was accompanied by a compromise understanding regarding vital questions of Lebanon's foreign relationships, about which Christians and Moslems generally held very different views. Most Christians, especially Maronites, attached the strongest importance to the continued independence of the country from her predominantly Moslem neighbour, Syria; correspondingly, they had traditionally looked to the West, especially to France, for both cultural and economic ties and for political protection. Furthermore, the very large numbers of Lebanese who had emigrated in recent generations to North and South America were overwhelmingly Christian, and their relatives and fellow-villagers who remained behind felt close bonds with them. Conversely, most Lebanese Moslems, especially the Sunnis, felt more kinship with their coreligionists in Syria and other Arab countries than with the Lebanese Christians, and regarded their identity as citizens of a Christian-dominated, Western-affiliated Lebanese state as somewhat irksome at best. Accordingly, the 'National Pact' of the politicians of 1943 sought to compromise between these loyalties, by assuring the Christians that Western culture, while assuring the Moslems that within this limit she would cultivate close relations with other Arab states and renounce all forms of European political protection. The provision for a Christian President and a Moslem Prime Minister, as well as the remaining division of offices, would stand as a practical guarantee of this compromise.

Bolstered by all these arrangements, Lebanon embarked on independence, and all was well as long as certain conditions prevailed. One was that the Sunni Moslems should be represented by a vigorous Prime Minister capable of defending their interests in the face of the extensive powers of the Christian President. Secondly, it was important that the elaborate sharing out of offices should not fall prey to a game of systematic manipulation by an overambitious President, again using these same powers; for this could produce a crisis, not between the sects, but within each of them, as confidence in the parliamentary and electoral system was eroded. A third danger was that the considerable immobility that inevitably afflicted the parliament and the administration might render the country incapable of responding to needs of social and economic reform as they arose. Fourth, and most important, Lebanon's tranquillity was bound to depend on a minimum level of good relations between the Western world, to which the Christian communities generally turned their faces, and the Arab world, with which the Moslems identified.

The lapse of the first three of these conditions led, in September 1952, to a major crisis in which President Bishara El-Khoury was forced to resign. In his place the Chamber of Deputies elected Camille Chamoun to a six-year term. Chamoun possessed a number of qualities that fitted him for success. A Maronite and a Lebanese patriot, he none the less enjoyed a reputation for favouring cooperation with the Arab states, and sympathizing, more than most members of his sect, with the aspirations of the Arab nationalist movement. Like many Lebanese politicians, he combined a modest provincial family background with cosmopolitan education and experience: education in both French and English, a successful law practice, a wife of Anglo-Lebanese parentage, periods serving as Minister of the Interior and Ambassador to the Court of St James, great personal charm, and, last but not least, a strong instinct for the Byzantine personal intrigues and shifting alliances of Lebanese electoral and administrative politics. It was this last quality that eventually contributed to Chamoun's downfall, for after a promising beginning he developed overweening ambitions and made more enemies than he could afford.

By 1957 all four of the conditions necessary for Lebanon's political prosperity withered away. The Prime Minister, Sami Es-Sulh, was an ageing and ineffectual Ottoman-educated politician of the coffeehouse variety, a man of considerable local experience and personal popularity but very limited in his horizons and incapable of grasping either the problems of rapid change in Lebanese society or those of an increasingly turbulent world beyond, which was increasingly dominated by the militant trend of Arab nationalism and the cold-war rivalry of the United States and the Soviet Union for influence in the Near East. Sulh was adept at the daily political game of patronage and favours and electoral manoeuvre; amid the great issues, he was out of his depth. Increasingly, he became an unwitting instrument of Chamoun, and lost the confidence of his own Sunni Moslem community.

Meanwhile, with the approach of the 1957 parliamentary elections, Chamoun developed an ambition to secure his own re-election to a new term, beyond the expiry of his first term in September 1958. The constitution forbade this, but the constitution could be amended for this purpose by a two-thirds majority vote of the Chamber of Deputies; in fact, there was a precedent for this, as Bishara El-Khoury had secured a second term in this manner after rigging the parliamentary elections of 1947, an act for which he had been roundly criticized by his opponents, including Chamoun himself.

In the pursuit of this ambition, and in his general taste for unbridled power, Chamoun made himself a raft of enemies of every religious denomination, and came increasingly to rely on relatively inconsequential figure-heads to represent certain sects in public office while their more prestigious rivals were shut out. Thus while Sulh held the Prime Ministry, more forceful Sunni Moslem figures such as Saeb Salam, Rashid Karami, and Abdullah Yafi were excluded and alienated; among the Druses, Chamoun cultivated the dull-witted, almost comically archaic Majid Arslan, thereby antagonizing Arslan's influential rival Kamal Jumblatt. Among his own fellow-Maronites, some of whom, such as Hamid Frangieh, had their own ambitions for the Presidency, Chamoun also made enemies. The Maronite Patriarch himself, to whom Chamoun declined to show deference, became an outspoken critic.

In the elections of 1957, a strong pro-Chamounist majority was elected – enough, seemingly, to ensure his re-election the following year. But in the process many of Chamoun's strongest opponents, including Salam, Yafi, Jumblatt, and Frangieh, lost their seats, while others such as Chamoun's

Foreign Minister, Charles Malik, secured election despite a glaring absence of any domestic political experience or popular following. Inevitably, charges of electoral corruption were widely raised, perhaps with some justification. And these were linked to other charges of corruption in the administration and of the great neglect by the government of the elementary economic and social needs of the more disadvantaged areas of the country, where, as it happened, a number of Chamoun's opponents were based. Although Chamoun never openly announced his desire for re-election, a vociferous campaign against it developed.

It may be that none of these elements of domestic conflict would have mattered very much were it not for the added ingredient of international conflict. The combination, however, proved explosive. Indeed, the international problem was critical enough to have jeopardized the survival of the most well-intentioned and well-regarded Lebanese government.

In the international arena, Lebanon was a victim of the aftermath of Suez. The Anglo-French-Israeli attack on Egypt in 1956 inflicted intense embarrassment on all those Arab régimes and groups who had customarily relied on cooperation with the two discredited Western powers; and despite the opposition of the United States to the Suez expedition, when the American government shortly afterward attempted to inherit Britain's lost influence through the medium of the Eisenhower Doctrine, friends and clients of the United States found themselves embarrassed also. Nowhere was this more clearly the case than in Lebanon, where large numbers of Christians attached to the independence of their country from its Arab neighbours suddenly found themselves isolated, and where the mass of Moslems were absorbed in a wave of enthusiasm for Gamal Abdel Nasser as the champion of pan-Arab unity and defiance of the West. As the allegiance of Lebanese Moslems was forcefully drawn to Cairo and Damascus, the fears of the Christians for the security of what they viewed as their little island of prosperity and civilization correspondingly increased.

This polarization was already dramatically symbolized only a few days after the Suez invasion, when President Chamoun rejected the advice of his two leading Moslem ministers, Abdullah Yafi and Saeb Salam, and refused to break diplomatic relations with Britain and France. A new government was appointed, headed by Sami Es-Sulh and including as its most notable member Dr Charles Malik as Foreign Minister. It was Dr Malik who, together with Chamoun himself, was to personify the controversial policies of the government from that point onward.

Malik had begun his career as a professor of philosophy at the American University of Beirut, after graduate study in Germany and the United States. He subsequently served for many years as Lebanese Ambassador in Washington and at the UN, and at the time of Suez had only lately returned to the American University of Beirut as the Dean of Graduate Studies. A brilliant and deeply cultivated man of great energy and strong convictions, Malik was temperamentally unsuited to the climate of Lebanese politics, and fitted in awkwardly with the brokers, fixers, rug-dealers, wardheelers, and village patricians who kept the machine running. Malik combined an outspoken religious piety with a fervent attachment to the mystique of Christian Lebanon, an unswerving belief in the virtues of Western and particularly American society, a hatred of godless Communism, and an attitude toward the international issues of the day that was indistinguishable from that of John Foster Dulles, with whom he had developed a close friendship. Nasserism, defiance of the West, neutralism in the cold war, pan-Arabism, all were anathema to him.

On the other side of the political fence, Malik had a rough counterpart in the person of Kamal Jumblatt. Different as the two men were in many ways, they shared the fatal trait of determined righteousness. Jumblatt was the scion of an ancient family of Druse landed patricians, which was no doubt the main reason he had been elected to parliament continuously since 1943. Yet, despite these trappings of feudalism, he emerged on the Lebanese political scene as a doctrinaire prophet of radical reform, not hesitating to reject national traditions and myths ordinarily considered sacrosanct by Lebanese politicians: free enterprise, intersectarian distribution of government jobs, the National Pact of 1943. To him these aspects of the 'Lebanese way of life' signified anarchy, grasping materialism, hypocrisy, corruption, and the enshrinement of national mediocrity. He had joined Chamoun in opposition to Bishara El-Khoury in 1952, but was alienated afterward by Chamoun's disinclination to accept his advice (he insisted that Khoury should be brought to trial on criminal charges, for example), and by 1957 he had become one of Chamoun's most unbridled critics.

The other leading politicians, both supporters and enemies of Chamoun, lacked Malik's and Jumblatt's ideological rigidity and were generally more disposed to adapt themselves to whatever popular and governmental pressures they perceived. In 1957 and 1958, however, these pressures inexorably pulled the politicians into opposing camps, in which the cultivation of their clienteles demanded an implacable attitude toward their opponents and made compromise impossible. The exclusion from Parliament of half a dozen leading members of the opposition, of course, made the problem much worse, and so did Chamoun's desire for a renewed term of office. But it was precisely the mentality of the Christian populace, and what they could observe of the Moslem mentality, that lent respectability to Chamoun's ambition: for he was now viewed by the insecure Christians as the indispensable man who, with the aid of the United States, would save their homeland from Gamal Abdel Nasser. And for the Moslem masses, accustomed to seeing Nasser's photograph pasted on every wall in their quarters of Beirut, Tripoli, and Sidon, and to hearing 'the Voice of the Arabs' on Cairo radio, it was Nasser who would save them from their depressed status in a Christian-dominated Lebanon and from the imperialist designs of the Western powers. These feelings on both sides were especially stimulated by the proclamation of the Eisenhower Doctrine early in 1957, and by the sudden merger of Syria and Egypt in the United Arab Republic early in 1958.

The key to understanding of the Eisenhower Doctrine is the realization that what was explicitly stated in its text only obliquely reflected its actual political significance, whether the latter was initially intended or not. The Joint Resolution of Congress of 9 March 1957, issued at the urging of President Eisenhower, declared that 'the United States regards as vital to the national interest and world peace the preservation of the independence and integrity of the nations of the Middle East. To this end, if the President determines the necessity thereof, the United States is prepared to use armed forces to assist any such nation or group of nations requesting assistance against armed aggression from any country controlled by international communism... The President is hereby authorized to use during the balance of fiscal year 1957 for economic and military assistance under this joint resolution sums not to exceed $200,000,000...'

Economic and military aid would be granted, in other words, to Middle Eastern governments that were judged to be responsive to the determination of the United States to defend them against the designs of the Soviet Union; and if they were attacked, American troops would be available for their defence as well.

The prospect of armed attacks in the Middle East by Communist-controlled forces was scarcely a likely danger in 1957, inasmuch as there were no Communist régimes in existence there. What did exist was an evident Soviet readiness to capitalize on the Suez episode, and on the general unpopularity of all the leading Western powers including the United States, in order to curry favour with Egypt and Syria and with Arab nationalist opinion generally. There was a corresponding fear in Washington that the Soviet Union would achieve some success in this, the more so because of a considerable American reluctance to compete directly for the favour of either the Syrian or the Egyptian régime, both of which were regarded as reckless and demagogic.

On the other hand, the remaining régimes of the area were generally well-disposed to American purposes, and an explicit show of American encouragement and solidarity would hopefully stiffen their resistance to the pan-Arab and neutralist appeals of Gamal Abdel Nasser, as well as to any notion of doing business with the Soviets. The Eisenhower Doctrine did not speak of this; but its mere issuance, however irrelevant its reference to 'armed aggression' by 'international communism', constituted an invitation to Middle Eastern governments to associate themselves with it and to accept a share of the proffered $200,000,000. Hopefully, the Syrians and Egyptians would find themselves isolated among neighbours who indicated their preference for cooperation with the United States rather than the Soviet Union; and the popular momentum gained by Nasser from his 'victory' at Suez would be stalled.

In quest of such results, apparently, Eisenhower lost no time after the passage of the Congressional Resolution in sending out a special emissary to explain its virtues to the governments of the Middle East. His most dramatic success was in Lebanon, where President Chamoun and Foreign Minister Malik welcomed the Eisenhower Doctrine enthusiastically: a joint communiqué of March 16 declared that both Lebanon and the United States 'consider that international communism is incompatible with national independence and constitutes a cause of permanent trouble for world peace and security'. This declaration brought a storm of criticism from the gathering opposition to the Chamoun régime. A rump session of parliament endorsed the government's action by a vote of 30 to one, but only after seven Deputies had resigned their seats in protest. This was soon followed by the formation of a group calling itself the United National Front, including political figures of all the major sects, Christian as well as Moslem, who were united in a common antipathy to Chamoun. These events signalled the beginning of the Lebanese crisis, although more than another year was to pass before the outbreak of violence.

In the Arab Middle East in general, the American effort to mobilize diplomatic support, symbolized in the Eisenhower Doctrine, was not a spectacular success. While neither the Syrian nor the Egyptian régime was popular with the monarchial governments of Iraq, Jordan, and Saudi Arabia, all of whom looked to London and Washington for support, they were put on the defensive by the appeals of Nasser to pan-Arab mass sentiment and his attacks on what he portrayed as the American attempt to organize the Middle East against him. A crisis arose in September and October 1957 when the Syrian government claimed (perhaps correctly) that the United States, together with its Turkish and Arab allies, was plotting its overthrow. This led to Soviet threats against Turkey and to the dispatch of Egyptian troops to Syria; the pro-American Arab governments were so embarrassed by the affair that they hastily issued declarations of solidarity with the hated Syrian régime. It was a signal diplomatic victory for the Nasserites and a humiliation for the United States. Several months later, Nasser cemented his victory with the Syro-Egyptian union, which he celebrated with a triumphal visit to Damascus. Tens of thousands of Lebanese streamed across the border to pay homage to him.

Meanwhile in Beirut, the Lebanese police uncovered a load of weapons concealed in the car of the Egyptian military attaché, whom they expelled from the country. Government leaders accused the United Arab Republic of arming the opposition; in return, opponents charged that the government was illicitly arming its civilian supporters. In addition to the United National Front, a predominantly Christian group of moderate critics of Chamoun (the Third Force) called upon the President to renounce the intention of securing re-election. The participation of many prominent Christians – including the Maronite Patriarch – in the criticism of the régime, and ultimately in some cases in supporting the rebellion itself, was of crucial importance. Notwithstanding the polarization of mass Christian and Moslem opinion to which we have referred, this participation provided a symbol by which the sectarian overtones could be considerably muted, if not altogether concealed. If prominent Christians as well as Moslems deplored the government's association with the Eisenhower Doctrine, and opposed the President's re-election, then perhaps a potential basis for restoring the National Pact and preserving Lebanon's independence existed after all, once Chamoun and his associates disappeared. We shall see later that it was precisely this consideraation that enabled the American intervention of July to find a satisfactory outcome.

The civil war began with the murder of an opposition journalist (a Maronite, as it happened) on 9 May 1958. The crime was promptly charged to the government, and almost at once opposition leaders called a general strike throughout the country. Within days, barricades had been erected against the authorities in Beirut's Moslem quarter of El-Basta, as well as in the predominantly Moslem city of Tripoli and elsewhere. Extensive areas in the interior of the country, mainly populated by Druses and Sunni and Shi'ite Moslems, were closed off to government personnel and patrolled by bands of armed followers of various rebel leaders. These areas included almost the entire frontier with Syria. Rebel spokesmen, who had heretofore demanded simply that Chamoun renounce a second term, now declared that only his immediate resignation would end the rebellion. (His term was due to expire on 23 September.) Members of the Third Force unsuccessfully sought to mediate: Chamoun clung stubbornly to his refusal to issue this or any other conciliatory statement, attributing the entire campaign against him to the instigation of the Egyptians, and the rebels, once behind the barricades, had passed the line of no return in their refusal to countenance Chamoun's continuation, however temporarily.

Despite repeated acts of violence in the cities, and a series of pitched battles between rebel irregulars and government gendarmes and armed civilian supporters in the countryside, as the weeks passed the two sides became deadlocked. The key to the outcome of the fighting was the Lebanese army, a modest volunteer force of perhaps eight thousand men who had had little experience of the sight of blood and whose chief function heretofore had been to march in Independence Day parades. Given the modest scale of manpower and armaments involved in the rebellion, the army would have had no difficulty in suppressing it had its commander chosen to do so. The latter, however, was inspired in his conduct at least as much by his own astute political judgment as by a desire to exercise his battalions. General Fuad Chehab, a Maronite Lebanese patriot and the descendant of an ancient family of mountain princes who had once governed the country, took the view that it could not properly be the role of the army to protect the government against its domestic opponents. (He had similarly refused to put the army at the disposal of Bishara El-Khoury in 1952, thereby precipitating the latter's resignation.) More than this, Chehab was acutely conscious of the fact that the army itself was composed of both Moslem and Christian officers and men, and that an ultimate test of its loyalty might only cause it to fall apart into factions, thereby perhaps destroying the unity and independence of the state once and for all. He therefore evaded Chamoun's repeated 'suggestions' that he suppress the insurrection, limiting himself to patrolling the fringes of some of the rebel-held territory and preventing the rebels from marching on the government's central offices, the international airport, military installations, and other selected key points. With this judicious and uniquely Lebanese behaviour, General Chehab progressively emerged as the most eligible compromise candidate to succeed Chamoun as President.

The government lost little time in appealing for international support by casting the responsibility for the insurrection at the doorstep of the UAR. It simultaneously appealed to both the League of Arab States and the UN Security Council, supporting its indictment with a long list of specific accusations. Not only had the UAR engaged in a long propaganda campaign against the Chamoun régime, thus stimulating disaffected segments of the population to revolt, but more significantly it was charged with 'massive infiltration' of weapons and men across the border from Syria into the rebel-held areas. There were some clear bits of evidence to lend credence to this charge: in the first days of the rebellion, for example, Lebanese border guards on the Damascus–Beirut road had seized the car of the Belgian Consul in Damascus, stuffed full of small arms and explosives; shortly afterward, a raiding party, apparently from Syria, had attacked the border station, killed the guards, and demolished the building. The UAR however, denied all responsibility and countered with the charge that Chamoun sought to escape his domestic difficulties by artificially internationalizing them.

A meeting of the Arab League in Bengazi, Libya, ended inconclusively after a few days, the Lebanese government having declared itself unsatisfied with a vaguely worded compromise draft resolution. The Security Council, after much debate in which the United States and Britain strongly supported the Lebanese contentions and the Soviet Union equally backed the UAR, finally passed a resolution on 11 June providing for the dispatch of a team of UN observers to Lebanon. By late June a skeleton group of observers was installed in Lebanon and had begun limited operations. The insurrection, however, continued unabated.

According to numerous reports, none of which can be conclusively substantiated but which have the ring of authenticity, early in the crisis the Lebanese government supplemented its appeal to the Arab League and the Security Council with private requests to the United States for armed intervention.[1] To this the United States refused to agree, but it did supply an airlift of small arms for police purposes almost immediately after the outbreak of the insurrection, and lent considerable verbal support to the Lebanese government's cause. Soon afterward it announced its decision to send a shipment of tanks, and on 18 May the State Department declared that the question of sending American troops was under consideration.[2] Meanwhile the United States Sixth Fleet in the Eastern Mediterranean was reinforced.

As the Lebanese crisis dragged on through June and into July, however, it became clear that the intention of the United States was to wait out events and hope for a compromise solution arranged in Lebanon itself. This policy seemed justified by the gradual decline of the level of violence in Lebanon, and by the rising speculation in early July that a compromise settlement, involving the convening of parliament to elect General Chehab to the Presidency, was in prospect. Prime Minister Sulh issued a statement on 28 May to the effect that his cabinet did not plan to submit a proposed constitutional amendment, enabling Chamoun's re-election to parliament; Chamoun himself, however, remained silent on this issue.

All calculations were shattered, however, on 14 July by news of the revolution in Iraq, where a military cabal suddenly overthrew the monarchy and liquidated King Feisal, Crown Prince Abdul Ilah, and Prime Minister Nuri Es-Said. Inasmuch as the deposed government had long been a close ally of Britain and more lately also of the United States, and a bitter rival of President Nasser and his régime – speculation had even arisen that Iraqi units would be dispatched to Lebanon to crush the revolt – the Iraqi revolution was an event of dramatic symbolic importance. The news was greeted triumphantly, not only in Cairo and Damascus, but also among the insurgents in Lebanon.

The government in Beirut, for its part, reacted with consternation. Within hours, President Chamoun appealed to the American Ambassador for armed intervention; within a few more hours, the decision was made in Washington to accede to the request. By the next day, 15 July, American Marines from the Sixth Fleet were streaming ashore on the beaches south of Beirut, with bayonets fixed. In the unique spirit of the Lebanese civil war, they were greeted at the water's edge by curious bathers and by soft drink vendors. The Marines found that General Chehab had his American-made tanks drawn up across the highway, poised to open fire; President Chamoun had neglected to discuss the American intervention with his commander-in-chief. The Ambassador's mediation overcame this handicap, however, and the convoy proceeded into Beirut: a Lebanese army jeep in the lead, followed by the Ambassador's limousine flying both Lebanese and American flags and bearing both Chehab and the Ambassador, and finally a contingent of American Marines.[3] The civil war had become internationalized.

A reading of President Eisenhower's own memories of the Lebanese crisis makes it clear in what oversimplified, even caricaturized, terms he viewed the developments there. No doubt outsiders who intervene in domestic or regional conflicts in far-off places, however humane and constructive their motives, are in one vital sense bound to be playing with fire: their leading statesmen, who are ultimately responsible for charting the policy of intervention, are likely to lack many dimensions of understanding of what the conflict is about and how their own involvement is likely to affect those on the local scene.

President Eisenhower can readily be forgiven a lack of intense interest in the details of Lebanese clan politics. It is a little startling, however, that the diplomatically experienced President of the United States should sum up his underlying premises about what was at stake as follows:

> Behind everything was our deep-seated conviction that the Communists were principally responsible for the trouble, and that President Chamoun was motivated only by a strong feeling of patriotism. He was the ablest of the Lebanese politicians and would undoubtedly agree not to be a candidate again for the Presidency if only he could be assured of a strong and sincere pro-Western successor.[4]

The State Department professionals, of course, took a more nuanced view. Robert D. Murphy, the Deputy Undersecretary of State sent by Eisenhower to Lebanon immediately after the landings, recognized the elementary fact that 'Communism was playing no direct or substantial part in the insurrection'[5] and saw Chamoun as something more than a patriot and an American ally: 'I regarded Chamoun as a good friend of the United States but I never really understood his motives. I felt that he was the victim of his own political excesses and that he had overreached himself in the brambles of Lebanese politics.'[6]

Still, Murphy's account, if more reflective of local realities than Eisenhower's, is a little flat. He breezed in and out of the crisis in the grand manner of the seasoned non-specialist, and viewed the Middle Eastern participants – Chamoun, Jumblatt, Karami, Chehab, the Patriarch, Nasser, Prime Minister Kassim of Iraq – with more than a touch of passing amusement.

We do not get a clear picture from any inside source – neither Murphy nor Eisenhower, nor others – of precisely what reasoning was engaged in by Washington in deciding to send in the Marines. Just what would they accomplish? Just what was feared might happen if they were not sent? What risks were envisaged if they were? How would these be dealt with? Under what circumstances would it be judged appropriate to withdraw them again? These are things we do not know. We can invent our own rationales; but not only are these no more than speculation they are likely to be too neat and too concrete. For what seems likely is that the decision to send in the troops was made, under the confused circumstances of the moment, without any precise scenarios or any precise definition of the mission. Rather, there was a generalized feeling on the part of the highest officials that 'something had to be done', that the United States had to establish a military presence as quickly as possible, that if she did not do so she would find herself without effective influence over the course of events in the area, while if she did, she would find that she had bought a little time and maintained some credibility, and would be better assured that whatever happened in the wake of the Baghdad revolution would not be entirely outside her control. Obviously the intervention would provoke anger in many quarters, but as long as the Soviet Union was in no position to respond materially (as Eisenhower rightly judged she was not), then 'doing something' was better than 'doing nothing'.[7]

In the last analysis, for Eisenhower, it seems to have been the Soviet Union to whom the United States was responding. ('Most skeptical of all [among congressional leaders called to the White House for a briefing] was Senator Fulbright, who seemed to doubt seriously that this crisis was Communist-inspired.')[8] However the local problems might work themselves out, in the grand picture the old joust between the White Knight of the Free World and the Black Knight of Communism was the only theme that mattered. In Eisenhower's hindsight, what was accomplished was that

Nasser learned that 'he could not depend completely on Russia to help him in any Middle East struggle, and he certainly had his complacency as to America's helplessness completely shattered'.[9] Eisenhower was hardly alone in seeing the intervention as a ploy on the cold-war chessboard. Walt W. Rostow, for example, in an article five years later, contentedly noted: 'At two points the forward momentum of the post-Sputnik Communist thrust was slowed down by major and successful United States actions: in the Lebanon–Jordan and Quemoy–Matsu crises of 1958.'[10]

The very large powers can afford to stumble in the dark on a good many occasions, however, as long as the other great powers are not there in the same room. Even assuming the vaguest and most ill-founded rationales for American intervention on the part of the President, in one essential respect his estimate that the Soviets would do nothing in response was all that really mattered: in the absence of the Soviet Union in the Eastern Mediterranean, an American exercise in military deployment, not devoted to outright assault on anyone (unlike Suez), ran no great risks. In this respect it might be compared to the American landings in the Dominican Republic in 1965, which was a messier operation involving some loss of life but involved no threat of the outbreak of war. Apparently, on that occasion also, the decision to intervene was made from one moment to the next by a President possessing only the skimpiest of information and the crudest image of the local realities. A mistake? Quite possibly; but one that the intervening power could rather easily afford to indulge in.

This writer happens to be convinced that the Lebanon intervention was not a mistake, however foggy the thinking that determined it. Whether or not anyone in Washington spelled out for Eisenhower the precise nature of events that he would have to be prepared to witness if he did not send the Marines, such events can be readily imagined in retrospect. Chamoun's prospect for finishing out his term until 23 September was fairly good on the eve of the Iraqi revolution, and so was the prospect that the Lebanese parliament would shortly agree on General Chehab as his successor and that with this, the violence would taper off appreciably. The events in Baghdad washed out those prospects at once, however, and replaced them with the opposite presumption: that Chamoun, unprotected from abroad, would find that what authority he held was dissolving all around him as various supporters deserted him and would end up, in a matter of days, being escorted out of the country by the Lebanese army or perhaps assassinated. Chehab might inherit the Presidency anyway – or perhaps not – but would do so in circumstances that would propel Lebanese politics away from, rather than back toward, their traditional equilibrium, amidst all the euphoria of Sunni Moslem and pan-Arabic popular sentiment. The rebel-dominated cabinet first put together by Rashid Karami after taking office late in September, which was withdrawn because of Chamounist objections, could have easily been outdone in militant partisanship by the kind of régime that might have been installed in the wake of a fleeing Chamoun in July. The whole stability and attachment to normality upon which Lebanon had prospered ever since independence, and constitutional politics with it, would have been very much in jeopardy.

More particularly, however, the short-term implication of Chamoun being abandoned to his fate would have been the abandonment of King Hussein to his. Hussein was confirmed in his rule, as it happened, by an airlift of 2,300 British troops from Cyprus. There is little question but that they never would have been sent independently of the dispatch of American troops to Lebanon. Would Hussein have survived in the absence of British forces? Perhaps. Would he have survived also in the absence of Chamoun's survival? It is much less likely. All that is certain is that, had he been forced out, in the chain reaction of the defeat of established régimes arising from the Baghdad revolution, the next step would have been the invasion of the West Bank of Jordan by Israel – a threat that the Israelis conveyed on several occasions, including the occasion of Murphy's visit to Ben-Gurion after he left Lebanon.[11] Such an event, less than two years after the Sinai–Suez War and only a few days or hours after upheavals across the Arab world, would have been about as dangerous and unwelcome to Washington and London as any that could be imagined. At a time when the overwhelming concern of the two Western powers was to keep further events in the Middle East under some measure of control, another Israeli–Arab conflict would only open up the prospect of total confusion.

Such was the risk to the United States government of doing nothing. Whether it was clearly envisaged at the highest levels or not, something of the kind was very likely sensed in a general way : the basic instinct that warns statesmen in the midst of crisis against losing control of events was presumably operating. But intervention carried its own risks. One commitment might lead eventually to others. Even though the American forces were sent to Lebanon at the invitation of the Lebanese government, their presence there would be widely resented – not only by Chamoun's enemies in and out of Lebanon, but even by some Lebanese who were well-disposed toward their government but baulked at the idea of outside forces being brought in. If the American troops went near the Syrian border they would run the risk of incidents with UAR forces. If they stuck close to Beirut, they would still run the risk of incidents with the local insurgents – particularly, but not only, if they were so stationed as to guard buildings of the Lebanese government. Any American move into the rebel strongholds themselves, aimed at positively suppressing the rebellion, would almost certainly meet with vigorous resistance – resistance that could readily be overcome, but not without killing a good number of Lebanese. Indeed, the very act of landing on the beaches entailed the danger of armed conflict, either with insurgents or with the Lebanese army itself, whose Commander, General Chehab, was certain to be greatly displeased.

Whatever the nature of the incident, any American shots fired at any adversary would present the danger of political and military escalation, rendering impossible the hoped-for compromise settlement of the Lebanese civil war, and creating even greater difficulties than the United States had already faced in dealing with the UAR and the new revolutionary régime in Iraq. King Hussein's tenure might be rendered even less secure, rather than more so, if American intervention in Lebanon led to violence. And once any such adverse effects occured, the American military commitment would either have to grow to undesired proportions or be abandoned under humiliating conditions.

These alternative risks were not equal: American inaction would leave the initiative and the ability to influence events entirely to others; American intervention might turn out to be messy and expensive, but not downright disastrous, given the clear superiority of American armed forces over those of anyone else in the area (the chance of a Soviet decision to intervene having been readily dismissed in Washington). The worst that might happen was that American forces would actually have to be used, but not that they would not prevail. The best that might happen was that they would not be employed in combat, but that their presence would calm and stabilize a deteriorating situation and enable Lebanese life (and with it that of surrounding states) to return to normal. And that is precisely what happened.

In order to minimize the risks of intervention, however, it was essential for the American authorities to aim only at the most modest possible objectives and employ the most modest possible tactics. The majority of the American troops were stationed outside the city in the surrounding olive groves, where there was little contact with the local population and, in fact, nothing at all for them to do. Some troops were stationed at the harbour and others at the airport, and a few others along the road connecting them. One or two tanks sat outside the gates of the American University, and another outside the American Embassy. Helicopters occasionally patrolled the shoreline and the Lebanese–Syrian frontier. But that was all: almost the only activity of the American forces was to keep themselves supplied and maintained. Their arrival in Lebanon had been occasioned by the Iraqi revolution, but they made no move to intervene in Iraq; their officially stated purpose was to uphold Lebanon's independence, but they made no move to take up positions on the frontiers. Clearly the hope of many pro-régime Lebanese, from Chamoun himself on down, was that the troops would mop up the rebels, but they carefully stayed away from rebel-held areas,[12] and renounced even the role of defending the Lebanese government against rebel attacks. After the passage of a few weeks, in which no more than one or two minor incidents occurred,[13] the troops were allowed occasional afternoon leaves to visit the safer areas of Beirut and provide a lively trade to the local shops and cafes.

This circumspect conduct of the American forces, calculated to avoid provoking the rebels, was accompanied by other policies that assured its success. For one thing, the build-up of armed strength was rapid and considerable: by early August it reached over 14,000 men, a figure much larger than that of the entire Lebanese army. It was discreetly intimated that the passive stance of the American forces would depend on the rebel leaders' success in restraining their own irregulars from acts of harrassment, and that otherwise the American forces would not hesitate to seize rebel strongholds.

More particularly, military circumspection was promptly paralleled by a conciliatory diplomatic initiative, both with regard to Lebanon and beyond it to her neighbours. On the heels of the Marines arrived President Eisenhower's special emissary, Deputy Undersecretary of State Robert Murphy, who plunged into intensive consultations with President Chamoun and his chief ministers, with the army commander Chehab, and also with the principal leaders of the rebellion: Saeb Salam, Rashid Karami, Kamal Jumblatt, and Hussein El-Oweini. Much to the dismay of Chamoun and the relief of his opponents, Murphy made clear the modest aims of American policy in Lebanon: not to use the troops to suppress the rebellion, which Chamoun's own army had declined to do, and least of all to enable Chamoun to renew his term of office, but only to exert a calming psychological influence that would enable the Lebanese, free of any real or imagined threat of intimidation or intervention from the UAR, to find a compromise formula to set their own house in order within the framework of their traditional institutions. In practice, this could only mean that Chamoun should continue to the end of his constitutional term on 23 September and that meanwhile the Chamber of Deputies should be convened as quickly as possible to elect as the next President the man whose election had already seemed assured before the events of 14 and 15 July had thrown everything into confusion: Fuad Chehab.

In retrospect, it appears that it was Murphy's mediation that made these arrangements possible. Chehab was duly elected on 31 July, with the sullen acquiescence of Chamoun, and was formally invested in office 23 September. Prime Minister Sulh left for an extended European holiday, and Foreign Minister Malik for the UN, where he was elected President of the General

Assembly. Chamoun retired to his heavily guarded seaside home south of Beirut. Rashid Karami, one of the principal rebel chiefs, became Prime Minister, and other opponents of Chamoun assumed other ministerial posts. All this happened with the American forces looking on unconcernedly. The Chamounists were furious. A counter-insurrection among Christian militants prolonged the crisis for a few weeks into October, when at length an emergency four-man cabinet of two Sunni ex-rebels (Karami and Hussein Oweini) and two Maronite ex-loyalists (Raymond Edde and Pierre Gemayel) was installed as a symbol of national reconciliation. The civil war was over. On 27 October, the last American troops were evacuated.

Many people, both in Lebanon and in the United States, wondered what the troops had been there for. Their role had been minimized, almost to the point of seeming to disappear altogether, so that the risks arising from their presence could be minimized. For some time thereafter, the most bitter feelings against the United States and its policies in Lebanon were harboured not within the Moslem community which had so angrily objected to American intervention in the first place, but among Christians who had welcomed it and now felt betrayed.

If we are to judge by results, these Christian resentments could hardly have been more ill-founded. Lebanon survived the civil war and reverted to its old ways of compromise politics, communal tolerance, and chaotic, re-laxed, prosperous and happy living. This was what the Christian Lebanese nationalists had looked to Chamoun to preserve for them in the first place, and it was what he had placed in jeopardy by his overweening ambitions and his disregard of the need to assure other communities a stake in the system. The American intervention had the effect of saving Chamoun's supporters from the consequences of his excesses, and of facilitating an outcome to the crisis in which Chamoun's successor, General Chehab, could devote his six-year term of office to the tasks of reconciliation and mild but necessary reforms.

Retrospectively, the American intervention in Lebanon appears to have been a rather special historical case. It proved to be a distinct political success; but it would not have succeeded in its purposes, and indeed would probably not have been attempted at all, were it not for a combination of special circumstances not all of which are likely to be repeated.

First of all, the United States possessed the logistical ability to place overwhelmingly powerful forces in Lebanon in a very short time. This involved not only the unchallenged presence in the Mediterranean of the Sixth Fleet but also the availability of a strategic reserve of American troops and equipment in Germany, staging bases in Turkey, the possession of an extensive airlift capacity, and – what may not exist another time – the willingness of the allied governments of France and Italy to have their territory overflown.

Second, the intervention had the advantage of having been expressly requested by the Lebanese government, which not only smoothed the diplomatic path of the United States at the UN and elsewhere, and allayed misgivings within the United States itself, but made it possible for General Chehab and the small Lebanese army to yield gracefully, albeit reluctantly, to an operation which effectively took matters out of their hands.

Third, the Americans were able to accomplish their essential objective by their mere presence in Lebanon, without having to engage in any hostilities with the rebels, since that objective entailed a compromise that was at least as welcome to the opposition as it was to the government. The conciliatory attitude displayed by American representatives toward the opposition, and their coolness toward the government that had invited them in, could only strengthen the conclusion, widely drawn in Lebanese society after the crisis was over, that never again ought the government to stray so far from the traditional path of compromise that either itself or its opponents would feel encouraged to seek armed support from outside the country. Thus, ironically, the very success of the intervention had the effect of making it unlikely that any future Lebanese government, even if faced with difficulties comparable to those of 1958, would feel able to appeal for American troops. Even as the first Marines were landing in July, in fact, some perspicacious Lebanese observers foresaw that Chamoun would not receive the positive American support he thought he had negotiated. Ghassan Tueni, editor of the independent Beirut newspaper Al-Nahar, a Greek Orthodox Christian and a member of the Third Force, observed:

> To certain Christians who still tell themselves that the age of protectorates and Crusades is not over, we say quite frankly that the Sixth Fleet did not land its troops to protect them, but to protect its own vital interests; and that its vital interests have no religion, but that if we must give a religious label to those with whom its interests lie, we should say that it is the Moslems with whom the West will try to make friends.[14]

Lastly, the success of the intervention was aided by the modesty of American intentions toward Lebanon's neighbours, particularly Iraq and the UAR, which reduced the extent of their hostile reactions. The troops stationed in Lebanon were not used as an instrument of pressure or intimidation against these states – a point on which Robert Murphy sought to reassure Prime Minister Kassim in Baghdad and President Nasser in Cairo on his visits to them after departing from Beirut,[15] and which made possible the General Assembly's compromise resolution of 21 August in which all the Arab states concurred. It was significant that although the troops were sent to Lebanon within the implicit framework of the Eisenhower Doctrine, the action amounted to the last gasp of that policy rather than a preliminary to any further steps. The Iraqi revolution and the Lebanese rebellion had rendered unworkable the policy expressed by the Doctrine, and there was little left to the United States but to restrict the damage as best it could. Hence the diplomatic atmosphere in the Near East, as it unfolded in the weeks following the intervention, was very different from what it had been in September and October of 1957 at the time of the Syrian-American crisis, in which the Syrians could genuinely fear that the United States was encouraging its Turkish, Iraqi, Jordanian, and Lebanese allies surrounding Syria to intimidate the Damascus régime and perhaps engineer its overthrow. In the summer and fall of 1958, following its intervention in Lebanon, the United States was already beginning, tentatively at least, to swing toward a policy of reconciliation and cooperation with the UAR.

What about international efforts to contain the civil war and external intervention? There is something of a myth that gained currency in the summer of 1958, and that has persisted ever since, to the effect that before American forces arrived on the Lebanese beaches on 15 July the international dimensions of the crisis had already been adequately taken care of by the UN through the passage of the Security Council's resolution of 11 June establishing the United Nations Observation Group in Lebanon (UNOGIL) and the functioning of that body on the local scene. According to this view, the reports of UNOGIL supplied sufficient assurance that no significant infiltration of men or arms to the rebels was occurring across the Syrian border; or at least the very presence and activities of UNOGIL served to discourage it. The American intervention, therefore, only served to intensify a quietening crisis, and more particularly to place obstacles in the path of the UN at a time when its representatives were in the process of making a constructive contribution to the restoration of peace in the country and tranquillity in the area.

This view came naturally to many critics of the American intervention who were motivated by instinctive enthusiasm for President Nasser or for the UN, or distaste for American foreign policy. Basically, however, its chief weakness is its disregard of the evidence. The Observation Group established by the resolution possessed no authority, few resources, and little familiarity with the subject they were being asked to investigate. By the time of their first report, on 3 July, they had barely had time to assemble a skeleton body of personnel and equipment consisting of 94 military observers, 74 vehicles, two helicopters, and a radio communications system, and to establish a handful of observation stations in government-controlled areas.[16] Representatives of UNOGIL had visited a number of rebel strongholds, but only by prior arrangements in each case with local rebel leaders and under rebel escort; only on 15 July, the day of the American landings, did they secure permission for general access to rebel-held territory. Their observations prior to their initial report were made only in daylight hours, when nothing consequential in the way of infiltration across the border could be expected anyway. In any case, they were in no position to observe the border, which was 324 kilometres long, only 18 of which was under government control.

In these circumstances, the initial report of UNOGIL is hard to take very seriously. Much of the report was given over to a recitation of the difficulties under which the Group laboured. ('The existence of a state of conflict between opposing armed forces in a territory to which an independent body of observers seeks free access throughout imposes upon that body an attitude of discretion and restraint if the express or tacit acceptance of its presence is to be obtained from those exercising authority or effective control on different sides in the conflict.') Nevertheless, commenting on the visits they were able to arrange to a number of rebel groups, they felt free to state: 'It has not been possible to establish where these arms were acquired ... Nor was it possible to establish if any of the armed men observed had infiltrated from outside; there is little doubt, however, that the vast majority were in any case Lebanese.'[17]

The second report, of 30 July, was a good deal more substantial, as by then UNOGIL had organized its operations more fully, improved its resources somewhat, and toward the end of the period, established observation posts in rebel-held areas; it also had undertaken night air patrols. The report indicated some unmistakable signs of activity across the border. For example:

> The greatest amount of traffic was observed on the Braghite–Halba road. On the nights of July 5–11, 50, 5, 20, 10 and 25 headlights respectively, were seen moving southwards in what appeared to be convoys at various times between 2100 hours and 2400 hours Lebanon Time.

> It cannot be assumed that all the existing traffic has been observed by air. The traffic along the above three roads has proved to be heavier at night than during the daytime. A large majority of the vehicles observed were moving southwards and westwards [i.e., into Lebanon].

> It has been observed that after the second night of aerial reconnaissance the lights of vehicles have been switched off or dimmed when an aircraft is in the vicinity. What appeared to be a strong flashing light was observed on a hill-top, presumably to warn the vehicles on the Braghite–Halba road of the approach of aircraft. Up to 6 July, the villages in this area were well illuminated at night. On successive

nights, however, aerial observations have established that the villages along this road have been blacked out, except for a few odd lights.[18]

The report added that it was impossible to verify on the ground the suspicions of arms transport arising from these observations. None the less, the report inexplicably concluded: 'The extent of the infiltration of arms which may be taking place has been indicated in the report. It is clear that it cannot be on anything more than a limited scale, and is largely confined to small arms and ammunition.' It added that 'in no case have UN observers, who have been vigilantly patrolling the opposition-held areas and have frequently observed the armed bands there, been able to detect the presence of persons who have indubitably entered from across the border for the purpose of fighting'.[19]

Generally speaking, these reports reflect a mixture of futility and fatuous-ness. It was clear that the observers, by their own account, were in no position to gather conclusive evidence concerning infiltration. There was ample opportunity for men and supplies to have passed unnoticed; where partial evidence was gathered, it could not be confirmed. Yet both reports, as can be seen in the extracts cited above, went so far as to draw presumptive conclusions that had the effect of minimizing the Lebanese government's case at the UN. It was hardly surprising that both the Lebanese delegation in New York,[20] and President Chamoun in Beirut,[21] should have taken strong exception to UNOGIL's reporting. In any case, somewhat absurdly, UNOGIL's resources and operations underwent their most considerable expansion only well after the arrival of American troops on 15 July and the election of General Chehab to the Presidency on 31 July, by which time the worst of the crisis was over and their mission had lost its relevance. Whereas on 15 July there were a total of 133 ground and air observers, the number climbed to 190 on 10 August, 287 on 20 September, and 590 on 14 November, the date of UNOGIL's final report in which they recommended the termination of their mission. Similarly, UNOGIL's air patrols flew approximately twice as many observation sorties in September-October as in July-August,[22] despite the fact that infiltration was no longer a significant issue.

Presumably, there is a rational explanation for this altogether pointless pattern, in which, in the manner of Parkinson's Law, the scope of the effort of the organization expanded as its practical utility declined. Given the limited nature of the UN's logistical and manpower resources, it may simply have required several months to build up the Observation Group, regardless of the urgency of their task. We should ask, however, what UNOGIL's func-tion really was, and how urgent, from the perspective of its own responsible officers and that of the UN Secretariat. The operation was proposed to the Security Council by the Swedish delegation as a diplomatic compromise enabling the Council to avoid a complete deadlock between Lebanon and the United States on one hand, and the UAR and the Soviet Union on the other. As in many such situations, it no doubt seemed more politic to those concerned with the prestige of the world organization to appear to be doing something than to be doing nothing – but especially if one did not come up with dramatic results that would suggest the need for further action and stimulate even greater controversy. To those primarily concerned with minimizing the international aspects of the Lebanese crisis so as to preserve what they could of a normal diplomatic atmosphere, the creation of UNOGIL was the equivalent of what governments and other large organizations do when they seek to evade an unwelcome controversy by appointing a committee of inquiry, where the matter will hopefully remain submerged until it has lost its urgency. Once the American troops had landed, however, it became important for UNOGIL to reassert its presence as best it could, so as not to let its peace-making role be usurped or overshadowed altogether.

What level of infiltration of men and arms actually occurred from the Syrian province of the UAR into Lebanon during the months of the crisis, and how much such assistance contributed to the rebels' military performance, is impossible to determine with any accuracy. The Lebanese government at the time sought at the UN to document its allegation that the infiltration was 'massive', but did so mainly from its own unverifiable sources. Individual citations of alleged instances have abounded. Murphy recalls in his memoirs, for example, that 'when our Marines tapped the telephone line between the capital of Syria and the Basta at Beirut, it was proved conclusively that the rebels were receiving outside support.'[23] Such references do not give us any very useful picture, however.

From my conversations in the years after the crisis with a good many persons of widely varying allegiances in Lebanon, it seemed clear to me that whether a significant amount of infiltration had occurred was not a serious issue among the Lebanese themselves. It was generally recognized that it had, however much the rebel leaders and spokesmen for the UAR had found it expedient to deny this while the crisis was still in progress. Indeed, given the great ease of carrying out infiltration and, at least up to 31 July, the vested interest of the UAR authorities in doing so, it would be inexplicable for them to abstain from it. Likewise, the violent propaganda campaign conducted by the UAR against the Chamoun régime from mid-1957 onward constituted an evident encouragement to disaffected elements in Lebanon to rebel, and if a number of Lebanese opposition leaders did not receive financial subsidies for their activities from UAR sources, given the familiar practices of inter-Arab politics over the years, it would be extremely difficult to imagine why they did not.

Thus, in seeking to find out whether infiltration was taking place, the UN Observation Group was playing a somewhat futile role, for it was asking a question the general answer to which was well known or could readily be surmised. That the observers failed to find the answer only added to the absurd nature of their activities; that those to whom they reported in New York understood this absurdity, and recognized that the main diplomatic purpose served by their activities was a largely symbolic one, made their role even more absurd. And yet even that symbolic purpose was not really accomplished; it might have been had the Iraqi revolution not occurred, but in the wake of that event it was the American intervention, rather than that of the UN, which prompted the Lebanese to negotiate an end to their quarrels.

A more interesting and important question, which UNOGIL did not investigate and could hardly have done so, was where the greatest stimulus for the Lebanese rebellion really lay: among the rebel leaders and followers themselves, or among those in Cairo and Damascus who lent encouragement. We have already seen that this is by no means a simple question, since various answers are possible on different levels. This, however, was the kind of question more germane to an analysis of the responsibility for Lebanon's problems in the spring and summer of 1968; and it was this question that government and opposition spokesmen were implicitly arguing about when they overtly debated whether infiltration was a reality or not. Had Chamoun brought his difficulties on himself, or had Nasser concocted them for him? Clearly there was an element of each; but clearly also, however substantial the role of the UAR, it was one to which the Lebanese insurgents themselves did not hesitate to appeal.

TEXT REFERENCES

1. See for example Qubain, Fahim I., *Crisis in Lebanon*, Washington 1961, p.131, footnote 1, quoting details from 'a highly authoritative Western source, who asked that his name be withheld', to the effect that Chamoun made two explicit requests to American Ambassador McClintock that US troops be sent.
2. Ibid., p.113, citing *Mideast Mirror* (Beirut), 25 May 1958, p.23.
3. For a detailed description of this bizarre episode, see Charles Thayer, *Diplomat*, New York 1959, pp.31–36.
4. Eisenhower, Dwight D., *Waging Peace, 1956–1961*, New York 1965, p.266.
5. *Diplomat Among Warriors*, New York 1964, p.450.
6. Ibid., p.454.
7. Eisenhower, op. cit., p.274: 'In Lebanon the question was whether it would be better to incur the deep resentment of nearly all of the Arab world (and some of the rest of the Free World) and in doing so to risk general war with the Soviet Union or to do something worse – which was to do nothing ... There was little doubt in my own mind as to the correctness of the decisions.'

8. Ibid., p.272.

9. Ibid., p.290.

10. Rostow, W. W., 'The Third Round', *Foreign Affairs*, October 1963, p.5.

11. Murphy, op. cit., p.462.

12. The press reported an incident in which two American soldiers in a jeep lost their way and strayed into the rebel-held quarter of Beirut called El-Basta. Local irregulars surrounded their car, disarmed them and took them to their chief, Saeb Salam, who served them Coca-Cola and gave them a kindly lecture about interference in the domestic affairs of foreign countries. They were then sent off in their jeep, minus their weapons.

13. The US government acknowledged the death of one man by sniper fire. If other casualties occurred, they were effectively concealed.

14. *Al-Nahar*, 16 July 1958.

15. Murphy, op. cit., pp.457–60.

16. UN *Doc.* S/4038, 28 June 1958, p.2.

17. UN *Doc.* S/4040, 3 July 1958, p.9.

18. UN *Doc.* S/4069, 30 July 1958, pp.7–8.

19. Ibid., p.21.

20. Official comments of the Lebanese government on the first UNOGIL report, 8 July 1958, *Security Council Official Record*, 13th year, Supplement for July, August and September 1958, pp. 18–27. Reproduced in M. S. Agwani, ed., *The Lebanese Crisis, 1958: A Documentary Study*, New York 1965, pp.216–27.

21. Chamoun was quoted by a British correspondent: 'It is rather difficult for me to comment on the activities of the observers here because they appear to be doing absolutely nothing. As far as I can see they spend their time at the Aero Club in Beirut, on the beaches and up at the Cedars.' *Daily Mail*, London, 6 July 1958. Text in Agwani, op. cit., p.215. Chamoun subsequently disavowed the quotation.

22. Fahim Qubain, op. cit., pp.149–52.

23. Murphy, op. cit., p.448.

5 THE CIVIL WAR IN LAOS

John Main

For more than 50 years, the government of France ruled the territories collectively known as Indo-China, until the Japanese occupation and the collapse of what was left of French administration in the area gave the Vietnamese nationalist movement, the Vietminh, an opportunity to assert authority in Tongking, Annam and Cochin-China. A fortnight after the end of the Second World War, they were in a position to announce the independence of their country as the Democratic Republic of Vietnam and set up a provisional government in Hanoi under Ho Chi Minh as President. The Laotian Independence Movement, unlike the Vietminh, was not a coalition of nationalist parties and did not have a dedicated corps of Communists to give it dynamism, purpose and direction. Its leader, Prince Petsarath, was popular personally, but there was in Laos nothing like the deep well of nationalist feeling which Ho Chi Minh could draw on in Vietnam. Powerful influences, including the King, were opposed to the idea of independence, and there were divisions within the movement itself over what was best for the country, on what support to seek abroad and where to find it.

When the Japanese surrendered, the French government were anxious to restore their position immediately, but were prevented from doing so because of an agreement reached at the Potsdam Conference, under which the whole of Indo-China as far south as the 16th parallel of latitude was occupied by Chinese troops. It was the end of February 1946 before the Chinese agreed to withdraw, and French soldiers and administrators were allowed to enter North Vietnam, by which time the Vietminh had secured control of most of the country. In the absence of any alternative, the French authorities were forced to negotiate and to give qualified recognition to the Democratic Republic in return for a Vietminh undertaking not to oppose the entry of French troops. Further negotiations continued for six months, but it was already plain that no basis for a permanent settle-

91

ment existed between the Vietminh who wanted complete independence and the French government who were determined to retain some foothold in Indo-China; and after a series of incidents at the end of 1946, the struggle which was to last for more than seven years began.

In north and central Laos, where the Potsdam arrangements also applied, independence had been declared in September 1945. A government was formed by Prince Petsarath which, with Chinese support, claimed jurisdiction over the whole of the country; but south Laos remained loyal to the French, and large areas of the north-east and centre were controlled by mixed groups of Laotian and French guerrillas on one side, and joint companies of Vietminh and Laotian partisans on the other. When agreement with the Chinese was finally reached, and the French forces began their march northwards, almost all resistance vanished. There was only one serious engagement, near the town of Thakhek on the river Mekong, at a point which controls the shortest road across Laos between Vietnam and Thailand; and it turned into a rout. By the time the French had garrisoned Vientiane and occupied Luang Prabang, in May 1946, all the leaders of the Laotian Independence Movement had fled to Bangkok where they were to remain in exile for the next three years.

The government of France now resumed their tutelage of the Laotian people. They proved conciliatory, and in 1949 a Franco-Laotian Convention was signed which recognized Laos as an independent state, but continued to impose a number of restrictions on complete autonomy. The French authorities retained the right, among others, to station troops in Laos, a privilege which became increasingly significant as the military situation in neighbouring North Vietnam deteriorated. The Convention of 1949, however, satisfied most of the demands of the leaders of the Independence Movement still exiled in Thailand, and they now returned to Vientiane to take their place in the political life of the capital. But there were two notable exceptions: Prince Petsarath, because the King refused to forgive him; and Prince Souphanouvong, his younger half-brother, who chose to seek the help of the Vietminh believing, as they did, that independence was not to be won from the French by negotiation, but by force.

The year 1950 was a crucial one in the history of the Indo-Chinese states. The Communist victory in China and the outbreak of the Korean War revolutionized the attitude of the United States government to the problems of South-East Asia which from then on was regarded as an area of potential Soviet and Chinese expansion. The forces of France were provided with American aid, and finance was made available to help create a Laotian army. In response to Chinese and Russian recognition of the Democratic Republic of Vietnam, the American government recognized the Laotian government, and in 1951 signed an agreement on economic aid which laid the foundation for United States involvement in Laos over the next decade. The years 1950 and 1951 were good ones for the Vietminh also; with a safe sanctuary in China in which to refit and retrain their soldiers, and ample equipment supplied by the Chinese armies, they were able to transform what had been up to now no more than efficient guerrilla groups into a regular military instrument. By the beginning of 1951, they had six divisions in the field; and, from 1952 on, French control was confined to the main Vietnamese towns and the routes between them.

The final crisis for the French began in April 1953 when Vietminh troops crossed the border into Laos, driving back the French and Laotian forces who were stationed in the north-eastern provinces of Phong Saly and Sam Neua, and at one point threatening the royal capital of Luang Prabang. Along with the Vietminh companies came fighting units of the Pathet Lao, a national resistance organization which had been established under Prince Souphanouvong early in 1950, shortly after he moved to North Vietnam from Bangkok. With the arrival of the rains, the Vietminh returned to their base in Tongking, leaving the Pathet Lao behind in Laos to continue to administer the regions which had been taken over. This was the beginning of the civil war in Laos that has continued, on and off, ever since. Well-disciplined and orderly, like the Vietminh themselves, the Pathet Lao cadres proceeded to put into practice the methods of population control which they had been taught by the Vietminh (who in turn had learned from the Chinese) was the most effective way of liberating their country. The royal government was now confronted with a serious collapse of internal security, but, obsessed, as the French were, by the Vietminh, they appear not to have appreciated the extent to which the Pathet Lao had become a factor in the political life of the country. The threat to the royal capital had caused consternation in Vientiane and the Laotian government appealed to the government of France for protection. Decisions were taken, predominantly based on fear of further Vietminh invasion, which led to the disaster of Dien Bien Phu. The failure to face up to the challenge of the Pathet Lao was to have its own particular consequences, some of which still persist.

Pressures on the French to grant autonomy to the governments of Cambodia and Laos had been growing in 1952, within these states and from a United States administration which found itself increasingly embarrassed at having to fight Communism in defence of a colonial power. At the same time, opinion in France had been moving in favour of an end to the war that had gone on too long and of negotiations with the Vietminh. Since any settlement, to have any hope of being successful, must include full independence for Vietnam, which could not then be denied to Laos and Cambodia, the two questions – independence and the negotiations with the Vietminh – were closely connected in the minds of the French; but not in American eyes. The United States government, while firm in its support of independence, was resolutely opposed to any kind of surrender to the Vietnamese Communists. An armistice was signed in Korea in July 1953, and it would seem that, about this period, the French government finally concluded that negotiations with the Vietminh were inevitable. An agreement to begin talks to remove all remaining restrictions on Laotian sovereignty was arrived at during the same month, and the following October, with Prince Souvanna Phouma, younger brother of Prince Petsarath and elder half-brother of Prince Souphanouvong, as Prime Minister, Laos for the first time became a completely independent state.

Because their military advisers believed that their position might improve in the spring, the French government delayed seeking a negotiated settlement on Vietnam until a meeting of the foreign ministers of the United States, Russia, France and the United Kingdom which was held in Berlin in February 1954. There it was accepted that the situation in Indo-China would be discussed in April at a conference in Geneva which was being called to consider the problem of Korea. The United States government was not at all happy about the decision. The view of their military advisers was even more optimistic than that of the French. They were of the opinion that, with American assistance, the war in Indo-China not only could, but must be won to prevent the whole of South-East Asia falling into Communist hands. After toying with the idea of direct intervention to save Dien Bien Phu, a course of action from which they were dissuaded by their allies who would not support it, the government of the United States concentrated their attention on organizing a collective defence pact for South-East Asia (SEATO); and despite American foreboding that nothing good could come of it as far as they were concerned, the Geneva Conference on Indo-China held its first session on 8 May 1954, the day after Dien Bien Phu fell, attended by delegations from France, the United Kingdom, Russia, the United States, China, Cambodia, Laos and North and South Vietnam.

One of the most interesting aspects of the discussions at the Geneva Conference in 1954, looked at in retrospect, is the way in which the delegations of France and the United Kingdom ignored the political complications of the Laotian question. What the French wanted was an end to the war, an armistice with enough supervision to guarantee respect for its terms. The British claimed to know that there were no resistance forces in Laos apart from the Vietminh, and took the view that hostilities would end as soon as foreign troops left the country. The Soviet delegation tried hard on a number of occasions to have the Conference move on from military matters to take up consideration of a political settlement, but the French were emphatic, maintaining that it was the first duty of the delegates to ensure that violations of the cease-fire which might lead to war breaking out again could not occur; with the result that international supervision became the central issue before the Conference. Several suggestions were made about who should be asked to oversee whatever settlement might be reached. The UN was proposed at one stage, but rejected because the Chinese, who had only recently had a bitter experience of the organization in Korea, objected. Eventually, a compromise was arrived at, and the governments of India, Poland and Canada were invited to make up an International Control Commission.

On 21 July, the members assembled to consider the draft Declaration with which the Conference was to end. They already knew that separate agreements had been made on the Cessation of Hostilities in Vietnam, Cambodia, and Laos, one for each state, incorporating individual arrangements for supervision by the International Commission. The Final Declaration took note of these arrangements and, in the case of Laos, of two unilateral Declarations made by the royal government, one dealing with general elections and the integration of the Pathet Lao into the national community, and the other with the future military status of the country. The Final Declaration – which contained clauses calling on the members of the Conference to respect the sovereignty and territorial integrity of Laos and to consult together in the event of any violations of the cease-fire – was accepted on behalf of their governments by all of the delegations attending except for those from South Vietnam and the United States, whose government nevertheless undertook not to try to upset the agreements by force or threat of force.

The International Commission for Supervision and Control in Laos took up its responsibilities in Vientiane as soon as the Conference was over, with a mandate based on the Agreement on the Cessation of Hostilities in Laos. Its task was to observe the disengagement, regroupment and withdrawal of the armed forces of both sides, including the evacuation of all foreign troops in accordance with an agreed plan and by a specified date. The Commission was also to make certain that, with one exception, no fresh troops or military supplies entered the country. No difficulties were encountered as far as French units were concerned who were easily identified and anxious to leave; and to begin with, at least, the Laotian army caused no trouble. On the Vietminh side, the cease-fire agreement had been signed by the Vice-Minister for National Defence on behalf of the Vietnamese People's Volunteer Forces and the Fighting Units of the Pathet Lao; the title of the former being a sop to the Vietminh who refused to admit that any of their regular soldiers were in Laos. Teething troubles, difficulties of climate and terrain, lack of transport and serious language barriers made the work of the Commission difficult, and yet there would seem to have been no doubt in the mind of anyone at the time that, by the date given in the agreement, there were no longer any foreign troops in Laotian territory and that their withdrawal had been completed without serious incident of any kind.

Two distinct, but related and far less tractable problems remained to worry the International Commission. The first concerned its responsibility for ensuring that no new troops or equipment came into the country. Check points could be established without great difficulty in the Mekong river ports and at other points of regular entry into Laos; but it was not at all easy, and in many districts impossible, to patrol every jungle path leading across the mountains along the border with Vietnam. At a later stage, when accusations of Vietminh interference in the internal affairs of Laos were renewed, the controversy was to become acute; but at the outset of the Commission's life, the greatest obstacle which stood in the way of its completing its work was the dispute between the royal government and the Pathet Lao about the interpretation of the Agreement on the Cessation of Hostilities in Laos and, in particular, Article 14.

This article stipulated that, after regrouping in each of the provinces of Laos, those fighting units of the Pathet Lao who did not choose to be demobilized locally should be moved into the provinces of Phong Saly and Sam Neua, pending a political settlement. The Pathet Lao read this to mean that, until the modalities of their reintegration into the national community had been agreed on, they were entitled to exclusive control over the two provinces which they had, in any case, administered – one wholly, the other to a large extent – since 1953. The royal government held a different opinion. As far as they were concerned, Laos was a sovereign, unified state, and it had been the clear intention of the Geneva Conference that they, the generally recognized government, would resume the administration of Sam Neua and Phong Saly after the cease-fire. Pending a general election, which in their view was what the Conference had meant by a political settlement, the royal government agreed that the Pathet Lao should have special representation in the administration of the two provinces, but under no circumstances could this be thought to justify complete control. The phrasing of the Geneva documents is sometimes ambiguous, as no doubt it had to be for agreement to be reached, but the real difficulty was not over words. It was a revival of the difference about the political status of the Pathet Lao which had cropped up on the first day of the Conference. Then the leader of the Vietminh delegation had demanded that representatives of the Pathet Lao and not only the Vientiane government should be seated. On that occasion the Pathet Lao had lost the argument, but it had not been disposed of. The Pathet Lao continued to act as if they were an alternative administration – which is what they considered themselves to be – and the royal government strenuously objected. Both sides repeatedly made complaints to the International Commission which encouraged them to negotiate.

For a time, the prospects of talks seemed promising. The Prime Minister was still Prince Souvanna Phouma whose ability to compromise and whose devotion to the cause of national reconciliation were well-known. He also had excellent personal relations with the leader of the Pathet Lao, his half-brother Souphanouvong. But in September 1954 his government fell, following the assassination of the Defence Minister in circumstances which have never been satisfactorily explained. The Prime Minister was succeeded by Katay Don Sasorith, a man in many ways his direct opposite. From the south, sympathetic to the Siamese, with an antipathy for the Vietminh, he regarded Souphanouvong as not much better than a traitor. He was also unusually determined for a Lao. After breaking off talks with the Pathet Lao, he told the army to take over the administration of the two rebellious provinces if necessary by force, and began to make preparations for holding a general election. The fighting units of the Pathet Lao reacted predictably, nearly always having the better of the exchanges. As the number of violations of the cease-fire grew, both sides protested repeatedly to the International Commission.

The Commission worked hard to check the allegations, and to bring the parties to the negotiating table. It even arranged a meeting between the principals on neutral ground in Rangoon. But, since neither side trusted the other, it was not possible for them to agree even on an agenda. On Christmas Day 1955, a week before the deadline set by the Geneva Conference, Katay's government held elections throughout the country except in the two provinces whose administration was the subject of dispute.

The International Commission divided sharply over whether the elections which the royal government had carried out were in accordance with the Geneva Agreements or not, the Canadian delegate arguing that they were and the Polish representative asserting the reverse. The Indian chairman, while he agreed that the Laotian government were sovereign and entitled to hold elections when and where they chose, nevertheless felt that, since no political settlement had been arrived at and the Pathet Lao had taken no part, the elections which had taken place were not of the kind contemplated by the Geneva Conference. Because they could not agree among themselves, the members of the Commission referred the matter to the Co-Chairmen, the Foreign Ministers of the United Kingdom and the Soviet Union, appointed at the outset of the Geneva Conference after attempts to agree on a single chairman had failed. Certain residual, financial responsibilities apart, they had been given no formal authority to guide or direct the activities of the International Commission. That power, if it lay any-where, rested with the Conference as a body. But, since it was obviously in-convenient to recall the Conference every time the Commission sought advice, it became the practice for the two Co-Chairmen to try to resolve any difficulties which arose. Whether the Co-Chairmen, bearing in mind that they had been chosen as spokesman for each side, could have given a joint ruling on the validity of the 1955 elections can only be guessed, for, before they had a chance to do so, negotiations with the Pathet Lao were reopened in March 1956. Laotian public opinion had come to look on Katay's policy of no compromise, as not only unsuccessful, but dangerous. Prince Souvanna Phouma was recalled in the expectation that he would come to an agree-ment with the Pathet Lao which he did in August of the same year. A broad settlement gave legal recognition to the Pathet Lao as a political party, provided for their participation in a government of National Union and promised supplementary general elections the following May. In return the Pathet Lao agreed to hand over the administration of the two provinces as soon as a government of National Union had been formed, and joint commissions were established to go into the details of the integration of Pathet Lao officials and soldiers into the royal administration and army.

With the firm foundation of an internal political settlement under him, Prince Souvanna Phouma turned his attention to foreign affairs. At Geneva, the Laotian government had undertaken not to pursue an aggressive policy, never to take part in a military alliance and to request no more military assistance than was required to defend the country – this last restriction, it was clearly stated in the agreement, to continue until a final political settlement had been reached in Vietnam as well as in Laos. Less than a year before, while he still thought that a military solution of the Pathet Lao problem was possible, Katay had signed an agreement with the United States government which had enabled him, among other things, to increase the size of the Laotian army from 15,000 to 25,000 men. To advertise the intention of his government to adopt a neutral course of action, Souvanna, taking Katay along with him, set out on a journey to the capitals, going first to Hanoi and Peking, and later to Saigon, Paris and London. Since there was no mistaking the attitude of the American authorities to his policies, he did not go to Washington; but Katay went, and when he returned, opened an angry campaign accusing the Prime Minister of weak-ness in dealing with the Pathet Lao. As if to underline Katay's contention, Prince Souphanouvong chose this moment to demand, as a condition of the Pathet Lao joining the government, that aid should be sought in China as well as the United States, which was too much even for Souvanna Phouma. He replied with a counter-ultimatum: either the Pathet Lao accepted the terms offered to them or negotiations would come to an end; and the Pathet Lao climbed down. The settlement, which came to be known as the Vientiane Accords, was signed on 12 November 1957. A week later, a government of National Union was formed which included two Pathet Lao ministers, one of them Prince Souphanouvong.

The International Commission had no sooner finished congratulating itself (with every justification) on the part which it had been able to play in bringing about the integration of the Pathet Lao into the national community, when it received a letter from Prince Souvanna Phouma, as Prime Minister, saying that the royal Laotian government had decided to ask the Commission to wind up its affairs. The date intended was 4 May 1958, the day of the supplementary elections, and the reason given that, with these elections, the political settlement envisaged by the Geneva Conference would be fully implemented. The Canadian representative accepted the decision of the Laotian government and proposed the dissolution of the Commission. The Polish delegate, on the other hand, argued that until a final settlement was reached in Vietnam there was still work for the Commission in Laos to do. The Indian, though mindful of the sovereignty of the royal government, believed, nevertheless, that only the Geneva Conference could dissolve a Commission which they had established. After long and often heated debate, the wish of the Laotian government prevailed and the Commission decided, the Polish delegate dissenting, to adjourn *sine die*.

Only three days after the International Commission decided to adjourn, the political settlement which they had so laboriously helped to create was, for all practical purposes, set on one side. Prince Souvanna Phouma and his government of National Union were forced to resign. The Pathet Lao had been sufficiently successful in the supplementary elections to seriously alarm the government of the United States who suspended their aid; and this, combined with pressure from the Committee for the Defence of the National Interests (CDIN), was enough to prevent Souvanna Phouma from forming another government. The CDIN was a ginger group of civil servants, mostly young, who relied almost entirely on the Army for their support. It had been formed to combat Communist influence – the first time the phrase was used in Laotian politics. While rumours of a military take-over circulated in Vientiane, the CDIN demanded, and were given, four seats in the cabinet of a new government formed by Phoui Sananikone, the leader of the Laotian delegation at the Geneva Conference and the only senior politician acceptable to the CDIN, since he had not been associated with the policies of former governments.

A month or two later, following a small-scale outbreak of fighting at a sensitive point on the border between Vietnam and Laos, Phoui's government was granted special powers to rule without parliamentary vote. In February 1959, they announced that the obligations of the Laotian government under the Geneva Agreements were at an end, and that they could no longer accept any restrictions on their freedom of action or any international authority other than the UN. The American government, in welcoming this statement, pointed out that they could now establish a military mission in Laos. One by one, the safeguards which Prince Souphanouvong had negotiated with his half-brother to protect the position of the Pathet Lao were being taken away. They were unrepresented in the government, and the national assembly to which they had been fairly elected no longer met. Any hope which they might have had of achieving power by constitutional means was rapidly disappearing. Matters came to a head when a Pathet Lao battalion, which had been encamped in the Plain of Jars awaiting reintegration, escaped into the jungle after an inept attempt by the Laotian army to take it over. The government announced that, the Pathet Lao having committed an act of open rebellion, only a military solution was possible. Prince Souphanouvong with a number of other Pathet Lao leaders was placed under arrest.

In July and August 1959, there were repeated allegations that Vietminh units were fighting on Laotian soil, and the royal government twice took their case to the UN. On the second occasion, the Security Council, in the face of strong Russian objections, decided to appoint an investigating sub-committee. Its report, issued in the first days of November, was inconclusive. There was no evidence, the committee found, to support the accusation that North Vietnamese forces had invaded Laos, although the Laotian dissidents appeared to be receiving varying kinds and degrees of support across the border from North Vietnam. What in fact was happening, now that the Vientiane Accords were as good as dead, was that the Pathet Lao, with clandestine help from the Vietminh, were busy re-establishing their administration in the north-east of Laos, as they had done in 1953.

A day or two after the sub-committee's report was published, the UN Secretary-General visited Laos to examine the situation for himself. On leaving after a week of talks, Mr Hammarskjöld's counsel to the Laotian Prime Minister and his government was that they should revert to a policy of neutrality and concentrate on civil rather than military development. While he was in Vientiane, the Secretary-General appointed a commission, with Sakardi Tuomioja, a Finnish diplomat and economist, as chairman to examine the country's needs and consider what the UN might do to co-ordinate and improve foreign economic aid. The result, a much needed, objective statement of Laotian requirements, followed by some technical assistance, mainly in the field of public health, was regarded by the Laotian Government as disappointing.

Mr Hammarskjöld's moderate advice made no appeal to the CDIN members of Phoui Sananikone's government. The situation, in their judgment, demanded an intensification, not a slackening of the pressure on the Pathet Lao. The rift between the Prime Minister, who was gradually coming to share the Secretary-General's assessment, and the fiercer young men in his cabinet grew and, on 30 December, he was forced to resign. To preserve a measure of constitutional propriety, the King appointed a provisional government under a respected elder statesman, but the acknowledged ruler was the army and, in particular, the Secretary of State for Defence, General Phoumi Nosavan, who now took over the task of ensuring the security of the elections due to be held in April 1960. The outcome was prearranged. Candidates supported by the CDIN were elected, often with bizarre majorities, while the few Pathet Lao supporters who had been brave enough to stand were credited with the minimum of votes. On 23 May, fearing that he might be brought to public trial, Prince Souphanouvong escaped with all his guards, and made his way to Sam Neua, once again firmly in Pathet Lao control. He went on foot, and the circumstances of his progress were such as to suggest that although the army might have won the elections, the Pathet Lao retained the support of the countryside.

Throughout 1959, the North Vietnamese government, as signatory of the Geneva agreement on Laos, complained frequently to the Co-Chairmen about the repression of the Pathet Lao and the increasing introduction of American forces into Laos. In passing these complaints on to the British government, the government of the Soviet Union proposed that the Co-Chairmen should take urgent steps to ensure that the Geneva settlements were observed, that the International Commission should be recalled and the royal government urged to co-operate with it. At the same time, the Russians, supported by the Chinese and the North Vietnamese, continued to denounce the intervention by the UN and its Secretary-General in Laotian affairs, and accused the United States authorities of trying to camouflage their interference in Indo-China under the UN flag as they had done in Korea. As far as the Soviet government was concerned, the Geneva Conference was the correct international instrument for dealing with the Laotian question, and it demanded that the Conference should be reconvened. The government of the United Kingdom took a radically different view. It argued that the Pathet Lao and not the government in Vientiane were acting contrary to the spirit of the Geneva agreements, and pointed out that it would not be in accordance with the sovereignty of the Kingdom of Laos which the Geneva agreements had specifically recognized to force the International Commission on the royal Laotian government against its will. The two Co-Chairmen found that they were unable to agree on any joint course of action, while the situation steadily worsened.

What finally led not only to the return of the International Commission, but also to the convening of a second conference in Geneva, was the crisis which developed when Captain Kong Le and the parachute battalion that he then commanded took over the administration of Vientiane on 9 August 1960. Several months of constitutional confusion, with *coup* upon *coup*, were followed by civil war. For the first time a great power became directly involved on either side. The Americans had been supporting the Laotian army for some time and, in November 1960, the Russians flew in oil, heavy weapons and ammunition to assist Kong Le's forces – the Neutralists, as they had been called. There were by now three political and military factions in Laos and two governments, one backed by the army in Vientiane, the other by the Neutralists and the Pathet Lao who had set up a joint military headquarters in the area of the Plain of Jars.

Whether or not the international machinery established by the Geneva Conference can be said to have worked in Laos after the adjournment of the Commission in 1958, there is no doubt that it broke down completely when one of the Co-Chairmen took an active part in the dispute on the side of one of the factions. By the beginning of 1961, the threat to peace in Indo-China was more rather than less serious than before the 1954 Conference opened, and the smaller powers, those who were not members of SEATO, began to press for new international action. At the end of January, most of the interested countries had accepted the idea of another conference but, partly because the Co-Chairmen could not agree on which of the two governments in Laos should be consulted, negotiations dragged on for another three months. The Pathet Lao and their Neutralist allies, taking advantage of the delay, made such spectacular advances at the expense of the royal army that the Thai government took fright and the Americans had to move additional troops to Thailand to calm them. But the wiser counsel that had been available in the United States for some weeks eventually prevailed; it was evident that neither the American nor the Russian authorities were willing to risk a confrontation over Laos. On 24 April 1961, the Co-Chairmen asked the International Commission to take up its work again and invitations were sent out for the Conference which assembled in Geneva on 16 May.

The 1961 Geneva Conference was not, strictly speaking, a continuation or revival of the Conference of 1954. In that year, only the great powers and the representative of those actually engaged in the fighting attended; in 1961, other governments – the Thai and the Burmese, both states bordering on Laos, and the countries of the International Commisssion (Canada, Poland and India) – were asked, making 14 members in all. Whereas the 1954 Conference had considered the situation in the whole of Indo-China, in 1961, Laos alone was on the agenda. There were other contrasts. In 1954, the Conference ended after three months, having completed the arrangements for an effective cease-fire; the 1961 Conference went on for more than a year, and a cease-fire, announced before the delegates convened, was ineffective. At the earlier Conference, military matters had taken precedence over political; now it was to be the other way round.

After a difficult opening period, when the Chinese delegation was particularly awkward, the 1961 Conference began to make a considerable movement forward, and by the end of the year, agreement was close on most of the key issues, including the delicate question of a fresh mandate for the International Commission. But further progress was barred because the three factions in Laos were unable to speak with a single voice and until they could be persuaded to do so, no final settlement was possible. The army, the Pathet Lao and the Neutralists all accepted in principle that they should form a government of National Unity which could send a united delegation to Geneva. But because neither of the extremes would accommodate the other, in practice they failed to bring this about. By June 1962, the Americans found themselves compelled to bring strong pressure to bear to break the deadlock. It had become increasingly clear that, with the Pathet Lao making a fresh gain almost every day, the Chinese and the North Vietnamese were in no hurry to arrive at an agreement, and the United States government decided to force the army's hand by cutting off their support. Negotiations between the leaders of the three factions were resumed and, on 23 June, a government of National Unity received the royal assent. One month later, on 23 July, the second Geneva Conference was brought to a close with a Declaration on the Neutrality of Laos approved by a united Laotian delegation. A protocol to the Declaration contained proposals for the withdrawal of foreign troops, a ban on the reintroduction of armed forces or materials, the elimination of military bases and of the use of Laos as a corridor or staging-post for attacks on neighbouring countries, a matter of great concern to the Americans, Chinese, North and South Vietnamese for different reasons. The protocol also included provisions affecting the role of the International Commission and the Co-Chairmen. No important changes were made in the membership or functions of the Commission, but its duties were spelled out in greater detail. The position of the Co-Chairmen was also clarified and their authority made formal.

Despite the increased definition of its Articles, the Geneva Settlement of 1961–2 had two considerable disadvantages. In the first place, the International Commission could act only with the concurrence of the Laotian government. This phrase, which had been adopted by the Conference after long debate and as a compromise, had been carefully chosen to avoid any suggestion of interference in the affairs of Laos. What had not been foreseen was that the unanimous consent of the Prime Minister and his two Deputies, each belonging to a different faction, would be needed before the government of National Unity could concur; and that this would mean that the army and Pathet Lao, not to mention the Neutralists, would have to be of one mind – for example, over a cease-fire violation – before the International Commission could carry out an investigation. In other words, each faction had been given the right to veto the working of the supervision machinery.

A second serious drawback was that, unlike 1954 when complex arrangements had been worked out and signed by all the fighting forces, in the 1962 agreement no provision had been made to implement the armistice. The result was that each side continued to administer its own zone, and, because no lines demarcating the areas had been determined, armed clashes were frequent. The International Commission, realizing that everything depended on an internal political settlement, tried hard to speed up the integration of the three administrations and armies, but without success. Only the Neutralists were interested in trying to come to an agreement on terms other than their own, and the Neutralists were the weakest of the factions. Their strength was further reduced when the Russian airlift, on which they had come to depend, was suddenly stopped and they had to look to Hanoi for support. When it seemed that the Pathet Lao were taking an unfair advantage of this situation, Souvanna Phouma appealed to the United States government for assistance, and supplies were flown into the Plain of Jars. The invasion of their sanctuary by American aircraft angered the Pathet Lao. It also aggravated the growing divisions among the Neutralists, some of whom had began to resent their increasing dependence on the Vietminh, while others welcomed it. This schism spread to Vientiane, and very soon there were two Neutralist factions, one supporting Prince Souvanna Phouma, the other Prince Souphanouvong. Shortly afterwards, provoked on one side by the army, and on the other by the Pathet Lao, fighting broke out between them.

The International Commission made a number of attempts to bring the hostilities to an end and to encourage the two Neutralist groups to negotiate, but since they could not obtain the concurrence of the government of National Unity, everything they tried met with frustration. The Co-Chairmen fared little better. Because they now had specific authority from the Conference, they were emboldened to play a more active part than they had hitherto done which made it possible for their Ambassadors in Vientiane to give direct support to the Commission on the spot; but, as in 1959, they found that they were unable to agree on either the facts of the situation or what advice to give to the Laotian authorities. They were successful in working together only once – when the army tried to oust Prince Souvanna Phouma in April 1964 and they insisted on having him restored as Prime

Minister. On every other occasion, their efforts at joint action failed. By the end of 1964, the general state of civil war in Laos was as threatening to peace as it had been in 1961, with both sides receiving arms and material from outside the country and the machinery for supervision not in a position to prevent it. The two Co-Chairmen continued for a time to exchange notes, and there was a renewed appeal for yet another conference which came to nothing. No one any longer expected that the Laotian question could be settled while the larger war between the armed forces of the United States and the Vietnamese Communists, which had just been extended into North Vietnam, continued.

The political settlement proposed for Laos in the Final Declaration of the 1954 Geneva Conference – an end to external interference and national reconciliation at home – did not make enough allowance for the divisions in the country, caused by the dynastic, regional and commercial jealousies of the great Lao families on one hand, and the growing influence of the Pathet Lao among the mountain peoples, the non-Lao element in the Laotian community, on the other. Neither did it take sufficient account of the enmities which had troubled South-East Asia for centuries. Prince Souvanna Phouma, like Prince Petsarath before him, had, in addition to his acute awareness of the need for mutual concession, an understanding of the aspirations of the ethnic minorities which was shared by no leading Lao politician other than Prince Souphanouvong; and together they might have proved capable of providing good government in a united country. They were denied the chance, not because Prince Souphanouvong was thought to be a Communist, but because he was known to be too dependent on the Vietminh. This ancient Lao fear of Vietnamese power and ambition was shared by their other neighbours, the Siamese.

At Geneva, the Laotian question was dealt with in the context of Indo-China rather than South-East Asia. This tended to hide what might otherwise have been obvious, that the government of Thailand had legitimate interests there, which it was bound to assert when French troops evacuated the country and left the long sensitive border along the river Mekong virtually unprotected. The Siamese had not been invited to the Conference and did not feel bound by the agreements. In what they judged to be their national defence, and using whatever means were available to them, they did what they could to stop the spread of Pathet Lao influence, not for ideological reasons, but because, as far as they were concerned, Souphanouvong was the agent of the Vietnamese. It was the government of Thailand which took the lead, after Kong Le's *coup* in 1960, in resisting every effort by Souvanna Phouma to keep the three Laotian factions together. And, although they agreed finally to attend the 1961 Geneva Conference, they did it reluctantly, opposing to the very end any attempt to come to terms with the Pathet Lao.

The third important weakness of the agreements of 1954 was that the United States government did not adhere to them. Between 1954 and 1958, American preoccupation with the forces of international Communism was at its height, and the authorities in the United States were in no mood to go along with any further extension of Soviet and Chinese influence in Asia. They were convinced, not without good reason, that the elections promised under the Geneva arrangements would give the Vietminh the opportunity to take power by constitutional means in South as well as North Vietnam, and they could not accept this. In Laos, a similar danger was not immediately apparent, but when it did arise in 1958, the government of the United States quickly found a means of circumventing it. In 1959, the Vietminh and the Pathet Lao, who had been ready to stick strictly to the letter of the Geneva agreements as long as there was the hope that eventually they would lead to the reunification of Vietnam and Laos under governments which they could dominate, found that the way was becoming increasingly blocked, and took to armed struggle again. From that time on, the settlements reached at Geneva were ignored by both sides. And they were ignored also by the Chinese who considered that the promise which they had been given that there would be no American bases in Laos was broken.

The primary reason for calling the Geneva Conference in 1954 had been to bring to an end the war in Indo-China, and the course of the negotiations was in large measure dictated by the determination of the French government to secure an orderly and safe withdrawal of their troops. As a result the International Commission in Laos was established in the first instance to police a settlement. The members of the Conference took it upon themselves to consult with one another in the event of any violation of the cease-fire, but they apparently did not foresee the kind of situation in which the Commission might find it necessary to seek the guidance or invoke the authority of the Conference, and made no provision for the Commission to do so. Although it became the custom for the Co-Chairmen to act on behalf of the members in this regard, it was clear from a very early stage that they could not speak for the Conference as a whole. Lacking any other source, the individual Commissioners began more and more to look to their own governments for advice, and gradually ceased to behave as the instruments of an international body. Nevertheless (as Mr Hammarskjöld surely realized) the machinery of the Geneva Conference had one considerable advantage over the Security Council, in that it did not exclude the two countries who were not represented in the UN, China and North Vietnam. On the contrary, they were directly involved, together with the Pathet Lao, in the search for agreement. The disadvantage was that its procedures were un-wieldy. Reconvening the Conference in order to send instructions to the Commission was a cumbersome thing unlikely to commend itself to over-burdened Foreign Ministers; and yet there can be little doubt that if the Conference could have been recalled in 1959, or even possibly in 1963 (as the Russians among others demanded), the situation in Laos would not have deteriorated as quickly as it did. Regular meetings of the Geneva Powers, provided they could have been held at decision-making level, to consider the reports of the International Commission and to give weight to its recom-mendations, were perhaps the only method by which the Conference machinery could have been rendered more effective, however awkward they might have been to arrange.

On each occasion at Geneva, the delegates failed to face up to the delicate question of relations between the International Commission and the Laotian authorities. In 1954, the matter had been barely considered. In 1961, after more than six months of discussion, the relationship was defined in such a way as to paralyse the Commission's work. It was characteristic of both Conferences that the majority of members took it for granted that they were dealing with the problems of Laos in their external context only. In 1954, they were persuaded that once outside interference had been removed, the Laotians could successfully settle their difficulties among themselves. In 1961, undue deference was paid to the domestic jurisdiction of the Laotian government. There has never been, in modern Laos, a central administration strong enough to command the conflicting loyalties of the many ethnic groups which divide the nation, and as long as this remains the case, it is not easy for any Laotian government to resist the foreign pressures which these divisions attract. Because the stability of Laos depends as much on internal as on external factors, any future attempt to settle the conflict there by international means is, like its two predecessors, almost bound to fail unless the interested powers can be brought to accept that the regulation of the internal as well as the external aspects of the Laotian question lies within their competence.

6 THE CIVIL WAR IN THE CONGO

Evan Luard

Of all the cases of international action in civil-war situations, the UN intervention in the Congo is in many respects unique. UN involvement, whether measured in terms of men or of money, was on a larger scale than in any other case.[1] It aroused more passionate and prolonged controversy than any other peace-keeping operation, and its financial consequences put the very existence of the UN in peril for a time. Throughout the entire course of the operation there remained intense differences of opinion among the UN membership, among factions in the Congo, and even among UN officials, on the main objective of the force. And, because UN forces were withdrawn long before the civil war was finally brought to a conclusion, it is to this day a matter of controversy whether or not UN intervention achieved any useful purpose. While few would doubt that, in the long run, UN intervention in Lebanon and Cyprus secured positive results many still consider that the effects of the intervention in the Congo have been negative. Certainly the political situation in the country was far more confused when the UN force withdrew than when it arrived. Many of the difficulties of the operation stemmed from the changing, but always ambiguous, role the force was called on to carry out. This ambiguity was present almost from the beginning.

The situation which originally gave rise to UN action appeared relatively simple. In the immediate aftermath of independence, granted on 30 June 1960, a mutiny took place among soldiers of the Congolese Force Publique in Leopoldville. There was rioting, looting and raping of women. The officers of the Force, who were entirely Belgian, were incapable of restoring discipline. In the face of lurid descriptions of the treatment of Belgian civilians, especially women, at the hands of the mutinous troops, Belgium flew paratroops to the two bases which it already had in the Congo and which it expected to retain under an unratified Treaty of Friendship. From there they were flown to other towns throughout the Congo, in an attempt to restore order and to supervise the evacuation of Belgian and other European nationals. Though in general this action took place peacefully, in two cases, at the port of Matadi and at Kolwezi in Katanga, about thirty Congolese were killed in fighting between Belgian and Congolese forces.

Meanwhile Belgian officers were dismissed from the Force Publique by the new government and replaced by Congolese. Its name was changed to the Armée Nationale Congolaise (ANC). A sergeant, Victor Lundula, was made Major-General and Commander-in-Chief. Joseph Mobutu became Chief of Staff. Its discipline remained poor or non-existent for the next two years.

On 10 July, when it became evident that this force was quite incapable of effective discipline or maintaining law and order, let alone evicting the Belgian troops, the Congolese leaders, Kasavubu (the President) and Lumumba (the Prime Minister and Minister of Defence), appealed to the UN for assistance. They informally asked Ralph Bunche, at that time visiting Leopoldville on behalf of the Secretary-General, if the UN could provide 'technical military assistance' to help them deal with the situation in which they found themselves. In New York, Hammarskjöld called together delegates from a number of African countries to consider the establishment of a programme of 'technical assistance in the security field'. A request was also made for American military assistance, but the American government wisely advised the Congolese leaders to obtain the help they needed from the UN. Vague requests for help were also made to the governments of Ghana and the Soviet Union, but these also contented themselves with vaguely reassuring replies and took no action.

In a cable to Hammarskjöld on 12 July, the Congolese government formally requested UN assistance to meet 'the external aggression' and the 'colonialist machinations' of the Belgian government. On 13 July, perhaps realizing objections could be made to the dispatch of a UN force for restoring the *internal* situation in the Congo, Kasavubu and Lumumba sent a further telegram to the Secretary-General, stressing that 'the purpose of the aid requested is not to restore the internal situation in the Congo, but rather to protect the national territory against acts of aggression committed by Belgian metropolitan troops.' The implication seemed to be that, as soon as Belgian troops were evicted, the force's role would be at an end.

On 13 July, Hammarskjöld, invoking for the first and only time in the UN's history Article 99 of the Charter[2] (since the new government was not yet a member of the UN and able to demand a meeting itself), called a meeting of the Security Council. On the next day the Council adopted a resolution calling on Belgium to remove its troops, and authorizing the Secretary-General to take the necessary steps, in consultation with the government of the Republic of the Congo, to provide the government with such military assistance as may be necessary.' In the light of the attitude subsequently taken by the Soviet Union, it is important to note that (though she would have preferred a resolution naming Belgium as an aggressor) the Soviet Union voted in favour of this resolution, including the call for action by the Secretary-General personally. No member of the Security Council voted against the resolution, though Britain, France and Nationalist China abstained. America and Russia were both prepared to support UN action, primarily as a means of keeping the other out.

On the day after the resolution was passed, the first UN forces – Ghanaian troops transported by British planes and Tunisian troops transported by American planes – arrived in the Congo. Three weeks later there was a force of nearly 15,000. The force's strength rose to nearly 20,000 by the end of the year and, after various fluctuations, remained at this level for two years. It declined to about 12,000 in mid-1963, to 6,500 at the end of that year and was finally withdrawn in mid-1964. The largest contributors were India, Morocco, Ethiopia, Tunisia and Ghana; other substantial contributors were Malaysia, Ireland, Indonesia, Sweden and Liberia. Guinea, Mali, the UAR and Yugoslavia had forces for a time but withdrew them within a few months after the overthrow of Lumumba. Morocco and Indonesia withdrew their forces temporarily but restored them later.   ,

When first dispatched, therefore, the force was intended primarily to expel Belgian forces. But because of the indiscipline of the Force Publique it was accepted even in the first Security Council resolution that the force should also give assistance in keeping order 'as may be necessary' until the national security forces could 'meet fully their tasks'. This additional assistance in restoring law and order, rapidly became necessary. After years of paternalistic Belgian rule, which included little political development or administrative training, the Congo had been hastened to independence in the course of less than a year. The decision to grant independence in June 1960 was reached only five months earlier. At the time of independence there were few university graduates and few trained administrators. There were no African officers at all in the army. There was no effective government machine. There were no strongly based political institutions. Above all, there remained deeply ingrained tribal traditions within the country which, in any case, being the size of West Europe, would have been difficult enough to rule at the best of times.

The result was that the eviction of Belgian forces was only a small part of the task that was to be performed if a viable and stable state was to be established in the Congo. Internal divisions appeared long before the last Belgian soldier was evicted, and soon became a far more serious threat to the integrity of the country. Katanga, enormously rich in copper, declared its independence on 11 July, even before the first formal Congolese appeal to the UN. Because of the powerful Belgian financial influence in that province, the concentration of the remaining Belgian forces there, and the powerful propaganda on Katanga's behalf among Western capitalist concerns, it was understandable that its independence was widely regarded as having been contrived with Belgian connivance. To end Katanga's secession was therefore increasingly regarded as an important part of the UN's task in restoring the integrity of the country.

But even the central government quickly became deeply divided. Before considering the UN force's role, it may be useful to sketch these political developments. Within two months of the UN force's arrival, there was open conflict between the President, Kasavubu, and his Prime Minister, Lumumba. Here too the divisions went back to long before independence. Each had been political leaders, representing different parties, drawing support from different sections of the country, and frequently in rivalry. They had been able to co-operate with some success in the crisis which immediately followed independence, but they found that their attitudes and methods increasingly diverged. Lumumba became increasingly resentful at being unable to give direct orders to the UN force, and especially at the refusal of the UN to take open and direct action by force against Katanga. He was outspoken and even intemperate in his personal relations with UN officials. He was increasingly prepared to invoke Soviet assistance as a means of bringing pressure to bear on the UN and its Western members. These actions, together with the abrasiveness of his personality, even in dealing with his own countrymen, brought him increasingly into friction with Kasavubu. On 5 September Kasavubu dismissed him as Prime Minister and appointed the President of the Senate, Joseph Ileo, in his place. Lumumba in turn purported to dismiss the President and appealed for the assistance of the workers and the Congolese army.

Officially, the UN was impartial in all such internal political conflicts. Nevertheless some action had to be taken to maintain normal life and prevent disruption. For a few days, when the political crisis was at its height, the Secretary-General's special representative in the Congo, Andrew Cordier, closed the major airport and the radio station, and so made it more difficult for dissident forces to converge on Leopoldville. This could perhaps be regarded (and sometimes was) as a form of intervention in the Congo's internal affairs, since it certainly strengthened the President and his supporters against Lumumba. But if it is assumed that the UN regarded the President as exercising superior authority to the Prime Minister, it could be justified as helping to maintain central control generally. In fact both Kasavubu and Lumumba protested equally vigorously against these actions. The airports were kept under UN control. The radio station was returned to the government on 2 September. On the same day Lumumba was placed under arrest by the army.

Two days later, on 14 September, a military *coup*, led by General Mobutu, dismissed the new government and established a 'Council of Commissioners' to take over the country, with Kasavubu still the President. This *coup* is sometimes said to have been inspired by the CIA.[3] Whether or not this is so, the new régime certainly had the support of the United States government (as has General Mobutu through the succeeding period). Mobutu quickly broke off diplomatic relations with the Soviet Union. On 1 December Lumumba was again placed under arrest. Not long afterwards he was handed over to the forces of Tshombe, his greatest enemy. Meanwhile, Gizenga, an associate of Lumumba, set up a rival Lumumbist régime in Stanleyville, which was accorded some recognition by the Soviet Union and other countries.

All this created additional difficulties for the UN and its officials. They did all they could to avoid taking sides: the Secretary-General's special representative in the Congo, Mr Dayal, in conferring recognition on the Chief of State and the parliament, seemed to deny recognition to the new government which had dissolved parliament. Partly for these reasons, there was increasing pressure, especially from Western countries but also from the Congolese authorities, for the removal of Mr Dayal, and in March 1961 he was recalled. In general UN officials dealt on a *de facto* basis with whatever authority they found in power at any one time. But the difficulty, inherent in any UN peace-keeping operation, of deciding what degree of co-operation there should be between the UN and the central government of the country concerned, in the Congo was particularly acute: because of the additional doubt on which was the central government.

Because of these various difficulties, the mandate of the UN force was progressively strengthened. Increasing emphasis was placed on the restoration of law and order, and the maintenance of the unity of the Congo. A new resolution of 22 July 1960, made clear that the objective was the 'maintenance of law and order' as well as the supervision of the evacuation of Belgian forces. On 21 February 1961, a further and much stronger resolution was passed in the Security Council, calling for 'appropriate measures', including 'the use of force, if necessary, in the last resort' to 'prevent the occurrence of civil war'. This resolution also called for the reconvening of the Congolese parliament, and demanded the reorganization of 'Congolese armed units' to bring them under discipline and control: a form of intervention in the internal affairs of a member state of a type very rarely attempted in UN history.

On 9 February 1961, the Congolese régime was put on a somewhat better legal basis by the replacement of Mobutu's Council of Commissioners by a civilian government led by Mr Ileo (who had originally been appointed by the President to replace Lumumba the previous September). The government's authority, however, remained strenuously disputed. The murder of Lumumba by Tshombe's forces on 21 February intensified hostility both at home and abroad. Mr Gizenga's rebel Lumumbist government remained entrenched in Stanleyville. Tshombe remained in control in Katanga. There was a serious rebel movement in Kasai under Albert Kalonji. To try to resolve these various conflicts, two conferences took place in March and April 1961, designed to establish a new constitution for the Congo that would provide for some degree of provincial autonomy. In July the parliament was recalled and a compromise government was formed under Mr Adoula. This appeared even to reconcile Gizenga, who was made Vice-Premier, though in practice he soon absented himself from Leopoldville again. In September and December the UN force was involved in two clashes with Tshombe's forces in Katanga. Though inconclusive, these perhaps helped to induce Tshombe to recognize the Adoula government, and to enter into discussions on the reintegration of Katanga with the country as a whole.

None of this, however, lasted very long. In January 1962, Gizenga once again established a rebel régime in Stanleyville. In June, the talks between the Adoula government and Tshombe broke down. In August, the Secretary-General announced his own plan of national reconciliation for the Congo, which received little response. In December, yet another clash between UN forces and those of Mr Tshombe in Katanga brought Katanga's secession to an end.

Even this, however, was not sufficient to restore normality. Though central government control in Katanga was re-established, and Tshombe finally left the country in June 1963, political dissension continued elsewhere. Gizenga continued in control of Stanleyville. In September, parliament was again adjourned indefinitely, after it became bogged down in increasingly sterile conflict. In October, support for the Stanleyville government was increased by the establishment of a National Liberation Committee in Brazzaville. In 1964, a new rebellion broke out in Kwilu, and later spread through other provinces. In June of that year, the final UN forces left, with the country more divided than ever. Only a few days later, by a final irony, Tshombe, against whom much of the UN's activity had been directed, became Prime Minister of the whole country amid general acclamation.

During the course of these developments the UN found itself entrusted with at least four major tasks. These characterized the different roles which a UN force may be expected to carry out in a civil-war situation (the UN would find itself with very similar tasks if called to play a role in Vietnam today). The tasks were: to expel the Belgians; to end secession; to prevent civil war among the major leaders and to maintain law and order generally; and to build up the administration of the shattered country. It may be useful to examine the success of the UN in dealing with each of these main problems.

The first and simplest task was to supervise the eviction of the Belgians. The withdrawal of Belgian forces sent to the Congo in early July 1960, began within a week or two on 17 July, and it was largely completed by 23 July. There still remained, however, Belgian forces in the two bases provided for in the draft Treaty of Friendship. These were at Kitona in the west, and at Kamina in Katanga. Belgium was far less willing to evacuate her troops from here. She used her military strength in Katanga to give direct assistance to Tshombe, and to prevent central government forces overrunning that province. She also established a Belgian technical mission in Katanga, which gave Tshombe support of other kinds.

Under strong pressure from the UN, Belgium did finally agree to begin evacuation of Belgian forces from Katanga on 12 August 1960. By the middle of September the evacuation of Belgium's official national forces was largely completed. Even then, however, a considerable number of Belgian officers were left behind to assist Katanga's army on an unofficial basis. At the same time, Belgian officials sought to obtain assurances of UN 'non-intervention' in Katanga's affairs: in other words, the UN would be allowed to come in if they did nothing to displace Tshombe or his régime. Because of actions of this kind, Hammarskjöld considered it an important part of the UN's task to eliminate the 'Belgian factor'. He even extended this aim to include the eviction of all Belgians, including civilians and technical advisers assisting the central government, whom that government wished to keep. It is not certain how far this policy could really be justified by the Security Council's mandate, and it was abandoned after April 1961. In any case some Belgians managed to stay on throughout in advisory capacities. Others returned in the second half of 1961 and subsequent years. By 1964 there were probably 40,000 Belgians in the Congo again, against 100,000 in 1960.

In the summer of 1961, after a change of government in Belgium, Belgian policy in the Congo changed significantly. The seconded officers helping Katanga's army were withdrawn, and Belgium gave its full support to the central government in Leopoldville. There remained, however, the more difficult problem of the Belgian mercenaries, about 300 at that time, acting entirely independently, and fighting on behalf of Tshombe. Recruitment of mercenaries, both for military and other purposes, had been undertaken in Belgium under official auspices by the Marissal mission in the first half of 1961. But after July 1961, with the new Belgian govern-ment, this policy was abandoned. The new government also agreed to the recall of the officers and NCO's seconded to the Katangese forces. On 28 August, the UN attempted a forcible round-up of all Belgian officers and mercenaries. This was halted on Belgian representation, in return for an assurance that the Belgian government would attempt to secure the return of both regulars and mercenaries. In the event, almost all the regulars and two-thirds of the mercenaries were repatriated.

The UN attempt to round up the mercenaries by force, in September 1961, was poorly executed and proved unsuccessful. But, in October, the Belgian government announced (as the British government had done earlier) that it would withdraw the passports of Belgian nationals who continued to serve in Katanga's forces. Though some mercenaries un-doubtedly remained, Belgium had been brought to cooperate generally with the efforts of the UN in the Congo. The first, but least difficult, part of the UN's task was completed.

The second, and far more difficult, problem was to end the secession of Katanga. From the beginning, after Tshombe had declared secession on 11 July, the UN supported the principle of its reintegration with the Congo. But at first it favoured attempts to do this by peaceful means. Since, at first, Katangese and Belgian forces joined in preventing UN forces from entering Katanga at all, there was little the organization could do. An attempt to send in a token force, on 4 August 1960, was prevented by Katangese forces.

Lumumba became increasingly impatient at the failure of UN forces to reconquer Katanga by force. He clashed sharply with Hammarskjöld, Bunche and Cordier upon the issue. He was reluctant to accept the argu-ment that the mandate of the UN force did not provide for enforcement action, or that the contributing countries would object to the force being launched on a war to subdue Tshombe. In its resolution of 9 August, the Security Council sought to bridge the gap by declaring that the entry of the force into Katanga was 'necessary', but that it should not be used to determine the political issues in dispute. This enabled a token Swedish force, accompanied by the Secretary-General, to enter Katanga and to occupy various locations. By 23 August, UN forces had occupied the two main Belgian bases of Kitona and Kamina. But Tshombe's attitude on secession remained unchanged. He continued to maintain powerful forces which restrained all attempts by the central government to re-establish control of the province. Lumumba, disgusted by the UN attitude, at one time called for the withdrawal of the UN force and began negotiations with the Soviet Union for the dispatch of Soviet military aid. If this request for a

UN withdrawal had been backed by the President (who himself, at a later stage, briefly called for the UN's withdrawal), the UN would have had little option but to comply, though there were some attempts to argue that the agreement of 29 June between the Secretary-General and the Congolese government which spoke of the willingness of the latter to co-operate 'in good faith' with the UN, gave it the power to remain even against the government's will. In any case the overthrow of Lumumba on 10 September saved the UN from this predicament.

The advent of the Mobutu régime did not, however, in itself make any easier the problem of Katanga's secession. Gradually the UN regional command headquarters in Elizabethville was built up, despite Tshombe's protests. Tshombe himself came into increasing conflict with Baluba tribesmen in the same region, whose leader, Jason Sendwe, favoured central government rule. United Nations garrisons were established in various towns, and neutral zones were used to separate the Baluba and Tshombe forces. In April 1961, Katangese forces led by mercenaries attacked Indian and Ethiopian troops of the UN force. In the same month, Tshombe was captured by Congolese government forces leaving a conference of Congo leaders. After some UN intercession he was released in return for a promise that he would take part in the July conference at Lovanium and would support a united Congo. Although Tshombe appeared to go back on his promise, and never finally attended the conference, he did subsequently agree to support the Adoula government which was then set up.

The new government, however, which temporarily united Lumumbist and Mobutu forces, still regarded the ending of Katanga's secession as its main task. The UN endorsed this aim in several resolutions. Tshombe began to negotiate for a loose federal structure which would give considerable autonomy to Katanga. In September 1961, there were sharp but inconclusive clashes (O'Brien's War) between UN forces and those of Tshombe. These stemmed from the attempt to round up Belgian mercenaries, and an ill-prepared effort to arrest Tshombe and his ministers, and so to end Katanga's secession. In December, after an abortive cease-fire of three months, during which there was another attempt by central government forces to conquer north Katanga and repeated incidents between Tshombe's forces and the Baluba refugees, there was further fighting between UN and Tshombe's forces, this time deliberately provoked by Tshombe. Although the UN military position was strengthened by the second incident, neither affected the basic political situation. Tshombe continued to haggle with the Adoula government for a considerable degree of autonomy though he professed to accept the principle of 'unity'.

After the December 1961 fighting, Tshombe agreed nominally to participate in drafting a new constitution, to send back his representatives to parliament, to place the Katanga gendarmerie under the Chief of State and to respect the UN resolutions on the Congo. However he quickly began to place his own interpretation on this agreement. For a year, there was virtually no progress. In August 1962, U Thant proposed a constitutional settlement highly favourable to Katanga, calling as it did for the sharing of tax royalties on a fifty-fifty basis between Katanga and the central government, and for the representation of Tshombe's party in the government. But this was not accepted by Tshombe and, in December, U Thant called for economic sanctions against Katanga including a ban on the import of Katangese copper by UN members. At the same time, repeated incidents in which Katangese had attacked the UN force, and increasing impatience both in the Congo and elsewhere at the continuation of secession, promoted increasing tension between Tshombe and the UN forces.

On 28 December, after repeated firing by Katangese gendarmes against the UN forces, the UN informed Tshombe that unless firing stopped, they would take all necessary action in self-defence to restore order. When the firing continued, UN forces proceeded to invest Elizabethville and the surrounding area. Tshombe fled. When he returned to Katanga, he agreed to the surrender of all weapons to the UN forces and to the end of secession. Most of the mercenaries left for Angola.

In all the UN's operations in Katanga, about 42 UN soldiers were killed and 200 wounded against around 300 killed on the Katangan side. In addition nearly 50 civilians are thought to have lost their lives. It is the only example so far in which UN forces have been used on a substantial scale in a civil-war situation. Without their action, it is doubtful if the reunification of the Congo could have been achieved except at a far greater cost in lives and far more slowly. External intervention by the great powers would have been encouraged, and war on a still greater scale might have been precipitated.

The third task of the UN was to deal with the political divisions in Leopoldville itself. After these first appeared, with the overthrow of Lumumba, the UN, as we saw earlier, had sought to remain impartial between factions. It never formally acknowledged the legality of the 'Council of Commissioners'. However, after the formation of the Ileo government and the death of Lumumba, UN officials were bound to deal increasingly with the only effective government. The Gizenga 'government', which was never formally recognized even by the Soviet Union,[4] had no power in Leopoldville, and the UN in any case had little reason to deal with it since there were no UN forces in the Stanleyville area at that time.

When the UN force was originally formed, the Secretary-General established an advisory committee to help resolve the political problems. In

November 1960, this in turn set up a Conciliation Commission to help resolve the conflict between political leaders in the Congo. It was originally composed of fifteen African and Asian states, but the UAR, Guinea and Mali subsequently resigned because the Commission failed to support Lumumba. In April 1961, the Conciliation Commission proposed the establishment of a 'federal form of government' under a parliamentary system. The UN force should be strengthened to enable it to maintain law and order more effectively, to prevent tribal warfare and to control undisciplined soldiers, and all foreign interference, especially military interference, should be brought to an end. Admirable though these aims were, there was little that the UN could do at first to implement them. But, after the failure of the two conferences in March and April 1961, UN officials gave all possible support to the conference held at Lovanium University, which finally resulted in the formation of the Adoula government. UN troops demilitarized the zone where the conference was held, and generally serviced and guided the meeting. They were active behind the scenes in promoting compromise. UN officials welcomed the agreement to form the government, and Hammarskjöld announced that he would deal exclusively with that government from then on.

The Security Council resolution of 21 February 1961, gave the UN force the authority to use force, 'if necessary, in the final resort' to prevent civil war. Once a widely recognized government had been established, this could be interpreted as authority to use force on behalf of that government against all challenges to its authority. Except in Katanga, however, the UN sought to avoid direct involvement of this sort. When Gizenga again broke away to establish a secessionist government at Stanleyville in December 1961, the UN itself took no direct military action. But the UN force did give some direct assistance to the Congolese government force which defeated the Stanleyville gendarmerie, and an Ethiopian platoon helped to disarm some of the defeated troops. A UN plane flew Gizenga back to Leopoldville, where he was handed over to the Adoula authorities. U Thant justified these actions on the ground of the general UN 'mandate to assist the central government in the maintenance of law and order and in the prevention of civil war'.

The other dissident movements in the Congo were smaller in scale, and won no international recognition. The Kalonji régime in south Kasai, which was proclaimed an independent state on 9 August 1960, was at no time recognized by the UN as having any legitimacy. It was neither negotiated with nor recognized by any outside government. But the UN force took no action comparable to that taken in Katanga. Some areas were conquered by Congolese forces in 1960. But most of it remained independent under its self-styled President until January 1962 when Kalonji was arrested in

Leopoldville. He was subsequently sentenced to two and a half years imprisonment, but was released and subsequently rearrested. The UN explicitly
refused to intervene in the case of Kasai, when requested to do so by the
Adoula government, though the situation was not basically different from
that in Katanga. Mr Robert Gardiner, the UN Director of Operations in the
Congo declared : 'We are neither a force of occupation, nor the administration of a colony.'

The UN was more directly involved in the pacification of the Baluba in
north Katanga. These were at various times involved in clashes with central
government forces, Tshombe's army and UN troops. They were sought as
allies by Gizenga as well as Mobutu on several occasions. The UN took
responsibility for evacuating large numbers (nearly 70,000) at the time
when Tshombe was actively attacking them. They took over the chief
Baluba town of Manoma and sought to protect it from Tshombe's forces.
In September 1961, there were 35,000 Baluba refugees in UN camps in
Elizabethville, and the number continued to grow. Finally, in July 1962,
after Tshombe's forces were weakened, 70,000 Baluba people were flown
back from Elizabethville to their home areas in north Katanga.

In 1964, further rebellions broke out in Kwilu, Kasai, north Katanga and
elsewhere, partly supported by the National Revolutionary Committee. But
by this time, the UN force was reduced to only half its previous size, and
was preparing to withdraw (originally it had been hoped it might withdraw a year earlier than it did). At that time a new Lumumbist régime was
firmly entrenched in Stanleyville under Mr Gbenye. The UN did not,
therefore, make any real contributions to the containment of these later
rebel movements. At the time its force finally withdrew in June 1964, a
substantial part of the country was in rebel hands. It was Tshombe himself, once the foremost secessionist leader, who finally succeeded in putting
down secession, after he was elected Prime Minister in July 1964. He was
largely successful in restoring unity with the help of the same mercenary
forces with which he had previously sought to prevent it.

The final task of the UN in the Congo was the building up of a more
efficient administration, and especially more effective armed forces, to
enable the country to maintain its integrity in the future.

So far as the armed forces were concerned, everybody agreed that a
condition of restoring order in the country was the reorganization of the
ANC. The UN was not itself well equipped for this task, however, nor did it
have the authority, under its mandate, to take such action, except at the
request of the Congolese government. In some cases UN forces did bring
about the disarming of the ANC, a force which often amounted to little
more than bands of armed men engaged in bandit operations. But UN

civilian officials turned down requests from some of the military commanders, such as General Alexander (the commander of the Ghanaian forces) for a systematic reorganization of the Congolese forces. In his Annual Report for 1962, U Thant said that 'more determined steps would have to be taken with regard to the training and reorganization' of the ANC; but he was careful not to state that the UN itself would undertake this task. Retraining and re-equipment of the force was finally undertaken by the United States, Israel and other Western countries: ironically it was the American government itself which had been most anxious that the UN should undertake this task and it was the Soviet Union which had opposed it.

The UN did, however, give substantial assistance in undertaking direct administrative tasks as well as in the training of Congolese to take over technical and administrative responsibility. A whole generation of officials was produced in three or four years. A number of the UN specialized agencies, such as the UPU and the ITU, also gave special assistance in training personnel and reorganizing services. As a result of these activities, by the time the UN force left in June 1964, the Congo was incomparably better equipped to face the problems it confronted than in 1960. Many would judge this the single greatest achievement, and prime justification, of the UN's actions in the Congo.

At first sight, the UN operation in the Congo was not a happy example of international action in a civil-war situation. At the time the UN force left, the country was in a state of considerably greater chaos and disorder than when it arrived four years earlier. Unity had not been restored. Secession had not been ended. And, although Belgian official forces had been removed, European mercenaries still remained active in various parts of the country. The UN was forced to leave through financial necessity (and despair at the hopelessness of the task) rather than because its mission had been accomplished.

This is, however, to take a somewhat narrow view of the operation and its purpose. Looked at in a wider context, the essential value of the UN operation was that it enabled certain vital assistance to be given in maintaining the integrity of the Congo without its government calling in foreign military intervention. UN forces were instrumental in bringing an end to the secession of Katanga with a far lower loss of life than would have occurred without its help. Essential economic and administrative assistance was given. And the UN presence gave constant moral and material support to the principle of the unity of the Congo, and so made a very significant contribution to ensuring that that unity was finally restored. Above all, as we have just seen, the UN helped the Congo to build up its administration, and even for a time its political structure, more effectively and with less controversy than any other outside assistance could have done.

Quite apart from this assessment of success or failure, which can in any case only be subjective, the Congo operation is of special interest in examining the role the UN can play in civil-war situations. The UN has never been so heavily involved in such a situation as there. And the operation raised in extreme form some of the problems always likely to arise in such cases.

One particularly critical problem in the Congo lay in determining how far the UN was committed to assist the central government against rebel factions. At first, UN spokesmen insisted vigorously that the UN would not and should not intervene at all in the Congo's internal disputes. Even in Katanga they were willing to deal with the Tshombe authorities on a *de facto* basis, and Hammarskjöld consistently declined to help Lumumba impose his authority in that area by force. When authority was disputed between Lumumba and Mobutu in the autumn of 1960, UN officials also declined to take sides. But this attitude began to be eroded as time went on especially after the formation of the Adoula government in July 1961. At that time, Hammarskjöld assured Adoula that the UN force had 'only one goal, namely to aid your government in the maintenance of public order'.[5] This implied assisting it against secessionist movements, as the UN force did, in effect, in Katanga in September and December 1961 and, more decisively, in December 1962. Again, as we saw, though not involved in fighting, the UN force gave Adoula's forces some assistance against Gizenga in January 1962. Thus, even though only a month or two later U Thant declared that the UN had 'scrupulously avoided' any interference in the Congo's internal affairs, by the very nature of its presence, in 'restoring law and order' or 'ending secession', it was increasingly constrained to give active assistance to the central government against its enemies and so to interfere.

A second related issue, which could also occur in any case of UN action in a civil war, but occurred in acute form in the Congo, concerned the use of force. At first it was clearly laid down that the UN force was a 'peace-keeping' force only, and would use force, if at all, only in self-defence. But successive Security Council resolutions strengthened this mandate. The resolution of 21 February 1961 authorized the UN to 'take immediately all appropriate measures to prevent the recurrence of civil war in the Congo, including arrangements for cease-fires, the halting of all military operations, the prevention of clashes, and the use of force, if necessary, in the last resort.' The Security Council resolution of 24 November 1961 specifically declared 'full and firm support for the central government of the Congo, and the determination to assist that government in accordance with the decision of the UN to maintain law and order and national integrity.' Each of these could have been used as authority for the UN to use force on behalf of the central government against rebel forces. In practice, however, UN spokesmen (with the exception of Mr O'Brien) continued to deny any such intentions. Even in February 1963, after the final action which ended the secession of Katanga, U Thant continued to declare that the UN respected fully the principle of non-interference in the internal political affairs of the Congo. When force *was* used, as in December 1961 and December 1962, it could always be justified on the grounds of 'self-defence', 'maintaining law and order', 'securing freedom of movement', 'expelling mercenaries', 'preserving the territorial integrity of the country', or 'preventing civil war'. Whatever the justifications, however, the *effect* of using force was to assist the central government against rebel forces. Since there was ample authority for such action in Security Council resolutions, it would have been simpler and more honest if the UN had said as much in so many words. That it did not was probably the result of the outspoken opposition to firm action of countries such as Britain and France, whose governments totally failed to show how the central government could be assisted to 'maintain law and order' against actively rebellious forces without such intervention on behalf of the government. The confusion that occurred, however, suggests the need for the mandate of any future UN force to be drawn up with far greater clarity than on this occasion.

The third general issue arising from the Congo experience concerns the degree to which the underlying political conflicts of a civil-war situation can be influenced, without resorting to the use of force, by the UN when it has been asked to give assistance. In this sense too, the UN became increasingly involved in attempts to influence the resolution of political differences. The Security Council resolution of February 1961 recommended the reconvening of parliament and the 'formation of a government based on genuine conciliation'. The UN gave some assistance and encouragement to the two conferences held in the spring of 1961. And the conference at Lovanium University, which brought the Adoula government to power was largely promoted by UN officials, who encouraged agreement behind the scenes and suggested constitutional formulas. Dr Bunche helped in the negotiation of the Kitona Agreement between Tshombe and Adoula in December 1961. In July 1962, UN officials prepared a new constitution for the country at the request of the central government. Finally, that autumn U Thant proposed his own Plan for Reconciliation, setting out a new political future for the Congo. It is doubtful if the UN has ever in any other case become so deeply involved in proposing internal political arrangements for a member country : in Cyprus the UN mediator has made *private* proposals to resolve the constitutional deadlock there, but for the UN to become publicly committed to a particular solution to a country's political problems was a significant precedent.

A fourth striking feature of the Congo operation was the remarkable degree of consensus it was possible to achieve in New York, given the highly contentious political conflicts involved. There were five main Security Council resolutions (14 July, 22 July and 9 August 1960 and 21 February and 24 November 1961) and one General Assembly resolution (20 September 1960). Not a single vote was cast against any of these resolutions. The United States and the Soviet Union voted together on every Council resolution except that of 21 February 1961, on which the Soviet Union abstained.[6] The chief abstainers were France and Britain, but they never pushed their doubts to the point of a veto. It is true that, as always, this degree of unanimity was achieved partly through careful ambiguity. But it did reflect the wide concern nearly everywhere to prevent external intervention, to end the secession of Katanga, and to support the central government against its opponents (even the Soviet Union gave its support to the Adoula régime after its establishment in July 1961).

The final, and most obvious, point, however, is that, if the UN is to be able to play a more effective role in the future, it must show greater patience and persistence in the task than it did on this occasion. If the operation could have been continued for only one more year, it might have been brought to an end under less inglorious circumstances than in fact occurred. The undignified conclusion was partly the result of general frustration and the disorganized political scene in the Congo, but mainly of purely financial causes. If such fiascos, which do much to reduce the authority of the UN in the eyes of world public opinion, are to be avoided in the future, some more satisfactory financial basis for peace-keeping operations must be found. If a permanent peace-keeping fund could be established, even if voluntarily financed, or if some general agreement for the financing of peace-keeping forces could be agreed, further failures of this kind might be avoided. Alternatively, if, from the start, the force had been financed from voluntary contributions (like later forces) it is possible that the financial crisis which ensued, in part the result of an attempt to include the cost of the force in normal assessments, might have taken more manageable proportions. The UN role in Cyprus, which has already continued half as long again as that in the Congo, and at a lower total cost, may perhaps provide a better model for future operations of the same kind.

There is no doubt, none the less, that the UN operation in the Congo vitally assisted that country to restore its unity and to rebuild its administration without being obliged to call for help from any particular external party, which in turn might have provoked outside help on behalf of other factions. This alone can perhaps be regarded as ample justification for all the wearisome endeavour, heart-ache and disillusion which the UN underwent in that unhappy country. At least the Congo did not become another Vietnam.

TEXT REFERENCES

1. The total cost of the Congo operation from July 1960 to June 1964 was $402 million, of which the United States provided $168 million, or 42%.
2. Article 99 of the Charter authorizes the Secretary-General to 'bring to the attention of the Security Council any matter which in his opinion may threaten the maintenance of international peace and security'.
3. Hoskyns, C., *The Congo Since Independence*, Oxford 1965, p.201.
4. Dallin, S., *The Soviet Union in Africa*.
5. UN Security Council Records, S/4923, of 13 August 1961.
6. The Soviet Union had, however, vetoed earlier resolutions.

7 THE CIVIL WAR IN YEMEN

Dana Adams Schmidt

The attempt in the early 1960s to bring peace to Yemen was one of the notable failures in the annals of the UN. It was a failure also of American foreign policy because the State Department was obviously behind the UN's principal movements. But it was a failure from which something could be learned.

Before going into these lessons it would be useful to give an account, as objective as possible, of what happened in and to Yemen in those early years of the 1960s.

The conflict with which the UN was concerned began with the overthrow, on 26 September 1962, of the Imam Mohamed al Badr of Yemen by a group of officers headed by Brigadier Abdullah Sallal. The Egyptian army moved in behind the revolutionary movement to support the newly proclaimed Republic. Saudi Arabia at the same time began to support the tribes of northern and eastern Yemen who remained loyal to the Imam, or who at least were responsive to the money and arms sent to them by the Saudis.

Although the Egyptians sent in up to 70,000 men supported by a strong air force, they were not able to subdue the Royalist tribesmen. They persisted, however, until the circumstances created by the Arab–Israeli war of June 1967 obliged them to abandon the whole enterprise and they completed withdrawal from Yemen on 7 December 1967. But this did not end the war which continued in a desultory way till May 1970, when a settlement was eventually achieved with Saudi Arabia's blessings.

This chapter is mainly concerned with the period in late 1962, in 1963 and 1964, during which the UN attempted to bring about a settlement and to deter foreign intervention.

The subject may be clarified by dividing it into five periods. The first, concerned with manoeuvring at the UN and international diplomacy, begins on 27 November 1962. On this date the Royalists asked the UN for an inquiry into the situation created by Egyptian intervention in Yemen. The second deals with the UN's first activities in Yemen, beginning on 1 March, when Ralph Bunche arrived at Taiz in Yemen. The third covers the setting up of a UN Observer Mission in Yemen, beginning on 30 April, when General von Horn set off on his first exploratory tour to set up a UN Military Observer Mission. The fourth comprises the operations of the Observer Mission beginning 4 July 1963 and ending 4 September 1964 later. The fifth covers developments after the UN's departure.

The first period begins with moves by the United States, soon taken over by the UN, towards mediation. On 27 November 1962, the Permanent Mission of the Royal Yemeni government in New York urged the UN to make an inquiry into whether or not the rebellion in Yemen was fostered from Cairo. The letter was circulated only to UN members and not taken to a competent UN organ for further action. But the Yemeni Republicans, who by this time also had a delegation at the UN, let it be known that they would have no objections to a UN on-site inquiry.

Two weeks later, on 11 December, King Hussein of Jordan also suggested that the presence of a UN team of observers might help in finding a solution. King Hussein proposed a plebiscite that would follow the establishment of an impartial 'United Nations presence' in Yemen. Before the UN Secretary-General could respond to these initiatives, he felt that it was necessary to decide which of the two rival delegations properly represented Yemen. While this was in a formalistic sense the most obvious step to take, it was probably the first basic error that doomed UN intervention to failure. By determining which of the two sides could be legally represented the UN prejudged the whole issue and gave the side which it recognized a marked advantage.

On 17 December, the Secretary-General provisionally received credentials claimed by the Yemen Arab Republic, signed by President Abdullah al Sallal, and dated 8 December; the final decision on this claim had to be made by the Assembly's Credentials Committee. Two days later, the United States, after three months of hesitation, announced recognition of the Yemen Arab Republic. UN acceptance of the Republican credentials became certain.

The Yemeni *coup d'état* of 26 September had taken place when the Kennedy Administration was eighteen months old. It is necessary to put oneself into the psychological context of the time to understand how anxious the 'New Frontiersmen' were to break away from the American association with reactionary and sometimes anachronistic régimes. Anxious to restore mobility to American foreign policy in the Middle East which had reached an impasse as a result of American association with Israel and of John Foster Dulles's opposition to Nasser, the new Administration welcomed the opportunity to recognize this new Republic which, under the protection of President Nasser, laid claim to liberal ideas.

The Americans were also motivated at the time by concern over Soviet and Chinese involvement in this area. Well before the revolution the Russians had built the deep-sea port at the principal Yemeni port, Hodeidah, and the Chinese had built an asphalt road from Hodeidah across the coastal plain and up into the mountains to the capital, Sana. Both countries were obviously anxious to capitalize on these investments in the post-revolutionary period. Were the United States to withhold recognition and to withdraw from its own big engineering project in Yemen, the road from Sana to Taiz in the southern part of the country, there would be no major Western power to balance the activities of the two Communist giants.

None the less, the State Department hesitated. One reason was that the situation in Yemen could not really be reconciled with the traditional State Department criteria for diplomatic recognition. From both the British Foreign Office and from independent sources, including dispatches to the *New York Times*, the Department knew that large parts of the country were supporting the Imam against the Republic. It was reported that the Royalists could not be sure of victory but that the popular support they enjoyed, the leadership provided by the royal family, the Hamad Eddin, and the material support of the Saudis, certainly gave them a chance.

Along with the announcement of United States recognition of the Yemen Republic, on 19 December 1962, the State Department published statements by the Republic and the Egyptian Government which were obviously intended to provide a plausible basis for this act and to answer critics in advance. The Republicans said in their statement that they would 'honour Yemen's international obligations, including all treaties concluded by previous governments, and abide by the Charters of the United Nations and the Arab League.' Yemen, it continued, intended to live in peace 'with all our neighbours' and it called upon Yemenis in neighbouring territories 'to be law-abiding citizens'. Furthermore, Yemen would 'concentrate our efforts on our internal affairs'. According to the explanation given in the American announcement, the State Department interpreted this, particularly the allusion to Yemen's 'neighbours', as a reaffirmation of the 1934 Treaty of Sana under which the Imamic government and Great Britain had given 'reciprocal guarantees that neither party would intervene in the affairs of the other across the existing international frontier dividing Yemen from territory under British protection' (that is, South Arabia as it then was, now known as South Yemen).

The statement of the Egyptian government consisted of the following assertion of intention to withdraw from Yemen:

> The United Arab Republic confirms and supports the full contents of the communiqué released by the Government of the Yemen Arabic Republic. The United Arab Republic is proud of having extended full support to the Yemen revolution since the early hours of its outbreak, a support in consonance with the existing agreements. Now that the Yemen Arab Republic has firmly established itself as the Government of Yemen and inasmuch as we deplore the continuation of bloodshed, the United Arab Republic hereby signifies its willingness to undertake a reciprocal expeditious disengagement and phased removal of its troops from Yemen as Saudi and Jordanian forces engaged in support of the dethroned King are removed from the frontier areas and as external support, including Saudi and Jordanian support of the Yemeni Royalists, is terminated, whenever the Government of the Yemen Arab Republic should make such a request. To this we pledge ourselves provided the foregoing conditions are met.

The State Department said that it had decided to recognize the Republic 'in believing that these declarations provide a basis for terminating the conflict over Yemen and in expressing the hope that all parties involved in the conflict would co-operate to the end that the Yemeni people themselves would be permitted to decide their own future.'

The Egyptian and Yemeni statements and the State Department explanations may be best described in the American slang phrase as 'soft soap', intended to grease the way to American recognition and to justify the decision which the State Department or, more accurately, the White House, had taken for quite different reasons. The statements bore little relation to reality. Military developments continued as though the diplomats had never spoken.

The effect of American recognition and the statements quoted was to set the stage for UN recognition of the Republic. The Credentials Committee of the General Assembly met on 20 December, the last day of the Assembly's Seventeenth Session. It approved a proposal by Guinea recommending that the General Assembly accept the credentials submitted by the Yemen Arab Republic. The vote was six to nothing, with three abstentions.

Later the same day, the General Assembly debated the Credentials Committee's recommendation that the Yemen Republic's credentials be accepted. Representatives of the Kingdom of Yemen and of Saudi Arabia opposed the report. The representative of the Yemeni Kingdom charged that 'the so-called Republican government in Yemen' was only a front for the expansionist moves of the United Arab Republic, and lacked the support of the Yemeni people. The UAR, he declared, had committed an act of aggression against the people of Yemen, an act of war contrary to the principles of the UN Charter. And the Saudi representative asserted that the 'self-proclaimed Yemen Arab Republic had virtually no chance of survival but for the presence of foreign troops.' Both the Yemeni Royalists and Saudi delegates urged that the Assembly delay its decision on the credentials pending an inquiry by the UN.

Taking a different approach, the representative of Jordan expressed doubt as to whether the Credentials Committee was competent to decide which government was legal. With two authorities in the land, the 'legitimate government' of the Yemen, and the authority claimed by Brigadier al Sallal, how could the General Assembly presume to decide which delegation had the right to be seated?

Speakers on the other side of the question were the representatives of Algeria, Bolivia, Iran, Mali, Somalia, the Soviet Union, and the UAR. The representative of the last of these said that 'since the emergence of the new and progressive revolution of the people of Yemen against the reactionary feudalist régime', the people of the country had been exposed to brutal intervention by a combination of reactionary forces in the Arab world. He said that the UAR had sent in its military forces only in response to the request of the Yemen Arab Republic and with the sole purpose of enabling the people to practise their inherent right of self-defence in a war launched against them from outside. He argued that it was inconsistent to say that the UAR was interfering in Yemen's internal affairs: the UAR had been duty bound to come to the aid of the Republic, the UAR could not remain indifferent to 'reactionary conspiracies designed to re-impose a monarchy which had for generations isolated the Yemeni people from the world and from civilization', and no one could challenge the authority of this government which had been chosen by the people and was the only government in full control of the country.

The General Assembly thereupon voted 73 to 4, with 23 abstentions, to approve the Credentials Committee's report. Some of those who voted for the report pointed out that their governments had already recognized the Republic, or expressed belief that events within Yemen were exclusively a domestic affair. Several, including representatives of France, Japan, Venezuela and the Philippines, said that their vote in favour of the report was without prejudice to their position on the Yemen representation question on which their government had as yet taken no decision.

The representative of the Yemen Arab Republic declared that the Yemeni Republic was democratic and progressive, dedicated to a policy of non-alignment and positive neutrality, and warmly thanked the Assembly for its recognition.

The UAR and the Yemen Republic on the one hand, and Saudi Arabia and the Royalists on the other hand, represented the political poles of the Arab Middle East : the revolutionaries versus the traditionalists. In Yemen they were pitted against one another in a shooting war and the United States found itself, embarrassingly, with moral and material attachments to both sides. While there were reasons for recognizing the Republic, and possible advantage to be drawn from co-operating with President Nasser, the weight of American interests in the Middle East was in Saudi Arabia with its huge Arabian American Oil Company. The initial American response was to try to appease the revolutionaries with economic aid and political recognition, while restraining them and, at the same time, implying willingness to defend the Saudis, though not the Yemeni Royalists, and attempting to bring about 'disengagement' of Saudi Arabia and the UAR.

President Kennedy led off with a letter to Crown Prince Faisal (who was then Premier and had not yet taken the throne), dated 25 October, saying : 'You may be assured of full United States support for the maintenance of Saudi Arabian integrity.' President Kennedy's move was inspired by a certain disarray in Saudi Arabia where some cabinet ministers, including some of royal blood as well as commoners, felt that the Yemeni revolution could have dangerous echoes in Saudi Arabia. While Prince Faisal never hesitated in his determination to support the Royalist cause, the less self-assured elements in the régime were also upset by a series of air raids on Saudi territory, the first of which was on the town of Najran on 25 October, the same day President Kennedy wrote his letter. The United States followed up the President's letter with a 'show of force' in the form of aerial demonstrations by American aircraft over Jeddah and Riyadh, and a courtesy call by an American destroyer at Jeddah on 15 January 1963. The purpose appeared to be to reassure the Saudis and to say to President Nasser : 'Thus far and no further.'

In London the debate over whether to recognize the Yemen Republic or not differed in nature from the American debate. For the British, vital interests were at stake. At the time, with the Conservative government still in office, no question of abandoning Aden, the great British military base, had yet arisen. Furthermore, the ruling sheikhs and sultans of the South Arabian Federation which formed the hinterland of the Aden base were acutely alarmed by the emergence of the Yemen Republic and the arrival of the Egyptian army. They were Shaffeis, members of a sect of the Sunni branch of Islam, and valued their relative independence. Hence they had in the past resented the pretentions of the Imam of Yemen as head of the Zeidis, a sect of the Shiah branch of Islam, and his claims to sovereignty over 'Southern Yemen'. But now they were all for recognition of the Royal government rather than the Republic. The only influential voices in

London in favour of recognizing the Republic were those of some Foreign Office officials who felt that sooner or later Britain would have to come to terms with Nasser, or who thought that Britain could curb temporary security for Aden by recognizing the Republic.

The British government decided not to recognize the Yemen Arab Republic, as did the Saudis, the Jordanians, the government of Iran, Turkey, and most of the governments of Western Europe with the exception of West Germany and Italy. The West Germans were motivated by the desire to forestall East German relations with the new Republic, and the Italians by the fact that they had for many years enjoyed especially close ties with Yemen and wished to preserve this relationship. The United States therefore found that its diplomatic colleagues in Yemen, apart from the West Germans and the Italians, consisted of the remaining Arab governments, Ethiopia, and the entire Communist bloc.

With the issue of recognition resolved, Secretary-General U Thant, after consultations with the Saudis, the Egyptians, and the Yemen Republicans, as well as the State Department, asked Dr Ralph J. Bunche, the UN Undersecretary for Special Political Affairs, to go on a fact-finding mission to Yemen and the UAR. Dr Bunche had distinguished himself as the mediator who brought about the Arab–Israeli Armistices of 1949 and U Thant understandably hoped that he might be similarly successful in Yemen. Unfortunately, Dr Bunche's mission was confined to one side only. The Secretary-General later reported that it was left open whether he would eventually go also to Saudi Arabia, but developments made this unnecessary. Nothing at all was said about consulting the Royalists.

Dr Bunche arrived at Taiz, the principal southern town of Yemen and the diplomatic capital, on 1 March, just when the Egyptian army was carrying out its most successful military operation into northern and eastern Yemen. He was met at Taiz, according to Sana Radio, by the diplomatic corps and by crowds carrying banners inscribed 'Down with British imperialism', 'Death to the British' and 'Death to Kings Saud and Hussein', while balloons with pictures of Presidents Sallal and Nasser were launched in the air. Dr Bunche was welcomed by similar demonstrations at Sana, the capital, and at Marib which had been occupied a few days before by the Egyptian army.

At private meetings in Aden after this tour, Dr Bunche showed that he had been impressed by what he saw, and had concluded that the Republican régime effectively controlled the country.

In Cairo on 6 March, Dr Bunche received from President Nasser assurances that he would gladly withdraw his troops from Yemen if the Saudis would only end their support of the Royalist tribes. It was the same line the United States government had been given in order to bring about recognition.

The same day, United States Ambassador Ellsworth Bunker began a related mission on behalf of the State Department in Riyadh. Mr Bunker is a veteran of the American Foreign Service on whom the State Department has often called for difficult special missions. In Saudi Arabia his task was based on a National Security Council policy decision, a product of Mc-George Bundy's 'Little State Department' at the White House.[1] In this select group Robert Komer, a Special Counsel at the White House, had successfully advocated what became known as 'Operation Hard Surface'. This was to consist, in Komer's words, of 'eight little planes', sent to Saudi Arabia to symbolize American protection in return for a Saudi commitment to halt aid to the Royalists. On this basis, the National Security Council hoped that Nasser could be persuaded to withdraw his troops and the embarrassing Yemen war could be brought to an end.

The American offer of protection was somewhat equivocal in that it never became clear whether the American aircraft were to be authorized to engage the enemy or whether they were really only symbols. But Mr Bunker had another string to his bow. He also offered Prince Faisal the assistance of the United States Army Engineering Corps in establishing a television network in Saudi Arabia. He somewhat nettled the Prince by suggesting that television and other forms of American aid, coupled with political reforms, would help in containing 'unrest and rebellion in Saudi Arabia'. But in the end the deal was made. Prince Faisal got the 'eight little planes' and the television experts, and Mr Bunker departed for Cairo where he heard President Nasser repeat the assurances previously given to Dr Bunche.

Dr Bunche's and Mr Bunker's missions proved the basis for a Disengagement Agreement which Secretary-General U Thant reported to the Security Council on 29 April. In his report he said that he had received from each of the three governments concerned 'formal confirmation of their acceptance of identical terms of disengagement in Yemen. The will of all three interested parties to ease the situation has been the decisive factor, of course, and they are all to be commended for their constructive attitude.'

While the agreement has not been published, the Secretary-General desscribed it in his report in the following terms:

> The Government of Saudi Arabia on its part will terminate all support and aid to the Royalists of Yemen and will prohibit the use of Saudi Arabian territory by Royalist leaders for the purpose of carrying on the struggle in Yemen. Simultaneously, with the suspension of aid from Saudi Arabia to the Royalists, the United Arab Republic undertakes to begin withdrawal from Yemen of the troops sent on request of the new

Government, this withdrawal to be phased and to take place as soon as possible during which the forces would withdraw from field activities to their bases pending their departure. The United Arab Republic has also agreed not to take punitive action against the Royalists of Yemen for any resistance mounted by them prior to the beginning of their disengagement. There would likewise be an end to any actions on Saudi Arabian territory by United Arab Republic forces. A demilitarized zone to a distance of twenty kilometres on each side of the demarcated Saudi Arabian–Yemen border is to be established from which military forces and equipment are to be excluded. In this zone, on both sides, impartial observers are to be stationed to check on the observance of the terms of disengagement and who would also have the responsibility of travelling beyond the demilitarized zone, as necessary, in order to certify the suspension of activities in support of the Royalists from Saudi Arabian territory and the outward movement of the United Arab Republic forces and equipment from the airports and seaports of Yemen. The United Arab Republic and Saudi Arabia have further undertaken to co-operate with the representatives of the United Nations Secretary-General or some other mutually acceptable intermediary in reaching agreement on the modalities and verification of disengagement.

The methods by which the agreement was to function were not specified in either the authorizing resolutions or the Disengagement Agreement, but were to be worked out between the Secretary-General's representative and the parties concerned. In particular, the Secretary-General reported to the Security Council that he had asked Major-General Carl Carlson von Horn, Chief of Staff of the UN Truce Supervision Organization in Jerusalem – he had earlier served as Commander of UN troops in the Congo – to visit the three countries in order to consult the appropriate authorities and report back on how best UN observers could help the implementation of the disengagement. In his book *Soldiering for Peace* General von Horn wrote:

> The Egyptians gave reluctant lip service to an arrangement that they were to stop fighting and bombing the Royalists as soon as the Disengagement Agreement came into force. They also agreed to the stationing of observers to ensure that their troops kept out of the buffer zone, and to supervise withdrawal of their units when and if this took place, from the whole country.

As to financing the implementation of the terms of the disengagement, the Secretary-General further reported: 'I have it in mind to proceed under the provisions of General Assembly Resolution 1862 (XVII).' This resolution authorized the Secretary-General 'to enter into commitments to meet unforeseen and extraordinary expenses in the financial year of 1963. Resolution 1862 (XVII) also provided that 'if, as a result of a decision of the Security Council, commitments relating to the maintenance of peace and security should arise in an estimated total exceeding $10 million before the eighteenth session of the Assembly, the Assembly shall be convened by the Secretary-General, to consider the matter.'

The Swedish General took off from Beirut on 30 April on an exploratory mission to find out what kind of observer force was required. In Cairo he heard from Field-Marshal Amer that the Egyptians really had no intention of withdrawing all their troops. 'Whatever international agreements might be reached,' the Field-Marshal told von Horn as the latter later recalled in his book, 'a security force would always have to be left to ensure the continuation of Sallal's régime.' And a few days later he heard in equally emphatic terms from the Saudi Deputy Minister for Foreign Affairs, Omar Saqqaf, that the Saudis were 'not prepared to accept any attempt by the Egyptians to leave security forces in the country when eventually their Army withdraws.' Von Horn understood, and wrote in his book: 'I doubt the Egyptians or the Saudis had any intention of seriously observing the terms of disengagement.'

The picture given on 27 May in Secretary-General U Thant's report on General von Horn's consultations was, however, somewhat different. It read as follows:

> The parties again confirmed to General von Horn their acceptance of the terms of disengagement in Yemen as set forth in my 29 April report, General von Horn's concern, of course, being primarily with the questions relating to the need for United Nations Observers and their functions in the proposed demilitarized zone and elsewhere, as provided in the terms of disengagement.
>
> General von Horn held discussions with the appropriate authorities of the three parties in Cairo, Jeddah and San'a, obtaining the views of the parties on the role, functioning, scope and strength of the proposed United Nations observation operation. He also carried out ground and aerial reconnaissance on both sides of the Saudi Arabia–Yemen border, visiting Qizan, Najran, Sada and Hodeida, and covering the proposed demilitarized or buffer zone, totalling approximately 15,000 square kilometres.
>
> On the basis of the information available to me, with particular reference to that provided by General von Horn, I have reached the following conclusions:
> (a) United Nations Observers in the Saudi Arabia–Yemen area are vitally necessary and could well be the decisive factor in avoiding serious trouble in that area; their presence is desired by all parties concerned; moreover, as the need is urgent, they should be dispatched with the least possible delay;
> (b) The terrain and climatic conditions in which the Observers will

have to function in some sectors will be extremely difficult and even forbidding, and considerable danger may be encountered. Problems of movement and logistics will be great. But the provision and stationing of Observers is considered feasible and can be accomplished;

(c) The total personnel required for the observation mission would not exceed 200. This figure would include a small number of Officer-Observers; a ground patrol unit numbering about 100 men, in suitable vehicles, carrying arms for self-defence only; crews and ground crews for about eight small aircraft, fixed-wing and rotary, for reconnaissance and transport: and personnel for such essential supporting services as communications, logistics, medical aid, transportation and administration;

(d) It is estimated that the United Nations observation function would not be required for more than four months;

(e) It is expected that at least some of the personnel required for this short-term observation operation could be recruited from the United Nations Emergency Force (UNEF), the United Nations Truce Supervision Organization in Palestine (UNTSO), and possibly the United Nations Military Observers Group in India and Pakistan (UNMOGIP), subject to clearance with the Governments concerned. I plan to designate General von Horn as Chief of the Yemen Mission.

. . .

(g) It is estimated that the total cost of the Yemen Observation Mission will be less than $1,000,000. It has been my hope that the two parties principally involved, namely Saudi Arabia and the United Arab Republic, would undertake to bear the costs of the Mission and discussions towards this end are under way. These parties, I am sure, will agree to bear at least part of the costs, in money or in other forms of assistance. If necessary, to cover part of the cost of the operation, I would proceed, as previously indicated, under the provisions of General Assembly Resolution 1862 (XVII).

The estimates based on General von Horn's report were released on 3 June in two parts: cost of the mission on the assumption that it will have a minimum duration of four months, 807,000 US dollars; additional cost of the mission per month after the first four months in the event the mission should have to be extended, 102,000 US dollars.[2]

On 7 June 1963, the Secretary-General reported to the Security Council that 'Saudi Arabia has agreed orally to accept "a proportionate share" of the costs of the operation, while the United Arab Republic agrees in principle to provide assistance, in an amount equivalent to $200,000 for a period of two months, which would be roughly half of the cost of the operation over that period as indicated in my report on financial implications. It is not precluded, of course, that an appeal to the United Arab Republic Government for additional assistance could be made at the end of the two months, should it be necessary to extend the operation beyond that period.' He announced that: 'It is now my intention, therefore, to proceed with the organization and dispatch of the mission without further delay, and I am instructing General von Horn to go to the area with a small advance party within a day or two.'

Not satisfied with these instructions, the Soviet Union asked for a meeting of the Security Council which from 9 June to 11 discussed the situation. On 11 June it adopted a resolution, co-sponsored by Ghana and Morocco, authorizing the establishment of the United Nations Yemen Observation Mission (UNYOM). The vote was ten to none with the Soviet Union abstaining. The members of the Security Council were especially concerned with the financial arrangements and with the proper distribution of authority between the Council and the Secretary-General.

The resolution noted only that 'the Governments of Saudi Arabia and the United Arab Republic have agreed to defray the expenses over a period of two months of the United Nations observation function.' Ambassador Adlai Stevenson explained the position of the United States: 'As to the financing of the observer operation, it is proper, in our opinion, that the Security Council resolution makes no provision therefore and merely notes that the parties have agreed between themselves to pay the costs for a limited time.' The Soviet Union found the wording of the resolution on the matter of finance unacceptable, presumably because the duration of UNYOM beyond a four-month period was left as an open option, while the mention of the source of finance referred only to the first two months.

The UNYOM began its operations on 4 July 1963. When its mandate came to be renewed, the Secretary-General reported to the Security Council on all matters, including finance. It may be noted that, in spite of (or because of) these very full reports, no further meetings of the Security Council were held on the question of UNYOM, nor was the method of financing further debated in the Council.

General von Horn's Swedish, Irish, American, Guatemalan, British and Canadian staff was supplemented on 4 July by a mobile reconnaissance unit of 122 Yugoslavs, whose handicap was that their every move was controlled by a political commissar who got his instructions through a secret radio in the Yugoslav embassy. For weeks the mission had no medical officer and its troops were delayed. It lacked food, it lacked transport on the ground and in the air.

But General von Horn's life in Sana was not all frustration. He was delighted to find placed at his disposal a fantastic automobile which had been given to the Imam Ahmed by King Ibn Saud. In his book he describes it as a huge Daimler 'on whose chassis a famous Paris coach builder had erected a magnificent body, with sumptous (but now somewhat faded) upholstery, armoured windows and windscreen, and a wealth of opulent fittings which included a huge mahogany cabinet with a positive plethora of drawers.' The General was delighted also to find placed in his custody a white stallion formerly the property of the Imam al Badr. On its back he went out in the early dawn to probe the status of the revolution by counting the number of heads of executed Royalists stuck on poles outside the city gate.

Most of the time, however, General von Horn bemoaned his task, in particular that of supervising the six-mile square demilitarized zone. From the aircraft in which he commuted between Sana, Najran, Jizan and Sadah, he looked down at a landscape 'that looked as though the earth had been hacked up with some titanic prehistoric rake, ... the least inviting terrain for observer teams I have ever encountered,' he thought. He wondered 'which is worse, the desert and broken, rocky country, or the savage, jagged peaks which rose as high as 11,300 feet.' Air patrols would be troubled by the cloud formation that hung around the mountains every afternoon in summertime, while UN jeeps could hardly penetrate the mountains whose villages recognize no authority.

The residence in Sana in the Imam al Badr's former palace, proved a mixed blessing. Because, as he put it, 'it must have been built exclusively for dwarfs. The lintels were so low that one might have imagined a tribe of Swedish trolls inhabiting the dark winding staircase and every corner had niches which must have once concealed a crouching Yemeni guard.' He found it necessary to acquire 'the Yemeni stoop, a sort of shuffling defensive crouching, particularly repulsive to an old guardsman like myself.'

Von Horn found many reasons for the failure of his mission. He thought that it might have succeeded had there been a 'swift and impressive assembly of an international force whose appearance would have made an impact.' But both sides had been given time for second thoughts and the opportunity had been missed. He complained also that the Secretary-General's original instructions were 'under no circumstances to enter into contact with the Royalist authorities.' This remained the rule, obliging von Horn to ignore repeated approaches by the Royalists, until UN headquarters was at last stirred into reconsideration by reports beginning in July 1963, of Egyptian use of gas against the Royalists. Thereafter von Horn was asked to make inquiries as might be necessary. He noted that the Imam 'held large sectors of the southern buffer zone where we were proposing to operate ... the Royalists were a force to be reckoned with and Egyptian army and planes had been able to achieve little results.' He found the Egyptian garrison at Sadah 'in lonely little groups, patently disillusioned and homesick for the gentler atmosphere of the Nile Delta.'

During UNYOM's remaining life there were exchanges of complaints to the UN Secretary-General and to the Security Council, between Saudi Arabia and Egypt, and between the Republican Yemen and Great Britain. While the exchange between the Saudis and the Egyptians was directly related to the Observer Mission's tasks, those between the Yemen Republic and Britain concerned events on the south-eastern border of Yemen with which the Observer Mission was not directly concerned. I will summarize them, however, because they are an inseparable part of the larger picture.

On 14 June 1963, Jamail M. Baroody, the Saudi delegate to the UN, reported to the Secretary-General several Egyptian air raids on his country's territory. In one of these on 8 June, he wrote, 'thirty lives were lost and 22 homes were demolished, aside from the wounding of a good number of people in the town of Jizan.'

The Egyptians replied on 20 June. Mahoud Riad, the Egyptian delegate, wrote the Secretary-General a letter the text of which included the following :

> It is no secret that aggression against Yemeni territory emanated from inside Saudi Arabia, huge sums of money were tendered to incite mercenaries and provide them with arms to fight the people of Yemen, centres were established in Saudi Arabia to train those mercenaries in sabotage and laying mine fields. Furthermore, a flow of arms and ammunition were sent across the frontier to entice tribes to rise against their Government. The armed forces of the Yemen Arab Republic and the United Arab Republic can undoubtedly deal with any military aggression against Yemen. Nevertheless, motivated by an earnest desire to avoid bloodshed and to restore peace to the area, the two Governments have, in good faith, accepted the terms of disengagement which provided for the establishment of a United Nations Observation Mission whose main aim is the termination of outside military intervention against Yemen. Obviously, therefore, the Government of Saudi Arabia should be the last to complain or protest.

The background of the exchange of complaints between the Republic and the British concerned tribal affairs as much as they concerned the political conflict between Republicans and Royalists. With good reason the Republicans and Egyptians suspected that some supplies were being smuggled to the Royalists from Aden through British controlled territory at Beihan and via the towns of Harib and Marib to the Royalist forces in the mountains. The fighting that has taken place from time to time since late 1962 around Harib and Marib has been largely over control of these supply routes to the mountains.

British officers attached to the Federal army of the South Arabian Federation, as well as regular officers of the British army and air force were almost all vibrantly pro-Royalist at that time and inclined to look the other way as supplies went by or even occasionally were diverted from British stocks.

In the first of the Republican complaints on 28 February 1963, about the time the British had been obliged to close their Legation at Taiz, President Sallal cabled the President of the Security Council a charge that British planes had dropped circulars on Republican forces warning them to withdraw from their positions or they would be bombed. He said this constituted an attempt to aid infiltrators coming from Saudi Arabia to help the dethroned Imam.

The British replied on 4 March 1963, explaining that they had acted only after incursions into the South Arabian Federation in the vicinity of Beihan by Republican forces. The circulars dropped were in fact warnings, they said, to the Republicans to withdraw. Only after this warning, they said, had artillery fire opened up to evict the Republicans. No tanks or bombs were involved, they maintained.

In another exchange in June, the Republicans accused the British of 'continuous armed aggression' on their borders and the British replied with a list of incidents which had been provoked by the Yemenis. Both sides threatened forceful steps to quell the other's alleged aggression. The exchange of accusations continued in August and September but without major military consequences.

In the spring of 1964, however, tension on the Harib front rose again and the British (on 20, 28 and 30 March) accused the Yemeni Republicans of air attacks on bedouin inside Federal territory. They admitted that in reprisals for an attack on a Federal guard fort near Jabal Bulaiz on 27 March, British aircraft had counter-attacked against a Yemeni military fort about a mile from Harib. The British said they had first dropped warning messages and had acted 'strictly in exercise of their rights of defence.' On 1 April, the Republicans demanded an urgent meeting of the Security Council. They charged that the British attack culminated more than 40 acts of aggression against their territory. The angry exchange of accusations ended in a compromise resolution stating that the Security Council:

1 *Condemns* reprisals as incompatible with the purposes and principles of the United Nations;
2 *Deplores* the British military action at Harib on March 28 1964;
3 *Deplores* all attacks and incidents which have occurred in this area;
4 *Calls upon* the Yemen Arab Republic and the United Kingdom to exercise the maximum restraint in order to avoid further incidents and to restore peace in the area;
5 *Requests* the Secretary-General to use his good offices to try to settle outstanding issues, in agreement with the two parties.

The vote was nine to none, with the United Kingdom and the United States abstaining.

This whole sequence of complaints took place outside the framework of the Observer Mission's functions and, in its last stages, after the Mission had been wound up.

As the days went by, General von Horn grew more and more bitter. On 16 June 1963, he had been told by the commander of the Egyptian troops in Yemen, General Anwar al Qadi, that there was still no overrall plan for a phased withdrawal. He lacked the means to deal with either side in the conflict, whether Royalist raids on Egyptian and Republican positions, or Egyptian air raids against Royalist tribesmen. He was distressed, as he wrote in his book, by the 'complete lack of interest by the UN towards any Royalist complaint about bombing and massacres in Royalist-held territory by the Egyptians.' And he concluded that 'in real terms the whole story of the Mission was one of calculated deceit. I, its Commanding Officer, had been misled, the general public had been deluded, and the Egyptians and Saudi Arabians had been taken straight up the garden path.'

At long last, on 20 August 1963, General von Horn resigned. But the Mission continued. He was replaced temporarily by his Yugoslav deputy and later by the Commander of the UN Emergency Force in Gaza until, on 5 November 1963, the Secretary-General appointed Signor Pier Spinelli, the Head of the UN European Office at Geneva as the new head of the Observer Mission.

At the same time, U Thant decided to withdraw the military components of the Mission, partly because they had not proved effective in enforcing disengagement, and partly because the Saudis objected to the continued assessment of their share of the Mission's expense.

Because the Saudis at the last minute agreed to pay another two-monthly instalment, U Thant partly reversed this decision, and extended the military mission's life in a new form. He withdrew the Yugoslav reconnaissance unit and sent in a new staff of military observers from Denmark, Ghana, India, Italy, the Netherlands, Norway, Pakistan, Sweden and Yugoslavia. U Thant's January report to the Security Council said that a headquarters staff and three observers were stationed at Sana, two observers at Sadah, one observer at Hodeidah, and one liaison officer at Jeddah. He said that the observers at Najran and Jizan were to 'maintain permanent checkpoints at the main border crossings into Yemen, temporary checkpoints on an irregular basis at the more difficult crossings, as well as patrols, in order to observe the nature of the traffic across the border.'

His report continued with the explanation that 'most United Nations patrols and checkpoints are accompanied by Saudi Arabian liaison officers who check cargoes as requested by the Observers. Occasionally Observers visit Royalist territory on the Yemeni side of the border, in order to check on the extent to which arms and ammunition may be reaching them from abroad, and the degree of fighting occurring between them and the UAR forces in Yemen. The Observers in Sadah, Sana and Hodeidah observe the extent to which the UAR forces are being disengaged from Yemen.' This allusion to activities in Royalist territory was a notable development, probably explainable by the UN Headquarters concern over the reports of the use of gas by the Egyptians rather than by any recognition that it was inefficacious and unrealistic to ignore one of the parties to the conflict. U Thant reported that in discussions with the Saudi, Egyptian and Yemeni Republican governments Pier Spinelli had sought 'areas of agreement between the parties which might, through bilateral discussions or otherwise, lead to further progress toward disengagement and toward a peaceful situation.' He thought the discussions encouraging.

The UN Mission struggled on, with squabbles every two months over the question whether the Saudis and Egyptians would continue their contributions. Finally, in September, 1964, the Saudis balked. They maintained that although the UN had found some unofficial traffic from Saudi Arabia into Yemeni territory they had 'faithfully and honestly' halted their support of the Royalists since the time of the original Bunker Agreement on 29 April 1963. The Saudis charged that there was no indication that the Egyptians had similarly respected the agreement. Far from declining, the number of Egyptian troops in the land had risen from about 20,000 in April 1963 to some 60,000 in the autumn of 1964. This was the Saudis' last word as far as the UN was concerned. U Thant was obliged to admit defeat. On 4 September 1964, at forty-eight hours' notice, he ordered the Mission to be withdrawn from Yemen.

During the ensuing period, Egypt and Saudi Arabia entered into direct diplomatic confrontation without benefit of UN mediation. A prolonged tacit truce developed on the military front. The United States, meanwhile, watched nervously from its diplomatic outposts in Jeddah and Aden. Its involvement was limited to urging the Saudis to refrain from again 'unleashing' the Royalists; United States relations with Egypt were at the same time deteriorating, partly, perhaps, because the Egyptians had remained so unresponsive to American urging that they withdraw from Yemen, but more realistically, perhaps, because of the Zionist pressures in Washington.

Left more or less to themselves, the Royalists and Republicans succeeded, on 2 November 1964, in holding a secret conference at Erkwit, a resort on the Red Sea coast of Sudan. They declared a ceasefire as of 1 p.m., 8 November, and planned a national conference of 168 tribal leaders for

23 November. But on 10 November the Egyptians resumed bombing. Instead of peace another round of the war got under way.

None the less, the Erkwit ceasefire was important. It prepared the way for two other conferences which attempted to end the war. The first was a meeting between King Faisal and President Nasser at Jeddah, 22 August 1965, which led to the Jeddah Agreement of 24 August as the basic document on which subsequent negotiations have all centred. Because of its great importance, I will quote in full the text of this agreement as broadcast by Cairo and Mecca radios:

> The aim of President Gamal Abdul Nasser and King Faisal in their talks in Jeddah was to make it possible for the Yemeni people to exercise their free will so that it could provide an atmosphere of peace, in addition to the removal of every cause of the transient disagreement between the United Arab Republic and Saudi Arabia, and to consolidate the historic ties between their two peoples.
>
> As regards the relation of the United Arab Republic and Saudi Arabia to the present situation in Yemen, King Faisal and President Abdul Nasser, having got in touch with all the representatives of the Yemeni people and their national forces, and having been acquainted with their wishes, consider that the just and safest means of facing responsibility towards the Yemeni people is through:
>
> 1 Giving the Yemeni people the right to decide and affirm their view to the kind of government they want in a popular plebiscite at a date not later than 23 November, 1966.
>
> 2 The remaining period up to the date of the plebiscite shall be considered a transitional period to prepare for the plebiscite.
>
> 3 Saudi Arabia and the United Arab Republic will co-operate in forming a transitional conference of 50 members, representing all the national forces and people of authority in Yemen, after consultation with the various Yemeni groups in accordance with the agreement to be reached. The conference will meet at Haradh (in Yemen) on November 23, 1965, and will undertake: determination of the systems of government during the transitional period and until the popular plebiscite is held; formation of a provisional cabinet to be in charge of the government during the transitional period; determination of the form and kind of plebiscite which will be held by November 23, 1966, at the latest.
>
> 4 The two governments adopt the resolutions of the above-mentioned transitional Yemeni conference, support them, and co-operate to ensure their successful implementation. They declare from now their acceptance of a joint neutral follow-up committee of both to be in charge of the plebiscite should the conference decide the need for the presence of such a neutral committee.
>
> 5 Saudi Arabia will immediately stop military aid of all kinds and the use of Saudi Arabian territory for operations against Yemen.

6 The United Arab Republic will withdraw all its military forces from Yemen within ten months, beginning on November 23, 1965.

7 Armed fighting in Yemen will be stopped immediately and a joint peace commission from both sides will be formed to : supervise the cease-fire through a special supervisory commission; supervise the frontier and ports; and stop all kinds of military aid. Food aid will continue under the supervision of the peace commission. The said supervisory commissions will be entitled to use all the necessary travel facilities within Yemeni territory as well as use Saudi Arabian territory, if necessary.

8 Saudi Arabia and the United Arab Republic will co-operate and act positively to ensure the carrying out of this agreement and impose stability in Yemen until the proclamation of the result of the plebiscite, by forming a force of the two countries to be used by the commission when necessary to prevent any departure from this agreement or any action to obstruct it or provoke disorder against its success.

9 In order to promote co-operation between the United Arab Republic and Saudi Arabia and enable this co-operation to continue beyond the present phase to the normal phase which should prevail over relations between the two countries, there will be direct contact between President Abdul Nasser and King Faisal to avoid any difficulty in the way of carrying out this agreement.

As envisaged in the Jeddah Agreement, the Haradh Conference of Royalist and Republican Yemenis took place in November 1965. But all in vain, for agreement still eluded them.

The Jeddah Agreement envisaged setting up a new caretaker government within three months, followed by the staged withdrawal of Egyptian troops and culminating in a great conference at Haradh in November to determine the future régime in the country. The most important thing about the Haradh Conference was probably that it took place, for it had no constructive results in any formal sense. It remains remarkable, however, that 50 delegates representing the two sides succeeded in spending nearly a month together rediscovering that they were all Yemenis, even if they could not agree on future political development. What kept them apart was not so much their own differences but the fundamental Arab disunity which they reflected. Royalists represented the traditional forces of the Arabian Peninsula headed by King Faisal of Saudi Arabia; the Republicans represented the revolutionaries whose most prominent leader was President Nasser of Egypt. And behind the two sides was, of course, disunity on the world scene, with the United States and its allies fundamentally on Faisal's side and the Soviet Union and the Communist bloc fundamentally on Nasser's side. It was difficult for Yemen to heal itself while the Arab world and the great powers kept tearing them apart.

After the Haradh Conference had broken down, the Royalists made steady gains in Yemen, provoking the Egyptians to increasing use of gas as a weapon. The fact that they did use it was amply documented by outside observers and by the International Red Cross.[3]

It is impossible to say what the military outcome of this struggle would have been, had it not been decided by the Israeli offensive in the Six Day War of June 1967. After that, the Egyptians were bound to withdraw. For the time being their neo-imperialist adventure had to be called off, as war confirmed by the terms of the agreement reached at the Arab Summit in Khartoum of August 1967. In a way, the Khartoum Agreement was a more meaningful reaffirmation of the principles originally laid down in the Disengagement Agreement of 29 April 1963, worked out as a result of the Missions of Ambassador Bunker and Dr Bunche.

Under the Khartoum Agreement, Nasser agreed to withdraw from Yemen and did so; Faisal agreed to halt his assistance to the Royalists and did so for a while. He resumed aid to the Royalist tribes, as he told me in an interview in February of 1968, when he realized that forces other than the Egyptians had taken over support of the Republicans. He was alluding particularly to the MiGs and other aircraft supplied to the Republic by the Soviet Union along with military supplies of all kinds which enabled them, in February 1968, to break the Royalist siege of Sana and to go on from there to regain most, but not all, of the country. Perhaps the greatest advocate of reconciliation in Yemen during all of the last few years has been Mohamed Ahmed Noman, the grand old man of Yemeni politics, who was supposed to have become one of a three-man Presidential Council in Yemen after President Sallal was overthrown more or less simultaneously with the departure of the Egyptians. Noman had kept his friendships on both sides and was the only one who could ever hope to head a compromise government. But for that very reason he found it impossible to assume office in Sana, and he instead went to exile in Beirut. He refused to identify himself with a government that rejected the principle and the spirit of reconciliation.

With the Egyptians and Sallal out of the way, the Republic shed most of its socialistic trappings. Under growing tribal influence it became more conservative and attempted to renew relations with Saudi Arabia and the Western world. Although there were those on both sides, such as the elder Noman and his son Mohamed on the Republican side, and Kamal Adham, King Faisal's son-in-law on the Saudi side, who attempted to bring about yet another reconciliation conference, to meet at Athens in the summer of 1969, this initiative too broke down. On the Republican side, President Abdul Rahman al Iryani persisted, in an interview I had with him in June 1969, on maintaining the haughty attitude that 'the door of the Republic is open and all the Royalists needed to do was to come home through that door.' He meant that, if they would ask forgiveness, he would pardon them. But this was obviously no solution for proud men or for the Zeidi tribes of the northern mountains whose Sheikhs felt that they had served their country well by fighting the Egyptians and who had no intention of asking anybody's pardon.

It is, however, possible that the Republic could have imposed itself totally on Yemen in the course of the year 1969 had the Saudis been willing to come to terms. For better or worse, the Royalists had fallen apart and most of the princes of the Hamad Eddin family had departed from Yemen and were living in Jeddah, Beirut and London. But the Saudis were not willing to let it go at that. As the Republicans moved forward and reoccupied Sadah in the north and other points even closer to the Saudi border, they became nervous. A Republican air attack on the town of Najran in November gave them a pretext for resuming military material support of those tribes who were still willing to fight the Republic. Under the leadership of Prince Ahmed bin Hussein, one of the few princes who consistently remained at his post in Yemen and who has a personal following among the northern tribesmen, the Saudi-backed Royalists were, during the winter of 1969 to 1970, engaged in a desultory siege of Sawdah. Prince Sultan ben Abdul Aziz reaffirmed for the Saudis their backing of Imam Mohamed al Badr, who was living at his villa at Taif in the mountains above Jeddah.

It seemed that the Saudis were determined to maintain the partition of Yemen, with a small so-called Royalist area in the north as a buffer between the Saudis and the Republic. I felt, during a visit to Saudi Arabia in December 1969, that the highest officials of the Saudi government did not trust Yemenis of any kind whether Royalist or Republican. They denounced the Royalists for taking Saudi money and wasting it on personal expenditures and they suspected the Republicans, no matter how conservative they might seem to be, of collusion with the Marxist 'National Liberation Front' régime of Aden. Only reluctantly did they agree, in mid-1970, to recognize the increasingly conservative Republican régime.

Whether the UN could have succeeded in setting Yemen on the road to real peace is doubtful. The presence of the UN mechanism seems to have been an excuse among the Yemenis for not establishing their own mechanism through which to seek reconciliation. It became a device for avoiding action or responsibility. Either side could say to its people: 'It is in the hands of the United Nations now.' And the UN could serve as a scapegoat for whatever problems or failures ensued. In other words, the UN became a foil in the politics of Yemen. As in the case of faith in God, people consistently appealed to it. Politicians exploited its mystique in the form of petitions to the UN, or telegrams of protest and appeal, instead of taking action related to the problem.

On a more technical level it was undoubtedly a mistake to make the Observer Mission dependent on the two disputing parties for its financial resources. The money should have come from an independent third source representing the whole community of nations. This was the immediate cause of the Observer Mission's demise.

Another important point is that the Observer Mission could not operate successfully while ignoring the existence of one of the parties to the dispute, namely the Royalists. In order to put itself in a position to solve this problem, the UN should have suspended judgment as to which was the rightful government of Yemen, but have declared itself willing to talk to both sides until their problem was sorted out. This rather obvious point was lost sight of because of the insistence of American policy-makers in regarding the Republicans as the only authority in the country. The Americans insisted on regarding the opposition merely as dissident tribes who had always resisted the central government; they refused in spite of contrary evidence to recognize the political substance of the Royalist side. It is this slant that foredoomed every UN move, from Bunche's first mission to Spinelli's last tour.

Finally, the Military Observer Mission might perhaps have succeeded in imposing its observer role and enforcing the terms of mutual disengagement, as General von Horn understood from the first, had it been endowed with adequate independent forces. Instead of operating on a shoestring with a few hundred men, the UN would have had to move in with several thousand. The international eye, if all-seeing, might thus have become a deterrent, but so long as it could see so little it had no chance.

TEXT REFERENCES

1. National Security Action Memo 227, 27 February 1963.

2. (a) Cost of the mission on the assumption that it will have a minimum duration of four months.

		US dollars
1	Salaries and common staff costs	58,620
2	Travel and subsistence	76,200
3	Transportation and other costs of military personnel (other ranks)	163,180
4	Rental and maintenance of premises	4,000
5	Operation and maintenance of transportation equipment	12,000
6	Rental of aircraft	322,000
7	Communications and freight	15,000
8	Miscellaneous supplies and services	9,000
9	Permanent equipment	147,500
	TOTAL COST	807,500

(b) Additional cost of the mission per month after the first four months in the event the mission should have to be extended

1 Salaries and common staff costs	14,650
2 Travel and subsistence	10,350
3 Transportation and other costs of military personnel (other ranks)	15,800
4 Rental and maintenance of premises	1,000
5 Operation and maintenance of transportation equipment	3,000
6 Rental of aircraft	54,000
7 Communications and freight	1,350
8 Miscellaneous supplies and services	2,250
	102,400

3. Schmidt, Dana Adams, *Yemen, The Unknown War*, London 1968, chapter 19.

8 THE CIVIL WAR IN CYPRUS

Anne Duncan-Jones

On 4 March 1964 the Security Council passed a resolution recommending the creation of a UN peace-keeping force in Cyprus, and the appointment of a UN mediator 'who shall use his best endeavours for the purpose of promoting a peaceful solution and an agreed settlement of the problem confronting Cyprus, in accordance with the Charter of the United Nations'.[1] When the draft of the resolution was laid before the Council, the representative of Brazil, Senhor Bernardes, who was one of its co-sponsors said, 'the stabilizing presence of an international peace-keeping force and the endeavours of an impartial and respected mediator open the best prospects for a settlement of one of the most complex and delicate problems the United Nations has ever faced'.[2] Five and a half years later that settlement is still eluding both the UN and the parties concerned. Was the peace-keeping force inadequate as a stabilizing presence? Have the endeavours of successive mediators been insufficient? Has the problem proved just a bit too complex and delicate for the rigid and clumsy machinery of the UN to cope with? These are some of the questions which must be answered in order to arrive at an understanding and assessment of the role of the UN in Cyprus, and of the events which have passed between the high hopes of March 1964 and the present stalemate.

The civil war in Cyprus was first brought to the notice of the Security Council on 26 December 1963, in the form of a letter from the government of Cyprus listing acts and threats against the 'territorial integrity and sovereignty of the state', and asking the UN to protect the Republic from unilateral military intervention or threat of such intervention. The intervention Cyprus feared was of course from Turkey, which after the intercommunal fighting had broken out on a large scale on 21 December had conducted military flights over the island, sending destroyers and troop carriers to within sight of the north Cyprus coast, and had been making conspicuous preparations for war. Turkey's 'right' to intervene militarily in the Cyprus dispute was a moot point. Under the Treaty of Guarantee (which was an integral part of the London Agreements of 1959 which established the Republic of Cyprus as an independent state), Turkey, together with Greece and Britain, guaranteed the island's constitution, and undertook to maintain its independence, territorial integrity and security. If in the event of any breach of the provisions of the Treaty, concerted action was to prove impossible, the Treaty reserved for the three powers the right to take action 'with the sole aim of re-establishing the state of affairs established by the Treaty'. As the present crisis had in fact been brought about by President Makarios's proposals, communicated to the Turkish Cypriot Vice-President on 30 November, to amend the constitution unilaterally, Turkey appeared to be justified in claiming that this was a clear-cut case for intervention on her part. But whether such intervention should take the form of a full-scale military invasion was another matter altogether, and Britain and the United States although reluctant to respond to Cyprus's argument that the constitution was foisted on Cyprus and that therefore the Treaties were not binding, were even more reluctant to stand by and watch Turkey invade Cyprus, inevitably exacerbating the situation and probably instigating a full-scale flare-up in the sensitive area of the Eastern Mediterranean.

The British government therefore decided to take direct action, and when an emergency meeting of the Security Council was called on 27 December to discuss the apparent imminent threat of invasion by Turkey, discussion was discontinued in order to allow Britain the chance to deal with the situation herself. A British peace-keeping force was hurriedly established and sent to help restore order on the island and a conference was called in London to settle the problem. It failed to do so. Makarios rejected the idea of a NATO peace-keeping force to replace the British which was put forward at the conference, and insisted that if an international force were to be sent to Cyprus it should be under the auspices of the UN.

Meanwhile, although the Turkish invasion had never materialized, due partly to American and British pressure, the situation within the island was deteriorating rapidly with increased violence on both sides. On 15 February 1964, the British government instructed their permanent representative, Sir Patrick Dean, to request an early meeting of the Security Council. The same day the Cyprus government asked the Security Council to proceed in the examination of its complaint. The two requests together formed the agenda for all subsequent discussions of the Cyprus question by the Council. Two points, therefore, are worth noting about these preliminaries. One is that Britain, whose responsibility the problem had been up to this stage, only laid it before the UN as a last resort, when it had decided that its own troops could no longer be expected to control the situation single-handed. Secondly, Cyprus itself was already committed in principle to the idea of a UN force, and had indeed, held out against considerable pressure from agreeing to any alternative course. So although the UN was at a disadvantage in taking on the problem only after everyone else had failed, it had a considerable advantage in having, in principle, from the very beginning the cooperation of the host country.

The debates in the Security Council dragged on for days with mutual recriminations flying in every direction, tedious arguments about the legality or otherwise of the disputed Article IV of the Treaty of Guarantee, Soviet obstructionism over procedure, and British pleas for a quick decision. But whatever may be the virtues of UN action in a civil-war situation speed of operation is not one of them. Sir Patrick Dean summed up the situation when he said:

> It is inevitable that any problem brought to this Council is complex and difficult. Nations in dispute seek, as they are bound to do by the terms of the Charter, to deal with their differences by peaceful negotiation. It is only when this fails, and when matters have reached the pitch where in other times there would have been a resort to war to solve them, that recourse is had to this Council. There are times when full discussion here has helped to point towards a solution. There are times when argument and counter-argument indeed begin to take on the aspects of a game of chess. But, in this matter there is not one of my colleagues around this table who is not aware that lives are at stake at this very time.[3]

The problem is not limited to the decision-making body of the UN; the executive arm faces similar difficulties. Even when debate eventually culminated in the Council's resolution of 4 March, calling on all members 'to refrain from any action or threat of action likely to worsen the situation in the sovereign Republic of Cyprus or to endanger international peace',[4] asking the government of Cyprus to take 'all necessary measures to maintain law and order and to stop violence and bloodshed',[5] and recommending the creation of a UN peace-keeping force in Cyprus and the appointment of a mediator, nothing could be done until the Secretary-General created the force, and found the mediator. Neither task was particularly easy. In addition to stipulating that the force was to be stationed initially for no more than three months before further recourse to the Security Council, Russian and French objections to establishing and financing another UN peace-keeping force had to be met by stipulating that the costs of the operation were to be met by the governments providing the contingents.

This was accepted by all Western countries in the belief that the United

States would foot the bill. But she soon made it clear that she would do no such thing. Initial approaches to Canada, Finland, Sweden, Ireland and Brazil were all met with a lack of enthusiasm because of the cost. U Thant was forced to make personal appeals for voluntary contributions from likely countries. On 7 March he wrote, 'It has already become clear to me that some of the governments providing contingents may not be able themselves to meet all of the costs involved.'[6] Eventually he succeeded in getting fairly widespread financial support including a million US dollars from Britain, and two million dollars from the United States.

But money was only half of the problem. Although there were then 115 members of the UN, only a handful of them were really qualified for the job. African or Communist troops would not have been acceptable to the Cyprus government, nor the troops of any NATO power. Meanwhile the situation was becoming urgent. On 11 March, Britain told U Thant that unless a UN peace-keeping force arrived in Cyprus in a very few days, all British troops would withdraw to the sovereign bases in the island. There was also an increasing danger that Turkey would become impatient with inaction and act on her implied ultimatum to invade.

Even when the offers to provide contingents were secured, they all had conditions attached. Canada stipulated that it should not be the only country other than Britain to send troops, Sweden wanted to be sure that it was not the only neutral country in force. Eire wanted assurance that its troops would not be used to impose political decisions or partition on the island. U Thant, working in an atmosphere of rising tension, somehow managed to satisfy these conditions. By 13 March he was able to inform the Security Council, to the relief of everyone concerned, that the peace-keeping force had been established. Canada, Ireland and Sweden had agreed to send troops (the Finnish offer was confirmed shortly afterwards), and a small advance party of Canadian troops flew to Cyprus that evening. On 27 March, under the command of General Gyani, from India, UNFICYP (as the force was thereafter called) became operational.

Whether this delay in setting up the force can be considered an intrinsic disadvantage of international action in civil-war situations, as compared with the speed with which United States or British forces could have gone into operation, is questionable. The latter, even if sent more quickly, would not necessarily have fared better. The only permanent legacy of the British holding operation between 21 December and 27 March and one which would have been better avoided, was the arrangement for the 'green line' (so-called because it was drawn on the map with a green chinagraph pencil which was lying on the table)[7] dividing the Turkish and Greek sectors of Nicosia.

What is not in doubt is that the vagueness of the force's terms of reference put UNFICYP at a grave disadvantage from the beginning. They owed their origin to the necessity of finding a compromise resolution in the Security Council which would be acceptable to all the parties concerned and would not be subject to the French or Russian veto. The resolution divided UN action on the island into two parts, the mediating attempt, and the peace-keeping operation. UNFICYP was to have three main functions: it was to prevent a recurrence of fighting, to contribute to the restoration and maintenance of law and order, and to a return to normal conditions. But how was it to prevent a recurrence of fighting – by shooting at both sides to stop them shooting at one another, or by talking them out of shooting at all? Whose 'law and order' were they responsible for restoring and maintaining – the Greek Cypriot government's, even if this extended to disarming the so-called Turkish 'rebels'? And what were 'normal con- ditions' – those of the unitary state that the Greek Cypriots wanted, or those of *de facto* partition that the Turkish Cypriots wanted?

These questions were never really answered. U Thant did issue an *aide-memoire* to all governments providing contingents to the force, setting out guide-lines for the force's role, and later, due largely to pressure from the British parliament, this was published. It established that the troops could only shoot in self-defence, and that they could not take any action which was likely to bring them into conflict with either Greek or Turkish Cypriots except to protect themselves, or to avert the violation of arrange- ments previously accepted by both communities. But it made no attempt to solve the basic dilemma: was the UN in Cyprus as the Greek Cypriots believed, to enforce the authority of the Greek Cypriot government, or was it there, as the Turkish Cypriots believed, to protect them from this authority? In view of this total divergence of views held by the two sides in the civil war about the role of the UN in that war, it is a remarkable tribute to the skill, tact and impartiality of the successive force com- manders, that UNFICYP was able to function at all, and moreover, to do so over a period of five years without losing the respect or approval of either side.

It is perhaps, in the execution of the first of its functions, the prevention of a recurrence of fighting, that UNFICYP has been most successful. Its chief weapon has been not its rifles, but its negotiating skills; and the success of the UN force in Cyprus in reducing what was, in the spring of 1964, a full-scale civil war into the comparative peace of today, is an object lesson in the power of words over arms. Impartiality is the first principle of the force, and each situation as it arose was treated on its merits. The basic policy was to preserve the *status quo ante* wherever possible and to do so, not by force, but by persuasion. The advantages and limitations of the application of these principles in practice is best illustrated by actual rather than by hypothetical examples.

In July 1966, trouble arose in the village of Mora, about 10 miles east of Nicosia on what used to be the main road to Famagusta, when the Greek Cypriot National Guard alleged that the Turks had constructed fortified posts about 600 yards north of the road with the apparent aim of taking over control of the flow of traffic. In fact it was later confirmed that they were old positions being reinforced but the Greek Cypriot forces nevertheless threatened direct action if the posts were not removed, and the situation was aggravated by the appearance on the scene of General Grivas, who had come back to Cyprus in June 1964 to take over command of the Greek armed forces on the island, and General Prokos, commander of the National Guard. UNFICYP had divided the island into six main areas, each one under the control of a national contingent. Mora was in the Finnish zone, and when the news of the incident reached Nicosia, the commander of the Finnish contingent, Colonel Koskenpalo, went immediately to the scene where he found a united force of National Guard and Cyprus Police with armed cars preparing to attack the Turks who were occupying the positions around the village. Having deployed a company of infantry, he first confirmed that the Turkish positions were old ones to hold up the attack until he had talked to the Turkish side, and then for several hours he drove backwards and forwards negotiating between the Turkish leaders in the village and the Greeks manning their posts. Eventually, he worked out an agreement under which the Turks would evacuate their positions and the Greek Cypriot forces would withdraw to the nearby Tymbou airfield. He then ordered a company of Finnish troops, including rifle and armoured units, into the area to maintain order. A major outbreak was thus averted.

Around the same time a similar incident arose at Melousha, fifteen miles south-east of Nicosia. General Grivas wanted to disarm the Turkish village fighters; but before he attacked he notified UNFICYP through the local liaison officer, of his plans. UNFICYP immediately began to negotiate both with the National Guard commander in the field, through the Swedish contingent commander, and at a much higher level in Nicosia with General Grivas, through Brigadier Harbottle, UNFICYP's Chief of Staff. Negotiations, Harbottle says, 'were taken to their absolute limit', but after nine hours' hard talking they eventually collapsed. The UN chief weapon had not prevailed this time. However, Harbottle, acting under instructions from the force commander was prepared to fight on more than one level. While he talked in Nicosia, UN troops were slipping in under cover of darkness, and reinforcements called in from neighbouring contingents. The plan was that if Grivas could be kept talking until morning, by the time daylight came he would be confronted with the UN force comprising a company of infantry, backed up by 14 armoured carriers and two troops of armoured cars interposed between his troops and the village. It was thought that Grivas could hardly give the order to attack while Harbottle was with him. This is exactly what happened; Grivas faced with the prospect of taking on forces considerably stronger than his own (and Harbottle had left no doubts that his forces were quite prepared to fight it out if necessary), did what most military commanders would do in the circumstances, and withdrew. In this incident, the UN won the day and succeeded once again in 'preventing a recurrence of fighting'. It did so not through conventional UN methods but through the negotiator's skill in outmanoeuvring Grivas (with a tactic which soldiers have employed for centuries).

In November 1967, at Kophinou, the UN failed to prevent, though they perhaps had created, a serious outbreak of fighting. As a result of that failure, 26 people were killed, 21 of them Turkish Cypriots. It was not the first incident of its kind. At Kokkina in August 1964, a Greek Cypriot attack on Turkish positions in the north-west coastal area, which provided their main link with mainland Turkey, had resulted in severe fighting followed, a couple of days later, by Turkish air raids on Greek Cypriot villages. A major flare-up was only prevented by a Security Council call for a cease-fire backed up by UN efforts in Nicosia, and international pressure, particularly from President Johnson, on Greece and Turkey.

At Kophinou, a major flare-up was not prevented; war in the Eastern Mediterranean was only narrowly averted. The incident began according to a familiar pattern. The mixed village of Ayios Theodorus, just off the main road from Nicosia to Limassol, was normally patrolled by CYPOL, the Greek Cypriot police. After an incident in which the patrol had been prevented by the Turks from returning home after visiting the Greek sector of the village, the patrol was suspended. The UN, following their policy of always preserving the *status quo* wherever possible, started negotiations and, six weeks later, the Turks gave some indication that they would be willing to accept UNFICYP's plan for the resumption of patrols. But by 14 November, in spite of the fact that a verbal communiqué from the Turkish embassy had said that an answer was on the way, the Cypriot government ran out of patience, and gave the UN at the near-by village of Kophinou, half an hour's notice that a patrol was going down to the village. It consisted of a police car, an armoured car, and some infantry in a truck, and it got through without incident. The Turks said that if the patrol was repeated, they would prevent it. The following morning it was repeated, none the less, but a Turkish cart blocking the road was removed on request.

A few hours later, at 12.30 p.m., UNFICYP at Kophinou were informed by the Greek Cypriots they were going down again. What followed is best described by U Thant in his report:

> When the patrol from Skarinou reached the entrance to the village, it found a tractor and a plough drawn across the road. Although there were no Turkish Cypriots around the tractor, some were seen in the area of a nearby school. At about 14.00 hours, the patrol from the Greek Cypriot sector arrived on the scene. When it reached the obstruction the soldiers debussed, removed the road block and deployed in the vicinity of the road junction at the north end of the village. Almost immediately there were about three shots and a burst of automatic fire.[8]

At that moment, the Greeks launched two major attacks, more or less simultaneously, one on Ayios Theodorus and the other on Kophinou. Three companies of the National Guard were involved, both villages were shelled, mortars and armoured cars were used. In the course of the fighting the National Guard violated two of the UN observation posts; at one, two soldiers from the British contingent were disarmed; at another, the radio equipment was damaged and soldiers' tents ransacked. The battle lasted until eight o'clock that evening, by which time a cease-fire had been arranged through negotiations in Nicosia.

The consequences of Kophinou are well known. Turkey once again threatened to invade. In the ensuing weeks the danger of a major war in the Eastern Mediterranean became a reality. Three trouble-shooters arrived on the scene; U Thant sent Dr Rolz-Bennett, NATO sent Signor Brosio, President Johnson sent Cyrus Vance. Under the provisions of the so-called 'Vance Agreement' Greece capitulated to most of Turkey's demands (although President Makarios stood firm on those which related to the disbandment of the National Guard and other internal security arrangements, which he claimed were the affair of his government alone); the illegal Greek mainland troops who had been assisting the Greek Cypriots were shipped back to Greece, and General Grivas was recalled to Athens – to the relief of many he was not to return. It is one of the strangest ironies about the whole Cyprus question that this bloody incident was directly responsible for shaking all parties concerned out of their complacency, and out of their fixed positions, and indirectly for the change of climate that led to the initiation of the talks that still continue.

Meanwhile, however, 26 people – most of them innocent civilians – lost their lives, and the question remains, why was not UNFICYP whose first duty was to prevent a recurrence of fighting, able to do just that at Kophinou? The answer is, basically, that UNFICYP misjudged Grivas's intentions. But they had no means of guessing that Grivas had moved large quantities of troops into the area, and was planning a full-scale military operation. With the advantage of hindsight, of course, it was abundantly clear that it was a well-planned military operation – the magnitude and speed of the operation proved that, as did the fact that Kophinou, which was in no way connected with the patrolling question, came under simultaneous attack.

Moreover, the scale of the retaliation against the two villages was out of all proportion to the importance of the patrolling incidents. Once the fighting had broken out, therefore, the UN was in no position to interpose physically in the fighting – and for the same reason that would have faced any other force in the circumstances, namely military inferiority. If they had some inkling of the build-up of Greek troops in advance, UN troops would perhaps have been moved into the area, but by late 1967, after successive reductions, UNFICYP troops were spread pretty thinly on the ground and it would have meant taking them off other essential duties, leaving patrols and observation posts elsewhere unmanned. The UN has no official intelligence service and has to rely on observation alone for its information. In such a situation this proved a serious disadvantage.

However, the UN role in the incident was not entirely negative. Once fighting had broken out it was subject to a running commentary by UN observation posts on all sides and was relayed straight back to headquarters in Nicosia. As a result, the negotiation of a cease-fire was facilitated by the fact that the UN commanders knew exactly what was happening on the battle front. They were thus able to present the full facts to Makarios immediately, who although he must have had some knowledge of what Grivas was planning, was taken aback when he realized it had got so out of hand. Secondly, no wild claims were able to be made afterwards about what had or had not happened; U Thant's report to the Security Council, based on that running commentary, was accepted as the definitive account of the incident. Thirdly, the UN presence on the scene, and the knowledge that they were being observed, may well have deterred Grivas and his men from even bloodier carnage.

Of all the conclusions to be drawn about the successes and failures of the UN in Cyprus, in preventing a recurrence of fighting, perhaps this, concerning the value of impartial observation, is the most important. The three incidents of Mora, Melousha and Kophinou have illustrated that in keeping the peace, negotiation is the UN's first weapon; that in some circumstances negotiation is effective only when backed up by good old-fashioned superiority of arms; and that in other circumstances when faced with a major outbreak of fighting, negotiations are useless, and the arms at UNFICYP's disposal are inadequate. But in these incidents, and in countless others in the force's five years on the island, the usefulness and adequacy of their role as observers has never been in question. Despite its failure, UNFICYP has reduced what in March 1964 when it first arrived was an ugly civil war, into a situation which U Thant was able to describe in one of his recent reports to the Security Council as 'generally quiet' with 'no major breaches of the cease-fire' and 'a substantial decrease in the number of shooting incidents'.[9] The credit for doing so is probably due more to the blue-bereted soldiers manning the observation posts, all over the island, than to any other single factor. By their presence there these soldiers have deterred both Greeks and Turks from starting incidents, and by their swift arrival on the scene prevented any that have occurred from escalating. And, on numerous occasions, tension has been lessened by the impartial accounts which they have given of such incidents afterwards, thus preventing mutual recrimination from reaching the point of hysteria. It is significant that when asked about the contribution of UNFICYP in restoring peace on the island, the leaders of both sides will mention first this role of impartial observation.

UNFICYP's degree of success in carrying out its two other functions, those of maintaining law and order and contributing to the return of normal conditions, is less easy to estimate. The maintenance of law and order is normally the function of governments, and as the relationship between the Cyprus government and UNFICYP has never been clearly defined, and has been subject to considerable fluctuations of goodwill, it is difficult to judge the extent of the UN contribution in this area. In a civil-war situation, law and order is inextricably tied up with the fighting between the two sides. Are the people who are refusing to comply with the government's concept of 'law and order' rebels when an international force must subdue, or entitled to respect equal to that accorded 'the other side' in the dispute?

The UN policy has been to avoid interfering with the police or judiciary of either side where incidents involving members of a single community are involved. If a Greek shoots another Greek or a Turk a Turk, the UN keeps well out of it. If, on the other hand, a Greek shoots a Turk or vice versa, the incident, as we have seen, may escalate with alarming speed into an all-out shooting match between the two sides. In this case, the UN must act as swiftly as possible 'to prevent a recurrence of fighting'; this it has done wherever possible.

The contribution to the return of normal conditions is subject to a similar ambiguity. The Greek Cypriot government saw Cyprus as a unitary state, albeit one containing a substantial minority to whom certain safeguards should ideally be given. The Turkish Cypriots saw Cyprus as a state comprising two distinct and separate communities which should each be allowed to govern and control their own community affairs. And this latter has been the *de facto* position since the civil war broke out in 1963. So what are normal conditions? Those of a unitary state or of a divided state? In quarrels over military fortifications and posts, UNFICYP has considered it its duty to preserve the *status quo*, as it was when it arrived. But, in civilian and political matters, the *status quo* could not in any sense be regarded as 'normal conditions'. On the whole, the UN tried to avoid a political interpretation of the phrase and concentrated on day-to-day economic and social problems, the solution of which would enable the two communities 'to resume their normal relations and make it possible for all Cypriots of both communities to go about their normal daily occupations anywhere in the island in greater freedom and unimpaired security.'[10] In his latest report to the Security Council, U Thant said: 'A great deal remains to be done to bring about real progress towards a return to normal conditions in civilian life.'[11] On the all-important question of freedom of movement, for instance, the Turkish Cypriots have stubbornly refused to open the important Nicosia–Kyrenia road, and Greek Cypriots still have to pass down the road at two specified times of day in a convoy, organized and patrolled by UNFICYP. Although contacts between the two communities are increasing and although theoretically the Turkish Cypriots are now free to go almost anywhere in the island (the only exceptions being a few restricted military areas), in practice they are still sticking to their own areas. The Turkish Cypriot refugee camps are still full and there is little movement between the two sectors of Nicosia. The inequality of economic opportunity between the two communities is still very marked and indeed increases with every week that passes.

It has been argued that the presence of the UN, itself, is a deterrent to the full restoration of normal conditions, and that in its anxiety to prevent outbreaks of fighting it has kept the two parties to the dispute further apart than is necessary. It has been said that, as long as the UN remains on the island, the situation will remain rigid; with the responsibility for preserving order taken out of their hands, neither side needs to take very energetic measures, or make any significant concessions, to restore normality. They can afford just to hang on and hope they will each get their own way in the end. Although there is some justification for these views, it would be a mistake to underestimate the contribution that the UN *has* made to restoring normal conditions on the island – or at least to creating conditions a great deal more 'normal' than those which it found on its arrival in March 1964.

Normal conditions are to a very large extent, of course, a natural consequence of the lessening of tension. And perhaps, UNFICYP's biggest contribution in this field has been through the indirect effects of the success discussed above, in preventing a recurrence of fighting and reducing armed confrontation. However, it has also been responsible for influencing more practical steps in this direction.

After the outbreak of the civil war in December 1963, an economic blockade was imposed by the government on the Turkish quarter of Nicosia. In July 1964, restrictions were stepped up when 'for some time all movement of supplies into the areas controlled by Turkish Cypriots in Nicosia, Lefka, Limnities and Kokkina was cut and a list of materials prohibited to the Turkish Cypriots was drawn up by the Government.'[12] At that time Señor Galo Plaza was U Thant's special representative in Cyprus: the post had been created in May to relieve the force commander of the burden of non-military and political negotiation. Señor Plaza immediately set about trying to persuade Archbishop Makarios to lift the blockade which was causing great hardship, and in some cases starvation. On 18 August, he succeeded in getting the government to allow food supplies to pass into the Turkish areas. In April the following year, after a shooting incident on the Green Line, in which shots were fired by a Turkish Cypriot found in a Greek-owned shop, the blockade on the Turkish quarter of Nicosia was renewed. Once again Turks were unable to enter or leave this area, and food supplies were cut off. After a protest to U Thant by the Turkish Cypriot leadership, supplies were later allowed in.

UN pressure on the government of Cyprus to take normalization measures takes different forms. For instance, on 23 September 1965, the day after Makarios had submitted an explanatory memorandum of Cyprus's recourse to the General Assembly, restrictions on sixteen items which had previously been denied to the Turkish Cypriots because of their strategic value, including boots and tyres, were lifted. UNFICYP can claim no credit for the move; but in that the Cyprus government placed great importance on the way its case was judged by the General Assembly, the UN, perhaps, can. Another factor to be taken into consideration is that when making a decision on whether to lift any given restrictions the government has understandably had to weigh up the chances of the other side taking military advantage of the move. Where UNFICYP has been able to obtain assurances from the Turkish Cypriots that this would not be the case, the decision has been facilitated. In September 1967, for example, after U Thant's special representative had obtained such assurances from the Turks, the government announced a plan for the relaxation of tension in the Limassol and Paphos districts. National Guard posts were to be left unmanned, and restrictions on travel and the purchase of items like cement and building iron were to be lifted.

However, it was not until after the Kophinou incident at the end of 1967 had shaken everyone concerned out of their lethargy, that really significant progress towards normalization began to be made. When all the shouting had died down, and U Thant had reopened talks with the parties in New York, Makarios announced, on 4 January 1968, a series of pacification measures to extend to the whole island except for the Turkish quarter of Nicosia. All check-points were to be abolished and restrictions lifted on the supply of goods still denied to the Turks. The Turkish quarter of Nicosia was excluded because it housed the headquarters of the Turkish Provisional Administration, the formation of which had been announced a few days before. Further pacification measures were announced on the twelfth, the day that Makarios broke the news that a presidential election would be held; and, on 8 March the last vestiges of the economic blockade, including those on Nicosia, were lifted. All check-points throughout the island disappeared, except for the Turkish-manned ones on the Kyrenia road. In spite of pressure from U Thant and his special representative, Osorio–Tafall, these remain although, on 23 August 1968, the Turkish leadership did announce certain readjustments to the timings of the convoy hours, and also said that it would consider proposals for the reactivation of factories situated on both the Greek and Turkish sectors, and individual applications from Greek civilians for entry into the Turkish sectors of the main towns in an unofficial capacity and on legitimate business.

From this history of the gradual lifting of restrictions in Cyprus and the consequent progress towards normalization, two points emerge. Firstly, with the exception of that mentioned above, most of the moves have been in one direction only, namely concessions from the Greek Cypriots to the Turkish Cypriots. This is partly because the Turkish Cypriots, perhaps because of their minority position, have been far more stubborn about hanging on to the advantages – like control of the Kyrenia road – which they do have, than the Greek Cypriots, and partly because there were far more restrictions imposed on them than by them, from the first. In 1964, when the Turkish mainland forces had failed to carry out their threat to invade, the Turkish Cypriots were in no position to impose restrictions on anyone. The fact remains that the blame for the lack of progress towards normalization since March 1968, lies squarely on their shoulders.

The second point, which follows indirectly from the first, is that UNFICYP as such is unable to do much to contribute towards normalization. The decisions for the gradual lifting of the economic blockade recounted above, had to be made by the Cyprus government – the UN could do nothing but persuade it that the measures were a good idea, though the persistent pressure of Osorio-Tafall and General Martola were vital factors. And if the Turkish Cypriot leadership refuses to move the road-blocks on the Kyrenia road, there is absolutely nothing that the UN can do about it. U Thant made the mistake once, of announcing in New York that an agreement had been reached whereby on the one hand the rotation of the Turkish army contingent would recommence and on the other hand that the road would be opened. Subsequent angry statements revealed that whatever the Turkish government had accepted, the Turkish Cypriot leadership had not been consulted about the 'agreement'. The road remained closed.

Where UNFICYP has been able to play a more direct role in the restoration of normal conditions, is away from the political battle-front in the social and economic fields. The UN Development Programme in Cyprus has been hampered by the fact that under its terms of reference it only gives technical assistance to governments, which in Cyprus has, to all intents and purposes, confined its activities to the Greek Cypriots. And it is the under-privileged Turkish Cypriot minority who need technical assistance most. Nevertheless, economic officers attached to each contingent in UNFICYP have done invaluable work in, for example, finding ways in which Turkish-owned factories in the Greek sector of towns and Greek-owned factories in the Turkish sector have been able to be opened up, or the machinery, at least, extracted for use elsewhere. Similarly in the countryside they have been able to help Turkish Cypriots harvest their fields in former mixed villages now dominated by Greek Cypriots, and vice versa. Even more important, over the past year participation in joint projects such as soil conservation and water development, have brought members of the two communities closer together. For, in the long run, the UN can only succeed in restoring normal conditions to Cyprus by increasing the contacts between the two communities. There is nothing 'normal' in the present state of partition in the island, where Greek and Turkish children are being brought up with no knowledge whatever of their counterparts on the other side. Removal of physical barriers can only go so far; mental barriers must also be dispensed with before normality will prevail. And the mental barriers are both the cause and effect of the failure so far to find a political settlement.

It was this political settlement, which the second part of the UN effort in Cyprus, that of mediation, was set up to promote. The mediator, the Security Council said, was to seek an agreed settlement 'in accordance with the Charter of the United Nations, having in mind the well-being of the people of Cyprus as a whole, and the preservation of international peace and security'[13] – a tall order and one which no one so far has succeeded in meeting. There have been three main attempts: that of the first mediator, Sakardi Tuomioja, that of Galo Plaza, and that of U Thant's current Special Representative in Cyprus, B. Osorio-Tafall.

Tuomioja arrived in Cyprus on 2 April 1964. His first round of diplomatic talks which took him to Athens, Ankara, London and Paris to report to U Thant, served only to convince him that the problem was so complex that it would take much longer to work out than was originally envisaged. There had been a second round of talks in Athens and Ankara, still with no sign of progress, and the Turkish Foreign Minister had told reporters: 'If the Cyprus situation continues like this, our going to Cyprus will be predestined.'[14] At this point the United States decided to take matters into its own hands. On 10 June, President Johnson, now convinced that the UN could not handle the problem, sent his Undersecretary of State, George Ball, to Athens and Ankara to ensure that Greece and Turkey did not go to war with one another. The United States was most anxious to avoid an open fight between two members of NATO in such a strategically important area as the Eastern Mediterranean. A fortnight later he held separate talks in Washington with the Prime Ministers of the two countries. These resulted in failure but, undeterred by Greece's insistence that any talks should be conducted through the UN mediator, Johnson then sent Dean Acheson to Geneva, where Tuomioja had set up his headquarters. The mission, the State Department said, was 'to provide assistance that may be appropriate in helping to resolve the Cyprus crisis'.[15] Acheson took with him a five-point peace plan, which he presented to Greece on 30 July. The basic provisions were that in return for immediate *enosis* (union of Cyprus with Greece), Greece was to cede to Turkey the island of Kastellorizon in the Dodecanese, the installation of a Turkish military base in Cyprus, the payment of compensation to Turkish Cypriots willing to emigrate, and the formation of two Turkish 'cantons' in Cyprus.

But Acheson had reckoned without Makarios. Any plan decided on by the American without consulting him would have been unlikely to meet with his approval; a plan which contained provision for a Turkish military base on the island was anathema to him. It is also doubtful if he genuinely desires *enosis*. He flew to Athens, attacked the 'self-styled mediators' in Geneva who are 'deflecting the Cyprus problem from its course',[16] and announced that the governments of Greece and Cyprus had reached a complete identity of views on handling the Cyprus problem. The plan was rejected.

A week later fighting flared up around Kokkina where the National Guard had attacked Turkish Cypriot positions; and in retaliation Turkish planes dropped napalm bombs on Greek Cypriots in the north-western coastal area. In the bitter aftermath of the fighting, Tuomioja announced new discussions with the governments concerned to take place almost immediately. On 13 August, Acheson discussed details of a new Geneva Plan with Tuomioja, but on the sixteenth, a few hours before Tuomioja was due to leave Geneva on a mission to Athens, Ankara and Nicosia to talk over the proposals, he had a heart attack. He died three weeks later; the talks in Geneva, which had never really got off the ground, broke down. The UN mediation effort was back to square one.

Whether it failed because of, or in spite of, American interference, is hard to say, because the Acheson effort and UN effort were inextricably intermingled with one another. Both made the same mistake: they supposed that the Cyprus problem could be settled between Greece and Turkey; that it could be discussed in Geneva in the context of international relations and without reference to the Cypriots themselves. They underestimated Makarios's influence on the Greek government, his determination to reject any proposals which he did not like the look of, and to hold out against a solution imposed on him from outside. They were too concerned with the preservation of 'international peace and security' and not sufficiently concerned with 'the well-being of the people of Cyprus as a whole',[17] and consequently they failed even to scratch the surface of the problem.

The second UN mediator, Galo Plaza, put the problem straight back into its proper context, that of the relationship between the two communities within the island itself. He spent six months, between September 1964 and March 1965, studying the situation and at the end of that time submitted a report which contained three main suggestions. Firstly, he said, the government of Cyprus should undertake to maintain the independence of Cyprus rather than leave the door open for *enosis*; secondly, there should be no physical separation of the two communities, but instead special measures should be taken to protect the rights of the Turkish minority and to give them proper voice in traditional communal affairs; thirdly, a UN Commissioner should be appointed to safeguard and act as guarantor for a settlement along such lines. In addition, he formally recommended that meetings between the parties concerned, with or without him, should take place as soon as possible. His conclusion, he said, could serve as a basis for such a meeting, which initially, at least, should be between representatives of the Greek and Turkish communities.

The plan was immediately rejected by Turkey, who objected strongly to being told that there should be no separation of the two communities. They informed U Thant that they considered Galo Plaza's mission as mediator to be terminated, on the grounds that he had exceeded his authority. Turkey considered Plaza to be prejudiced, and held that he had no business to put forward ideas for a final solution, but should have kept to procedural methods of bringing the parties together. They were opposed to the idea of community talks, because they felt that such talks would be hopelessly weighted against the Turkish Cypriot community. U Thant refused to accept this interpretation; in fact, by endorsing the document unreservedly, and failing to take into account the feelings of the parties concerned, he exacerbated the situation. A stalemate followed until after the UN General Assembly debate in December, in which the government of Cyprus due largely to the successful lobbying of its Foreign Minister, Spyros Kyprianou, scored a great moral victory by securing the adoption of a resolution which called on 'all states to respect the sovereignty and unity, independence and integrity of Cyprus and to refrain from any intervention against it'.[18]

Four days later Plaza finally submitted his resignation. His service, he said, 'could no longer contribute to the cause of mediation'. In a sense, Turkey was right; he had exceeded his brief. His plan for Cyprus made excellent sense – indeed the future he foresaw for the island, as an independent unitary state, but with real safeguards guaranteed by the UN for the minority, is that which the parties themselves have more or less come round to now – but his job was to mediate, not to judge. He failed to take into account the realities of the situation. It may have been the ideal solution in theory, but it was not at that time a possible one; and no solution, however sensible in theory, is any good without the agreement of the parties to the dispute.

After Plaza's resignation, the mediation effort went into abeyance for some time, with Makarios refusing to accept the appointment of a new mediator on the grounds that mediation was not complete: far from further mediation being necessary, what was needed was the implementation of Plaza's Report. Carlos Bernades, U Thant's Special Representative in Nicosia, made some attempts to break the impasse, but he met with little success. The emphasis shifted away from the UN to a direct Greco-Turkish dialogue which continued on and off from June to December 1966. 'In order to avoid doing anything which might be interpreted as imperilling a successful outcome of the talks,' U Thant said, 'all other efforts towards a solution have been temporarily suspended.'[19] In September 1967 a Greek-Turkish summit was held on the border between the two countries; the outcome was negative. It was hardly surprising; the Greco-Turkish dialogue had never got beyond the form of a double monologue.

Meanwhile, however, Osorio-Tafall, who had taken over as U Thant's Special Representative in February of that year, was busy establishing contacts with the leaders of both sides and biding his time for a more propitious climate to get talks going between them. He had to wait some time, for it was not until all parties agreed to accept the 'good offices' of the Secretary-General, in the aftermath of the crisis of December 1967, that the mediation effort was able to gain momentum again. Both sides were now in a better position to make concessions to the other: the Turkish Cypriot leadership had been strengthened by Turkey's moral victory over Greece; and the Greek Cypriot leadership was strengthened by the disappearance of Grivas and Makarios's sweeping victory over an *Enosis* candidate in the Presidential elections in January. Moreover the nearness of war during those tense days in November and December, had made everyone realize that some new effort must be made, and made as soon as possible.

After preliminaries in New York, Osorio-Tafall succeeded in winning acceptance in principle for his idea that talks should be held between a leading representative of each community: the obvious candidates were Glafkos Clerides, a moderate, and the President of the House of Representatives, and Rauf Denktash, the Turkish Cypriot leader who had been exiled from Cyprus since 1963, and who had been deported back to Turkey after attempting to enter the island illegally in December 1967. The two men had practised at the Bar together before the civil war broke out and, even allowing for their political differences, had a great deal in common. Denktash was allowed back to Cyprus in April. The first contact between the two men was made at a secret dinner party given at Osorio-Tafall's house on 22 May. One preliminary point that the two sides had been unable to agree about was the venue for the talks. The Turks insisted that it should be outside Cyprus, believing that they would be subject to unfair pressure within the island; the Greeks insisted that, as the problem was a Cypriot one, it should be Cyprus. Osorio-Tafall solved this one very neatly by suggesting that a preliminary meeting should be held abroad, after which the announcement of the formal opening of the talks in Cyprus should be made. This was done: Clerides and Denktash flew to Beirut on 2 June, and were much photographed having 'preliminary exchanges in a friendly atmosphere'; the talks opened formally at the Ledra Palace Hotel on the border between the two sectors of Nicosia on 24 June. This way the honour of both sides was vindicated.

The talks began in what Osorio-Tafall called 'an atmosphere of rising expectations, not only in Cyprus but elsewhere',[20] but since the initial burst of goodwill on all sides, progress has been slow. In March 1969, two sub-committees were appointed, one on the Legislative and one on the Independent Authorities, but these have achieved next to nothing so far. The only advantage they have had is to bring Greek and Turkish officials and politicians together again thus reducing the 'communications gap' which had existed between the two sides since the outbreak of the civil war. Clerides and Denktash continue their two-man talks; after the summer recess they came back in August 1969 to continue with the local autonomy question, which has proved by far the greatest stumbling block so far.

The Greek Cypriots are prepared to cede the Turks autonomy in education, religion and cultural affairs, and in local government on a village basis. But beyond village level, they want local government to be organized on a conventional geographical basis, decentralized and extending outwards, as it were, from the Ministry of the Interior. The Turkish Cypriots say that this would mean effective domination of Turk by Greek at all levels and want local government to be organized on community lines, and run by a Turkish Communal Chamber in Nicosia. This, Makarios says, amounts to 'federation', and he fears that once that had been established, 'it would be easy to achieve partition at a subsequent stage'.[21]

The two concepts are poles apart and so far neither side shows any sign of being prepared to make any concessions to the other. However, as U Thant has said recently, it will be a shame if the parties were to allow a deadlock to develop over 'such admittedly difficult issues as local government'.[22] Much of the trouble boils down to terminology. For example, 'local government having power to legislate' might be objected to; 'authority to regulate' might not. Despite the difficulties at the time of writing both Clerides and Denktash remain convinced that reason will prevail in the end, and that, somehow, a compromise solution will be found. Both realize that the price of failure would be high.

Indeed it is no exaggeration to say that on the outcome of these talks hangs the whole success or failure of the UN mission in Cyprus. We have seen how UNFICYP has succeeded, by and large, in de-fusing the situation on the island. It has acted – as it was expected to act – as a 'stabilizing presence'.[23] But this success is subject to the law of diminishing returns; extremists on both sides, always a potential source of renewed armed conflict, are beginning to get restless again, and until there is a settlement neither side is in a position to deal with them as firmly as they ought. Unless things get better soon, they may well get worse, and the UN force cannot remain in Cyprus to 'hold the ring' indefinitely. In a recent Security Council meeting on Cyprus (which extended the mandate for another six months) UN representatives called UNFICYP 'a milestone in international cooperation' and 'a model from which a great deal of valuable experience could be gained for use in future peace-keeping operations'. Certainly, as far as the functioning of the force is concerned, it has been entirely successful. The only defect of the operation has been the way in which it has been financed; the deficit, which has steadily built up, has been a permanent source of worry to U Thant and has proved once again that voluntary contributions are an unsatisfactory method of paying for a peace-keeping operation. Nevertheless the ultimate success of UNFICYP can only be judged in the last resort by the situation it leaves behind when it pulls out – and that depends on the result of the mediation effort.

Of all the mediation efforts made by the UN in Cyprus the present one, in the capable hands of Osorio-Tafall, certainly stands the greatest chance of succeeding. Osorio-Tafall's initial contribution was to change the situation from a static one to one that moved, however slowly. Since opening the talks, he has kept well out of them, believing wisely that it is best to reserve intervention by a third person as a last resort in the event of imminent breakdown. His tactic all along has been to encourage the two sides to deal with one another, to try to find some measure of agreement –

however small – on which to base the search for settlement. The mandate of the mediator was to promote an *agreed* settlement, not to impose a UN settlement – which is what both Tuomioja and Galo Plaza were attempting to do. Cyprus has learnt, from bitter experience, the futility of imposed settlements.

The UN may not have the power and influence which the United States or even Britain can bring to bear to force disputing parties to settle their differences. But although this may be the greatest weakness of UN action in civil wars, it is also, in a sense, its greatest strength. Free from the domestic pressures which govern the foreign policy of sovereign nations, its actions in Cyprus have been governed solely by the (albeit conflicting) interests of the parties themselves. Thanks to the smooth operation of UNFICYP, which has encouraged the force contributors to continue with their support, there have been no pressures for a quick settlement, which without the whole-hearted support of both sides might be in danger of collapsing at a later date. Tafall, by leaving the parties to get on with it, has ensured that if mutual distrust can be overcome, and a settlement does emerge from the talks, it stands the best possible chance of being a lasting one. Whether that settlement emerges at all depends on the Cypriots – and in the final resort it is by their reactions that the success of the UN in Cyprus will have to be judged.

TEXT REFERENCES

1. Security Council Official Records, 1,100th meeting, 4 March 1964.
2. Ibid.
3. Security Council Official Records, 1,098th meeting, 27 February 1964.
4. Resolution adopted by Security Council at its 1,102nd meeting. S/5575.
5. Ibid.
6. Letter from the Secretary-General to all members of the UN.
7. Stephens, Robert, *Cyprus: A Place of Arms*, London 1966, p.185.
8. Secretary-General's Report to the Security Council, 16 November 1967, S/8248.
9. Secretary-General's report on UNFICYP, 3 December 1968–2 June 1969. S/9233.
10. From a statement by Osorio-Tafall, issued as a Press Release CYP/521, 25 June 1968.
11. Secretary-General's report on UNFICYP, 3 December 1968–2 June 1969. S/9233.
12. Secretary-General's Report on UNFICYP, 15 September 1964–12 December 1964. S/6102.
13. Resolution adopted by Security Council at its 1,102nd meeting. S/5575.
14. *The Times*, 6 June 1964.
15. *New York Times*, 6 July 1964.
16. *Daily Telegraph*, 31 July 1964.
17. Resolution passed at 1,100th meeting of Security Council, 4 March 1964.

18. Report of the First Committee of the General Assembly (A/6166).

19. Secretary-General's Report on UNFICYP, 11 June 1966–5 December 1966. S/7611.

20. *Cyprus Bulletin*, 1 July 1968.

21. *Cyprus Bulletin*, 27 July 1969.

22. Secretary-General's Report on UNFICYP; 3 December 1968.

23. 1474th Meeting of Security Council. Provisional Verbatim Records 10 June 1969.

9 INTERNATIONAL LAW AND CIVIL CONFLICT

Rosalyn Higgins

To what extent does international law have anything to say about civil wars? And is what it says either germane or effective?

International law has traditionally been concerned with relations between sovereign states. But it has long been recognized that an internal war may have international repercussions, and international law has therefore sought to provide some guidance on what relations other nations may pursue with both the government and the rebels.[1] Equally, international law has long had an interest in promoting minimum standards in the conduct of hostilities; and in recent years it has come to be acknowledged that at least some of the rules devised must apply to internal, as well as to international war.

This being said, it must immediately be added that there is considerable controversy as to the content of the relevant rules of international law; that there is no clear normative guidance at all in a multitude of hitherto unforeseen situations which do, in fact, arise in internal war conditions in the contemporary world; and that even those norms which are clearly identifiable are frequently breached. These three points are closely related. If the basic rule is that international law forbids intervention in the civil strife of another state, does it yet allow assistance to the legitimate government? Or only if the rebels are assisted by another outside agent? How relevant is the fact of the existence of a prior treaty with the endangered government? May arms be supplied to either side? While different authorities may be cited to provide answers to questions, all that is truly clear is that the answers are uncertain, that particular circumstances can be picked out to justify answers either way. Moreover, there are new reasons both for and against intervention which states now find compelling, and which the law (which has painted with a broad brush) has not taken into account: intervention to give sustenance to a similar ethnic group which is being persecuted; intervention to protect a particular balance of power in the area;

or even UN intervention for certain purposes. This leads in turn to the third point which we have mentioned – that compliance with the law is far from satisfactory. Because there is no central superior authority to provide definitive answers, states must decide for themselves what the legal rules are, and what specific rules apply to the particular circumstances of their conduct. Both parties to a civil war, and their supporters, can come to the battlefield claiming support from international law.

International law, then, has a legitimate and increasing interest in civil war – but is inadequate to the task. Nor are international lawyers unaware of this. Some at least among the younger generation of academics have in recent years been directing their attention towards internal war problems, paying special heed to the question of intervention by third parties.[2] International law relies on several sources[3] for its authority; but at least some of these – judicial decisions, international treaties – are exceedingly scant in regard to civil war. Consequently, the role of eminent legal authors, as an acknowledged subsidiary source of international law, is particularly important. And so, of course, is state practice.

Among these lawyers, Professor Richard Falk of Princeton University has done pioneer work, and has analysed convincingly the inadequacy of the old legal order so far as internal conflict is concerned.[4] Traditional international law acknowledges two categories of civil conflict, with different legal consequences flowing from each. Where a status of insurgency exists, there is in effect an international acknowledgment of an internal war, but third parties are left substantially free to determine the consequences.[5] Where country A, noting a civil war in country B, acknowledges the rebels as insurgents, it is regarding them as contestants-at-law, and not as mere law-breakers. But it is still free, under traditional international law, to help the legitimate government, but should desist from helping the rebels.[6] However, the criteria for the recognition of insurgency are elusive, and an eminent legal authority, Sir Hersch Lauterpacht, has asserted that 'any attempt to lay down conditions of recognition of insurgency lends itself to misunderstanding. Recognition of insurgency creates a factual relation in the meaning that legal rights and duties as between insurgents and outside states exist only insofar as they are expressly conceded and agreed upon for reasons of convenience, of humanity, or of economic interest.'[7] Traditional law seems to provide no more guidance than to say that a recognition of insurgency puts no duty of neutrality upon the recognizing state. It does not clearly spell out whether its freedom to deal with each of the parties still remains absolute.[8]

Traditional international law also speaks of the status of belligerency. This is rather more precise than the status of insurgency, and entails the meeting of four criteria : first, the existence within a state of a widely spread armed conflict; second, the occupation and administration by rebels of a substantial portion of territory; thirdly, the conduct of hostilities in accordance with the rules of war and through armed forces responsible to an identifiable authority; and fourth, the existence of circumstances which make it necessary for third parties to define their attitude by acknowledging the status of belligerency.[9] This is rather more useful as a guide for conduct, one might think, than the elusive concept of insurgency. But, there are all too few situations today to which all four of the required criteria apply. The Nigeria-Biafra war clearly fulfils the first two points, but hardly the third; and the same may be said of Vietnam. Yet, clearly, these are in any normal sense of the term civil wars, with belligerent parties, in respect of which third parties may have to take some sort of stand. Yet the recognition of belligerency entails significant consequences, for once it has occurred the recognizing state is required to be neutral in the domestic conflict, and to aid neither the rebel nor the government. And they in turn are entitled to take certain measures to ensure this.

But it must be said that, because the four criteria seem not to cover contemporary situations, and because governments do not wish to harness themselves to the legal consequences of a recognition of insurgency or belligerency, recognition of this status has lost all practical significance. One has merely to look at the conflicts in Nigeria and Vietnam to see the total irrelevance of any formal acknowledgments of this sort by outside states. Yet the whole law of intervention – the degree to which outside parties legally may or may not intervene – depends upon the status of the protagonists in the civil conflict. The law is manifestly unsatisfactory. There is a traditional rule of non-interference following upon a recognition of belligerent status. To this basic rule there are claimed exceptions (to which we shall return below). But the criteria for the initial grant of recognition are unclear; states have for years avoided an express bestowal of status on the parties to a civil war; and consequently, it is impossible to establish in any objective way the validity of claims made by third states as to their right to intervene on behalf of one side or the other.

The traditional rule may have been of non-interference, except in the case of certain exceptions. The exceptions, claimed by governments every day, may now be thought to be more numerous and relevant than the basic prohibition. Governments may advance a variety of claims as to why in the particular circumstances, the basic prohibition notwithstanding, it is bound to intervene – humanitarian reasons, the existence of a treaty, the prior intervention on the other side by another country, and a myriad others. There is no central authority which can pass judgment on the legitimacy in principle of those claims, or on their applicability to the real facts of the situation.

We may thus restate the position so far. Traditional international law decreed that intervention in a civil war was prohibited, save for certain exceptions. But whether a situation is or is not a fully civil war depends, in the legal sense, on a cluster of criteria one or more of which are invariably lacking. And as to the exceptions claimed, there is no impartial authority to decide either whether there are such exceptions, or whether they apply in a particular case. All of these factors, therefore, militate in favour of intervention to such a degree that one may wonder whether contemporary international law – in which state practice plays a large part – really does basically prohibit intervention in civil wars.

To analyse the present situation further, it may be helpful to examine the legal arguments advanced by nations concerning intervention; and then to see whether there is any hope of providing an impartial authority which can pronounce on the validity of those.

A state deciding to intervene in a domestic conflict in another nation, may advance one or more of the following contentions:

1   *That it may assist the government because the violence has not yet attained the status of belligerency*

But we have already mentioned that the granting of a status of belligerency rests upon criteria which are not, unfortunately, wholly realistic in contemporary conditions; and that in fact formal recognition of this status rarely occurs nowadays. This is not, of course, to say that sporadic violence can never be distinguished from civil war. The Nigerian-Biafran conflict manifestly reached the proportions of a civil war (though, showing the outmoded nature of the traditional law, there has been no granting of 'belligerent status' to Biafra) and, if third parties wish to intervene they must justify the intervention on grounds other than the minor status of the conflict. In the fighting which occurred in the Lebanon in October 1969, between Palestine guerrillas and the Lebanon government, the violence could not have been said to have reached the status of full civil war. The inefficacy of traditional international law is shown by the fact that, in legal terms, neighbouring Syria could give aid to the Lebanon government but not to the guerillas. The actual facts were the other way around.

Any intervention on behalf of the government must, of course, be by invitation of that government. There are those who feel that, so long as there is no international procedure by which to establish the support commanded by the rebels, this doctrine should be looked at very cautiously.[10] The point is also made that, if it is necessary to call in foreign help, the outcome of the conflict would without it be uncertain, and consequently there is a doubt as to which side would ultimately establish itself as the legal representative of the state.[11]

Although this type of intervention still occurs, states have perhaps become more reluctant to engage in this type of action unless they have a specific commitment to the beleaguered government (as did the United Kingdom to President Nyerere during the army mutiny of 1964), or unless they can be confident (as apparently can France in francophil Africa) that no international opprobrium is likely to ensue.

II *That it may sell arms*

Whereas states may not legally provide arms or munitions to the rebels, nor allow their territory to be used as a base for rebel activities, they none the less may continue to provide arms to the lawful government, certainly until belligerency is recognized. Given the virtual lapse of the doctrine of recognition of belligerency, it has become common practice for states to ignore the traditional requirement of neutrality, and to continue supplying arms, even in a major civil war, to the government. A clear example of this has occurred in the Nigeria-Biafra war. It was impossible on the facts to deny the existence of a civil war in that country, and traditional law prohibited the provision of arms to either Biafra or the Federal government. The fact that a third party recognized the Lagos government as the legitimate government is irrelevant to this point. Yet the British government has stressed time and again that it was entitled, indeed bound, to provide arms to the recognized government of Nigeria. The degree to which the traditional notions of legal obligation have become obscured was evidenced by a statement of the then Commonwealth Secretary :

> Neutrality was not a possible option for Her Majesty's Government at this time. We might have been able to declare ourselves neutral if one independent country was fighting another, but this was not a possible attitude when a Commonwealth country, with which we had long and close ties, was faced with an internal revolt; what would other Commonweath countries have thought? [12]

Yet the Commonwealth Secretary himself classified the situation as a 'civil war'. The implication of this curious statement would seem to be that all Commonwealth governments may expect tangible support from Britain through the supply of arms, irrespective of the status of the internal conflict in which they may be engaged.

One should also note that the supply of arms to the rebels was clearly forbidden under international law – though those countries which did recognize Biafra, and some which did not, obviously felt themselves free to engage in such sales.

The pressure to sell arms to a government faced with civil war is very great where a treaty to provide arms already exists. If country A is a traditional supplier of arms to country B, A will be gravely embarrassed if civil war breaks out in B. Though A's legal duty may be to be neutral, there is nothing it can do that will have neutral results. The United Kingdom was well aware that, if it withdrew its traditional arms supplies to Lagos, it would in these circumstances effectively be taking action against Lagos. It is also argued – and Britain has made the case – that, if a traditional supplier withdraws its arms, it may in fact be prolonging the war, because the rebels will be securing arms also.

International law does not clearly state whether a treaty to supply arms may, or must, be held in abeyance while there is a civil war. However, most arms-supply treaties will now contain clauses covering this point, and in respect of those which do not, the doctrine of *clausula rebus sic stantibus* may be thought relevant. This legal doctrine suggests that the validity of the treaty is altered when the fundamental circumstances change.

III   *That it is aiding against a war of secession*

Domestic conflict may occur when rebels seek to control the metropolitan government. But equally, it can occur when a particular group seeks not to impose its authority on the territory as a whole, but to secede. Outside parties frequently intervene in such a situation either on the side of the government, or on the side of the rebels. Those supporting the government will speak of the undesirability of secession; and those supporting the rebels will speak of the desirability of self-determination. Though it is not usually advanced as a claim of law, in the strict sense, arguments concerning the undesirability of secession are frequently heard. There would seem to be no merit in the suggestion that there is a legal distinction between civil war and secession, that is to say, a distinction which forbids intervention on behalf of the government in the former case, but not the latter. When British support of the Lagos government was under discussion in the House of Commons, it was suggested that the delivery of arms was permissible. 'However, the position could change if the struggle took on the character of a genuine civil war . . . [Is] it not still a fact that this is a matter of secession rather than a civil war?' [13] The correct rejoinder was offered: namely, that this is an invalid distinction, for the events in Nigeria are in effect 'a civil war over the issue of secession'.[14]

As a matter of policy, however, most nations regard secession in another as undesirable; and there are those who have interests in discouraging either secession in general, or the case in particular, and consequently see fit to intervene on the side of the government. Nations which have different ethnic, religious and tribal groups within their borders, and are anxious about separatism, are inclined to oppose secession when it occurs elsewhere. The position of Iraq, India and Kenya may be cited. The issue is not one only of political principle, but of the allocation of economic resources, for it frequently occurs that the seceding region is the locus of the nation's major natural wealth. At the same time, the ex-colonial powers of Europe are equally disinclined to see secession flourish in Africa. They played a major part in moulding the nations which have come to independence, and have every reason to believe that a proliferation of yet smaller and less viable entities is not in the public interest. The United Kingdom, one may add, feels a particular burden in this respect with regard to the newer Commonwealth.[15]

Yet the question remains to be answered: by what right do external powers take it upon themselves to decide the optimum political and economic unit for another nation? If a people wish strongly enough to form a separate political community, the matter is one to be resolved between them and the larger unit of which they form a part. It is a curious contemporary form of colonization for a foreign state to impose, through intervention, its preferences as to the unity of the country concerned.

This viewpoint, it may be noted, does not require a decision as to whether there is or is not a right of secession under international law. If a region has voluntarily entered into an agreement whereby it is to become part of a larger political structure, the legal principle of *pacta sunt servanda* would carry weight, and the federal government will have an interest in its ability to share the resources of the country. However, if the federal government is clearly unable to honour its reciprocal pledges to the region, and especially if it is manifestly unable to provide fundamental freedoms and protection to the peoples of the region, a claim to secession will inevitably arise. It is not, however, for third parties to sit in judgment on these questions.

The obverse is also true. Nations are not free to encourage, let alone foment, a secession movement. Assistance to seceding movements is given in a variety of ways: by masterminding the military aspects of the secession (as in Katanga); by supplying arms (as in Biafra); and by recognizing the seceding government. Biafra undoubtedly possessed the status of a belligerent, which required other nations to be neutral. However, some went further, and recognized Biafra as an independent state – which in legal terms it clearly was not – and such action was an intervention in the civil war.

IV *That intervention in a civil war is necessary on humanitarian grounds*
Intervention for humanitarian purposes is not, of course, limited as a phenomenon of civil wars. States have long claimed the right to intervene in another country if the government of that country is unwilling or unable to protect foreign nationals, or particular ethnic groups with which the foreign country feels close affinity. In a civil-war situation the inability of a government to protect foreign nationals is likely to increase. Intervention on these grounds is clearly open to abuse, as there is no impartial agency to determine the *bona fides* of the necessity for such action. The United Kingdom initially claimed that it was entering Suez in 1956 to protect British nationals; and the United States made a similar claim in respect

of its action in the Dominican Republic in 1965. Should the possibility of such abuses prohibit the legal validity of such a claim? A number of eminent scholars have recently affirmed the legality of a circumscribed right of humanitarian intervention, so long as it is limited in duration and not directed at the political balance in the country concerned.[16] None the less, so far as international practice is concerned, opinion seems to be moving away from this form of intervention.[17] Even the strictly limited United States-British-Belgian intervention in the Congo in 1962 was severely criticized by many governments, even though they acted in rebel-held areas with the co-operation of the Congo government, and even though they speedily withdrew after rescuing the trapped missionaries. The Turkish insistence upon its right to protect its community in Cyprus (a right claimed to be treaty-based, as well) has equally found little favour in the international community.

v *That intervention is needed to protect authority in one's sphere of interest*

This, clearly, is a major cause of intervention, though the claim is hardly a legal one. Given the nuclear confrontation, intervention within one's own sphere of interest is increasingly tolerated by the nuclear powers, and to a certain degree, by those non-nuclear powers who are not directly involved. In Eastern Europe the Soviet Union has seen either possible moves towards neutralism (Hungary 1956) or even a more liberal form of Communism (Czechoslovakia 1968) as a threat to its own security and grounds for intervention. In the case of Hungary the Soviet Union claimed an invitation to intervene from the government – though these were not the acknowledged leaders of Hungary. In Czechoslovakia an invitation was also alleged, though those extending it could never be identified. The United States intervened in internal disorders in the Dominican Republic in 1965, claiming that Communists were among those otherwise likely to come to power. The United States found no major legal restraint against intervening in another nation's domestic matters; and of course the Monroe Doctrine formalized the interest of the United States in preventing the formation of Communist governments in the Americas.

While the nations of the world – both individually and collectively at the United Nations – condemn such sets of intervention, it is widely appreciated that they are likely to continue to occur, and that no effective measures can be taken against them. Interventions by the super powers within their immediate spheres of interest have almost become part of the fabric of community expectations.

vi *That intervention is needed to counterbalance other interventions*

Where a single country intervenes on one side in an internal war, it is highly likely that other foreign interventions will follow. A state may feel compelled to respond to another intervention representing competing values. It is clear that, if high stakes are involved, a prior intervention is in practice felt to legitimate a counter-intervention, a basic rule of non-intervention notwithstanding.[18] One of the great difficulties, of course, is that of assessing objectively which is the initial intervention. Did Egypt support for the Yemen Republicans precede or follow Saudi support for the Royalists? Did the United States massive military aid to South Vietnam precede or follow major infiltration from North Vietnam? Each side has its own answers.

One may also note another disconcerting tendency to counter-intervention: if state A intervenes on behalf of one side in a civil war, not only may state B feel, for various reasons, the necessity of intervening on behalf of the other side; but state X, wishing for the same outcome as state A, may feel compelled to intervene on the same side as state A in order to lessen state A's influence with its chosen side.[19]

THE ROLE OF INTERNATIONAL BODIES

Clearly, many of the problems in providing a legal system for intervention in internal conflict arise from the decentralized nature of the world community. We live in a horizontal legal order – that is to say, the law relies, in very large measure, for its efficacy and enunciation on sovereign, equal states. There is no superior legal body with greater authority. Those international organizations which entail some diminution of national autonomy, and which evolve some legal life of their own, represent a very small step towards a vertical legal order. What role can they reasonably be expected to play in improving the legal position in intervention in civil wars?

We have already made certain observations which may be recapped here: that recognition of the status of the protagonists in a civil conflict, from which status the application of international law flowed, rarely occurs today. Third parties thus lack precise legal obligations in their dealings with the warring parties. Many of the alleged 'exceptions' to the basic rule of non-intervention are unclear and dubious as a matter of law. And, it may also be here added, the decentralized assertion of claims by nations makes it virtually impossible to standardize what is permissible and what is impermissible. Whereas some states intervene while still paying lip service to the basic principle of non-intervention, others – such as the Communist and anti-colonial powers – see certain sorts of interventions as compatible with international law.[20] Their revolutionary ideology provides guidance to a new set of legal claims. The other great difficulty following from a decentralized system is the lack of an impartial authority to establish the precise sequence of events. There is thus no one to pronounce authoritatively on which side foreign intervention occurred on first, for example. This is an extremely important *lacuna*, for a high proportion of foreign intervention is based on the claim that a prior intervention has already taken place.

International bodies such as the UN have been limited in the role they can play, because their constitutions specifically prohibit intervention in the domestic affairs of their members.[21] At the same time, they have not been wholly without authority; where third parties become heavily engaged, a civil war can be said to have become international; only where there is a threat to international peace the UN may act. Further, recommendations, even if not direct action, may be taken if human rights become endangered in an internal war.[22]

Suggestions have been made as to the role which the UN could play. Professor Falk, in his pioneer writings on this problem, has urged, realistically, that where one nation intervenes in a civil war, the law should acknowledge a response of counter-revolution by another nation.[23] He goes beyond this by suggesting that some types of social change can only be achieved by internal conflict, and that their achievement can only come about if assisted from outside. The UN could promote these ends: '. . . there is a need to promote certain social changes by organizing and encouraging external participation in anti-government insurgencies, but that this participation must itself be legitimated by a centralized process of decision and implementation.'[24] Professor Norton Moore, after suggesting a more detailed breakdown as to what types of intervention should be regarded as permissible or impermissible, also authorizes a legitimating role for the UN.

> An intervention in internal conflict is permissible if specifically authorized by the General Assembly or Security Council, even though in the absence of such authorization it would be impermissible. Conversely, if the General Assembly or Security Council specifically calls for cessation of a particular intervention, continuation is impermissible, even though in the absence of such prohibition it would be permissible.[25]

These views suppose two things: first, that such a collective control of the question of intervention is preferable to the present highly unsatisfactory pattern of unilateral intervention; and second, that the Assembly or Security Council will be able to act in accordance with criteria and in order to promote objectives of value to the world community. There are, in this writer's view, such grave doubts concerning the second proposition that even the first may be in issue. Undesirable though the frequency of unilateral intervention may be, that intervention none the less takes place within an understood framework. The legitimating intervention by the UN might well change the frame of reference very radically. Both Professor Falk and Professor Norton Moore seem to envisage a legitimating role for the Assembly, as well as for the Security Council. It needs no emphasis that these are very different bodies. The results that one can achieve in the one are by no means the results that one can achieve in the other. The Security Council, with its core of permanent members, each having the veto, has moved cautiously on the issue of civil war. On the anomalous question of Rhodesia (where there is domestic – in the constitutional sense – conflict, though not civil violence) intervention on behalf of one side has been authorized. But even here the intervention has been in the form of economic and diplomatic sanctions, rather than direct military measures. In the case of the war in Angola and Mozambique, the Security Council has called for an arms embargo against Portugal. And it has demanded an arms embargo against South Africa, even though no internal war yet exists there. The General Assembly (which is not able under the Charter to take decisions legally binding on its members), has taken altogether a bolder view. When violent revolution has occurred against a colonial power, it has frequently shown itself sympathetic to those seeking their independence. The present interest of the majority of the General Assembly leads it to a position where it will lend its support to colonial peoples who are waging a war against their colonial masters and to legitimate third party intervention on their behalf by urging UN members to give 'all moral and material assistance'.[26] But this is a very blunt tool, for such a legitimating function fails to distinguish between those dependencies which have been promised independence by a specific date (Aden) and those who have been told they are to remain an integral part of the metropolitan power (Angola); between those nations who had a good trend in granting independence with all due speed (the United Kingdom) and those who do not (Portugal); between those who have shown some concern for human rights (the United Kingdom) and those who have shown none (South Africa); and between those claims to decolonization which are based on a prior, disputed territorial claim (Gibraltar) and those which are not (Mozambique). General Assembly practice so far leads one to believe that, if it were granted the functions of authorizing intervention in a civil conflict, it not only would encourage those desirable processes of change which otherwise are resisted, but also would approve of intervention on behalf of non-democratic groups so long as their opponents were sufficiently tainted with the colonial brush. The handling of the Aden and Gibraltar cases give one little grounds for confidence.

To be sceptical of the desirability of a General Assembly legitimating role is not, of course, to deny any role at all to the UN. In the field of colonial wars (insofar as these are deemed civil wars) the constant pressure for independence has, on the whole, been desirable. It is useful that these matters should be debated, and that states should be held publicly accountable for their administration of dependent peoples. The UN performs a valuable task in continuing to press for human rights, and to bring international diplomatic and economic pressures to bear.[27] And even if the UN is not to be given the role of legitimation of intervention, it can itself intervene in certain situations. We have talked so far of internal conflict arising from colonial situations. But internal war also occurs through a breakdown of the constitutional machinery, bringing a flight from law and order in its wake. When this entails international repercussions the UN has intervened – on the invitation of the government concerned. Its mandate has usually been to restore law and order and to protect the state concerned from international pressure. In the Congo, much of ONUC's efforts were directed to removing Belgian influence in seceding Katanga. The Security Council also formally forbade intervention by other nations.[28] So far as restoring peace is concerned, UN forces have been fairly successful, as the operation in Cyprus since 1964 bears witness. However, the United Nations has been considerably less successful in finding long-term political solutions.

United Nations forces intervene in 'law and order' situations on the express understanding that they will be neutral in the domestic conflict, and not affect its outcome. But their very presence, and the fact that their efficient operation requires them to deal with the government, is a boost to the position of that government. In situations such as the Congo and Cyprus, it is inevitable that UN intervention will lessen the chances of success of the rebelling minorities. Ironically, therefore, we may note that the UN already has been quite efficient in a prevention-prohibiting function; and that this works in quite the opposite direction from the legitimating function envisaged by Professors Falk and Moore, for it freezes the possibility of change, and encourages the continuation of the *status quo*. While neither Professor Falk nor Professor Moore would probably regard the Congo or Cyprus as situations in which they would wish to see social change through legitimized resolution, the point of principle none the less remains.

One could wish also that the UN had been more successful in resolving the knotty problem concerning the unit to which self-determination applies. Self-determination – that is to say, the right of a people to choose their own economic, social and political decision – is in this writer's view by now established as a legal right.[29] What is far from clear is the 'self' to whom this applies. Is it a legal right applying only to dependent peoples? Are the Turks in Cyprus entitled to a self-determination separate from the wishes of the majority of that island? And how small is the unit, either of persons or territory, to which it can apply? Are the peoples of Gibraltar entitled to self-determination? Or does the territorial claim of Spain, if it could be proven, have the greater legal importance? Again, UN practice has shown little clear guidance dealing with cases on an *ad hoc* basis.[30] Yet, if intervention to support aspirations for self-determination is to be approved, one must understand in what ways the situation in South-West Africa, Hungary 1956 and Cyprus are perceived as similar or different. [31]

The UN can, to be sure, play a useful part in publicly declaring where a conflict is or is not an internal war. If the UN deems it mere local riot – and the more so if, in Professor Moore's terminology, it is not authority oriented [32] – certain legal consequences follow. If a situation is authoritatively deemed a civil war, an obligation of neutrality then follows. And, in so far as a breach of that obligation rests on an accusation of prior intervention by another nation, fact-finding bodies initiated by the UN can play a helpful part in unravelling the sequence of events. Clearly, also, the UN has indirectly to attest to the status of the protagonists to a civil war when it is presented with two sets of credentials both purporting to speak as the government. Who can doubt that the resolving of this diplomatic problem was of major importance to Kasavubu in 1960, the Yemen Republicans in 1962, and to the Iraq revolutionaries in 1958?

The UN's major role, then, seems to be threefold: first, to intervene itself, physically, where internal conflict has led to a breakdown in internal order which in turn has external repercussions; and in so doing to prohibit any other third party intervention. Second, to acknowledge that this is frequently a formula for freezing the *status quo*, and to use all the means at its disposal to urge change and to point to unjust social and political conditions. Third, to clarify and perhaps limit the options for unilateral intervention by third powers by pronouncing, in a clear and consistent manner, the legal status of the parties to a civil conflict.

Many of these tasks, of course, a regional organization can do as well; and in some cases it may be that peaceful settlement may be promoted even better at a local level. At the same time, one should be aware of the danger that too large an authority granted to a regional organization can result in an imposed hegemony of economic, social and political ways of life. Further, government in the region will necessarily view any attempted rebellion or secession against the likelihood of its occurrence in their own country.

THE CONDUCT OF CIVIL WAR HOSTILITIES

International law plays a small enough role in controlling the methods of hostilities in international law; and in civil war its role is still smaller. Yet the reasons underlying the rules of war conduct apply equally to internal war. Lauterpacht observed as early as 1946:

> A clearly ascertained state of hostilities on a sufficiently large scale, willed as war at least by one of the parties, creates *suo vigne* a condition in which the rules of warfare become operative ... Once a situation has been created which, but for the constitutional law of the state concerned, is indistinguishable from war, practice suggests that inter-

national law ought to step in in order to fulfil the same function which it performs in wars between sovereign states, namely, to humanize and regularize the conduct of hostilities as between the parties.[33]

However, the rights and duties of the laws of war and of neutrality of third parties have continued, in practice, to rest at least upon a recognition of belligerent status. The impact of international law here has been very limited. Where it has made some small inroad into internal war has been in the provision of a basic humanitarian code of conduct.

Article 3 of the four Geneva Conventions of 1949 [34] provides:

In the case of armed conflict not of an international character occurring in the territory of one of the High Contracting Parties, each Party to the conflict shall be bound to apply, as a minimum, the following provisions:

1   Persons taking no active part in the hostilities, including members of armed forces who have laid down their arms and those placed *hors de combat* by sickness, wounds, detention, or any other cause, shall in all circumstances be treated humanely, without any adverse distinction founded on race, colour, religion or faith, sex, birth, or wealth, or any other similar criteria.

To this end, the following acts are and shall remain prohibited at any time and in any place whatsoever with respect to the above-mentioned persons:
(*a*) violence to life and person, in particular murder of all kinds, mutilation, cruel treatment and torture;
(*b*) taking of hostages;
(*c*) outrages upon personal dignity in particular humiliating and degrading treatment;
(*d*) the passing of sentences and the carrying out of executions without previous judgment pronounced by a regularly constituted court, affording all the judicial guarantees which are recognized as indispensable by civilized peoples.

2   The wounded and sick shall be collected and cared for. An impartial humanitarian body, such as the International Committee of the Red Cross, may offer its services to the Parties to the conflict.

The Parties to the conflict should further endeavour to bring into force, by means of special agreements, all or part of the other provisions of the present Convention. The application of the preceding provisions shall not affect the legal status of the Parties to the conflict.

This requires the application of certain humanitarian rules, irrespective of whether the rebels have been recognized as belligerents either by the government or by third parties. It also provides the basis for Red Cross interventions, showing that they are not to be regarded as unfriendly acts.

Unfortunately, the results have been very poor: while the Red Cross has been able to get a footing (as in Guatemala 1954, in Costa Rica 1955 and Nigeria – in spite of the ups and downs of its relations with the Federal government – in 1968–9), paragraph 1 of Article 3 continues to be ignored in practice. Neither have the parties, as recommended in the second part of paragraph 2, endeavoured to make agreements to bring into effect other parties of the 1949 Conventions. The Article itself is certainly a step in the right direction – its application is not based on reciprocity by the other party, nor does it depend upon the fulfilment of a technical definition of a civil war.[35] But nations have been all too reluctant to acknowledge the application of Article 3 to conflicts in which they find themselves involved – Britain denied its relevance to the pre-independence conflicts in Kenya and Cyprus, and France to Algeria. France allowed some relief activity by the Red Cross and Britain, going further, permitted the Red Cross to visit detainees in Cyprus in 1955 and in Kenya in 1957. But both governments made it clear that these invitations to the Red Cross arose not from any obligation under Article 3, but as a gratuitous act of sovereignty.

In Vietnam the situation – with clear violations of humanitarian behaviour by all sides – has been particularly confused. The United States regards the war as an international one, and thus insists that the entirety of the Geneva Conventions (and not just Article 3) apply. North Vietnam, South Vietnam, and the United States are all legally bound by the Geneva Conventions. North Vietnam has insisted that aerial attacks by the United States, the use of napalm and indiscriminate bombing were breaches of the Conventions; and that accordingly American airmen would be treated as common criminals. Nor has it given permission for visits by the International Red Cross. There have also undoubtedly been breaches of the Convention in the South though there is evidence that the United States has somewhat restrained the excesses of South Vietnam.

CONCLUSION

In conclusion, therefore, it is clear that international law, though frequently invoked so far as the methods of war are concerned and though providing a basis for international concern in the form of the Red Cross nevertheless plays only a small part in regulating international interventions in civil conflicts. If one would look behind the legal rhetoric to the reality (and it is only by doing this that a more realistic legal order can be built), it is clear that the law has to be restated. Counter-intervention has come to be accepted, as well as the supply of arms to both sides. Effectively accepted as well is help given to a government faced with a local mutiny, and even assistance given to so-called liberation movements. Majority condemnation of these can no longer be expected. More in doubt is intervention, however brief, for humanitarian purposes. The area we can clearly define as illegal is surprisingly small: intervention in a purely civil conflict on behalf of unrepresentative rebels; intervention in a purely civil lonflict on behalf of an undemocratic government against a representative rebel movement; and intervention on behalf of a government merely on the ground that the territory it governs must remain one unit. In controlling this problem international organizations can surely help – not as arbiters of desirable and undesirable intervention, but rather in determining the facts which will limit the unilateral choices that can be made.

TEXT REFERENCES

This chapter is closely based upon a chapter which the author has written for Volume IV of *The Future of the International Legal Order*. This volume, to be entitled *Conflict Management*, is scheduled to be published in spring 1971. Her thinking upon this question has been advanced by the comments of colleagues at a conference held in Princeton, May 1968, in connection with the preparation of the above volume.

1. Silvanie, H., *Responsibility of States for Acts of Unsuccessful Insurgent Government*; Weber, J., *Problèmes de droit international public posés par les guerres civiles*; Wehberg, H., 'La Guerre Civile et le Droit International' 1 *Hague Recueil* (1938) 1; Wilson, G., 'Insurgency and International Maritime Law', 1 AJIL (1907) 46; Pinto, R., 'Les Règles de Droit International concernant la Guerre Civile' *Hague Recueil* (1965) 451; Castrén, E., *Civil War*, Helsinki 1966.

2. Falk, R., 'Janus tormented: the International Law of Internal War', *International Aspects of Civil Strife* (ed. Rosenau, J. N.) Princeton 1968, pp.185–92; Moore, J. N., 'The Control of Foreign Intervention in Internal Conflict', *Virginia Journal of International Law* (1969) pp.209–340.

3. These are commonly regarded as being recounted in Article 38 (1) of the Statute of the International Court of Justice: '. . . (a) international conventions, whether general or particular, establishing rules recognized by the contesting states; (b) international custom, as evidence of a general practice accepted as law; (c) the general principles of law recognized by civilized nations; (d) . . . judicial decisions and the teachings of the most highly qualified publicists of the various nations, as subsidiary means for the determination of rules of law.'

4. Falk, R., *Legal Order in a Violent World*, Princeton 1968, pp.119–22.

5. 2 Whiteman M., *Digest* p.487.

6. Hyde, C. C., *International Law Chiefly as Interpreted and Applied by the United States*, 2nd edn., Boston 1947, vol.1, p.204.

7. Lauterpacht, H., *Recognition in International Law*, London 1948, pp.276–7.

8. Ibid., p.176.

9. This last point is made by Falk, 'Janus tormented etc' op. cit.

10. Higgins, R., *The Development of International Law through the Political Organs of the United Nations*, Oxford 1963, pp.210–3.

11. Raestad, A., *Ned. Tid. Int. Ret.* (1938) 0.5; Hall, W. E., *A Treatise on International Law* 8th edn, London 1948, p.347.

12. *Hansard*, 27 August 1968, col.1146.
13. Ibid., col.1443.
14. Ibid., col.1437.
15. Ibid., cols.1443-44.
16. Moore, J. N., 'The Control of Foreign Intervention in International Conflict', op. cit., p.261-4; Lillich, R., 'Intervention to protect Human Rights', p.8 (unpublished paper presented at a regional meeting of the American Society of International Law at Queen's University, 22-23 Nov. 1968; McDougal, M., and Reisman, M., 'Response by Professor McDougal and Reisman', 3 *International Lawyer* (1969) p.494.
17. And for a more cautious view, see Higgins, R., *The Development of International Law* etc. op. cit., p.220.
18. Professor Falk suggests that this should be made explicit: 'Offsetting participation by nations in internal wars may often be more compatible with the notions of non-intervention than is an asymmetrical refusal to participate.' 'Janus tormented etc' p.207. See also Halpern, Manfred, 'The Morality and Politics of Intervention' in *International Aspects of Civil Strife.* (ed. Rosenau) p.249-88.
19. This, of course, had been a major motivation for British intervention in Nigeria on behalf of the Federal government: 'The Russians have already secured a political foothold in Nigeria by supplying military aircraft and bombs, which we refused to supply. If we cut off our arms supplies, Russia would be only too willing to fill the gap and gain the influence which we would lose.' *Hansard*, 27 August 1968, col.1448.
20. Thus the Czechoslovakian delegate to the UN thought that 'it was essential that the principle of non-intervention should be applied in international law in such a way … [as not to weaken] … The provisions of international law designed to help those countries still under colonial rule.' GAOR 18th session, 6th Committee, 802nd meeting.
21. Article 2 (7) of the UN Charter prohibits intervention in matters which are essentially under the domestic jurisdiction of a nation, except where provisional or enforcement measures under Chapter VII are concerned.
22. Article 55 of the Charter refers to the principle of equal rights and self-determination of peoples; and Article 56 states: 'All Members pledge themselves to take joint and separate action in cooperation with the Organisation for the achievement of the purposes set forth in Article 55.'
23. See above, fn.18.
24. op. cit., p.235.
25. Moore, J. N., 'The Control of Foreign Intervention in Internal Conflict', *Virginia Journal of International Law* (1969).
26. And see also Security Council resolution S/253, 29 May 1968.
27. See Luard, Evan, *Protection of Human Rights*, London 1967.
28. For full background, see Hoskyn, Catherine, *The Congo since Independence*, Oxford 1965; Lefevre, E., *Crisis in the Congo: A United Nations Force in Action*, Washington 1965.
29. Higgins, R., *The Development of International Law*, pp.90-196; see also Fawcett, J., 'Human Rights and Domestic Jurisdiction' in Luard, Evan, *Protection of Human Rights*.
30. For an attempt to deal with some of these questions, see Moore, op, cit.
31. One of the most useful functions of Professor Moore's excellent study is to provide a model for deciding, in internal war problems, whether two

situations are 'like' or 'on all fours'. He correctly perceives that this must be at the heart of any legal system on intervention. Op. cit.

32. Professor Moore distinguishes between civil violence aimed at replacing government structures, and those with a different purpose, Ibid.

33. Lauterpacht, H., op. cit., p.246.

34. On the Wounded and Sick in the Field; On the Wounded Sick and Shipwrecked at Sea; On Prisoners of War; and on Civilians during War.

35. For some comments, see Castrén, E., op. cit., fn.1, p.85; Jingling, R., and Ginnare, R., 'The Geneva Conventions of 1949', 46 AJIL (1952) p.395–6; McDougal M., and Feliciano, F., *Law and Minimum World Public Order*, pp.536–7.

10 UN PEACE-KEEPING FORCES IN CIVIL-WAR SITUATIONS

General H. T. Alexander, CB, CBE, DSO

Before discussing the military execution of UN operations it is as well to be clear on the various types which are possible.

(a) Truce Supervisory Operation. The UN is repeatedly employed in a truce supervisory role; for example, the Pakistan/India dispute in Kashmir and the confrontation between Israel and the Arab States. In this context UN observers have no real function except that of reporting and, by their presence, trying to influence the actions of the opposing parties.

(b) Korean War Type Operation. In this type of operation, a major power leads and organizes a military force. It is an unlikely situation for the future. Many of the remarks made later in this chapter will not apply to this kind of operation since the major power has the military organizing ability to make things run smoothly.

(c) Congo Type Operation. The Congo type operation can be classed as major intervention by a large 'disorganized' force aimed at the prevention of escalation, that is the intervention by major powers. In the Congo the UN intervention took place at the request of the Congo government. This type of operation in a civil-war situation such as this book is concerned with is very possible again.

(d) Cyprus Type. The intervention took place with the agreement of both disputing parties and fortunately for the UN there was already a British force *in situ*. This made the smooth operation of the forces much easier, since there was already an administrative organization on the ground, together with a command organization. The reasons for this intervention were the same as for the Congo type, i.e. to prevent escalation but there are not many part of the world in which the UN would be fortunate enough to find an organized, sophisticated force already on the ground.

My personal experience of peace-keeping and operations by the UN is confined to the Congo, and the study of possible UN intervention on the

Nigerian scene, although of course I have read the case histories of other operations. My brief and exciting, if not always exhilarating, experiences have caused me constantly to moderate my criticism and to try to apply the words of Spinoza : 'I have made a ceaseless effort not to ridicule, not to bewail human actions, but to try to understand them.' Those who are called upon to take part in UN operations are well advised to keep his words constantly in mind. What I am about to say may at times seem very critical of the UN, but one has always to remember the political background against which military operations take place. By this I mean that practically every member nation has a political interest which does not always coincide with the interest of the UN itself as a whole, nor with that of the country where UN intervention has occurred.

United Nations operations are greatly affected by the degree of responsibility exercised by the government of the country in which the UN forces intervene. Governments vary in their degree of responsible behaviour, as do their prime ministers. Although UN commanders in Cyprus may at times have been uncertain of the Turkish or Cypriot attitudes, they at least knew they were dealing with responsible men. In other situations commanders have not had the same certainty. In the case of the Congo, Premier Lumumba may have been likeable and intensely loyal to his country, but he certainly did not possess the sophistication and experience required of a prime minister. As an example, I can quote an actual incident which took place in the Congo. During the first few days of the operation, Premier Lumumba was constantly urging early evacuation of the Belgian forces, and seemed to think this was a matter which could be effected within hours. In the end he appeared to lose patience and sent for me. He threatened that unless the Belgian forces were all out of the Congo by 4 o'clock he would appeal to the Russians to intervene. I asked him whether in that event he would take responsibility for law and order, since UN forces had not yet arrived in adequate numbers to relieve fully the Belgians. His reply was quite simple. 'No General, this is a military affair.' I glanced at the clock and said, 'What time did you say that the Belgian forces had to be out of the country?' He replied, 'By 4 o'clock.' As it was by then 4.15, the whole matter was totally irrelevant.

United Nations operations are further affected by the intensity of cold-war activity. One sees from time to time British Members of Parliament of both parties stating that the cold war is easing off. I suggest that this is wishful thinking. Neither Russia nor China have any intention of easing their effort in the cold war. The fact that the great powers may still be pursuing cold-war aims will clearly affect the ability of UN forces to control civil-war situations.

Earlier I reviewed the types of UN operations in the past and touched on the possibility of their occurring again in the future. As I have said, it is very likely that UN forces will be called on to intervene in domestic conflicts in an area where both the major power blocs have an interest. By their intervention the UN forces may prevent escalation into a major conflict. Both in the Far East and on the African continent, a small country may call upon the UN to protect it from invasion from a more powerful neighbour. In Africa it is also possible that UN forces will be requested to intervene in areas of tribal conflict, such as the Nigeria war. It is more than likely that small countries will often prefer intervention by the UN rather than intervention solicited from a major power. They feel that if they appeal to a major power this may bring cold-war rivalries into the area.

If small countries in principle prefer the UN it is very important that UN operations do not become discredited : that is, that they are shown to be effective in producing solutions. The make-up of the forces may have to vary in each instance depending largely upon the political acceptability of the forces offered by nations prepared to contribute. But, whatever the make-up or role of the forces, it is important for the future credibility of these operations that certain deficiencies which have been shown to exist in the past are put right. I propose to discuss what I think to be the most important of these deficiencies.

Whatever the circumstances of the intervention, the aim must be clear from the start. In civil-war situations this is especially necessary as different factions may want the force to do different things. Soldiers, sailors and airmen have been taught that no operation is likely to succeed unless everybody is clear what they are trying to achieve. In the case of the Congo, the aim was abundantly clear to the UN Secretary-General and to Dr Bunche. I quote from the written instructions issued to all UN personnel arriving in the Congo. 'The United Nations force is in the Congo to help the Government of the country maintain law and order.'

For various reasons, the aim was by no means clear to the government of the Congo, some of the great powers and some contributing nations. Some examples of interpretations put upon the purpose of UN intervention were: (a) to eject the Belgians – Premier Lumumba; (b) to support the existing Lumumba government against all rivals – President Nkrumah of Ghana; (c) to unify the Congo by force – some African countries; (d) to make the UN ineffective – some Western powers; (e) to promote chaos – the Russians.

The attitude of countries or power blocs is always strongly influenced by self-interest. It is all the more important that all the contributing nations, the soldiers on the ground and the commanders understand the aim, again especially in a situation of civil conflict. Unless this is the case, the doubts and misconceptions and the ineffective orders and the muddle which occurred during the Congo are likely to occur again. National leaders must be made to understand that once they have contributed forces to serve with the UN they themselves have no right to issue orders to such forces. If they consider that the UN troops are not operating in accordance with the agreed aim, their only solution is to withdraw their contribution, but they cannot and must not be allowed to issue orders direct.

Having got the aim clear, it is then reasonably simple to identify the crux of any particular problem. In the Congo, the aim, as I have said, was to help the government of the country maintain law and order. With this in mind, what was the problem? To the UN officials, the problem seemed quite straightforward, to establish Premier Lumumba's government so that it could function sensibly and properly. In their view, other outstanding problems would then fall easily and conveniently into place. What they forgot were two major aspects. Firstly, that Lumumba was a very volatile character. He might be sensible one day and highly unpredictable the next. Therefore, it was essential to establish an atmosphere in which one could handle the Premier.

Secondly, it was hardly likely that such an atmosphere could be created when there was a force of some 25,000 or so national soldiers, the Force Publique, roaming officerless throughout the country without discipline and without morale, but well-armed. On my arrival in the Congo it seemed to me that, if the aim of the operation was to be achieved, the first requirement was to get this force under some sort of discipline and obeying some sort of orders. I suggested therefore that they should be persuaded to keep their arms under lock and key when not requiring them for military duty. This is a normal state of affairs in any well-organized military force. With the agreement of Dr Bunche and the Congolese government I started implementing a control of arms. But later Dr Bunche accepted Lumumba's argument that to tell his national army what it should do was an interference in the national sovereignty of the country, with the result that the Force Publique was allowed to continue its rampaging and carrying of arms at all times. There was therefore, never any chance of restoring law and order to such a country in civil conflict, particularly when the orders to the UN forces were so restricted.

Commanders serving under the UN are generally faced with a problem in making orders to troops precise. When soldiers are employed purely in support of their own country's policy, either at war or in aid of the civil power, it is relatively simple to frame satisfactory orders, since soldiers under these circumstances are permitted to use the degree of force necessary to achieve the aim. The political overtones of operations under the UN make the issue of precise orders much more difficult.

Any civilian or, in fact, anybody getting killed by UN troops causes a political uproar; therefore UN forces must never use more force than is necessary to achieve the aim of the operation. On the other hand, unless they are allowed to use this degree of force, the aim is unlikely to be achieved. There are examples in the past of orders being vague and loosely worded. This is usually perfectly satisfactory when you are dealing with sophisticated troops commanded by experienced officers who can interpret orders to suit the circumstances. It is not so satisfactory when you are dealing with less sophisticated soldiers, for example, Africans, who are extremely obedient but have been taught to obey orders precisely and have neither the education nor experience to use what may be called their 'discretion'.

The orders to UN troops during the Congo operation included the direction that 'peaceful persuasion' was to be used as often as possible when coping with incidents, and implied that the offensive use of weapons was not to be resorted to. These directions caused many unfortunate incidents and casualties which could have been avoided had those framing the orders in New York been men of military experience who understood the practical difficulties of operations in the Congo. For example, at a place called Port Franqui, a young, inexperienced British officer lost his own life and that of some 90 Ghanaian soldiers simply because, instead of opening fire when his troops looked like being overwhelmed, he tried to use 'peaceful persuasion' to pacify the Congolese soldiers.

In case it should be thought that these criticisms are unfair, the following are examples of orders issued to troops in the Congo. 'The UN force, it should be emphasized, is in the Congo at the invitation of the Congo Government. It is in the Congo as a friendly force. It is a peace force, just as the United Nations Emergency Force (UNEF) has been a peace force, and most effectively for four and a half years along the line between Egypt and Israel.' In fact, of course, there is no real comparison between the role of the UN forces in the Congo and those of observers on the line between Egypt and Israel. 'The United Nations force is armed, but its arms are to be used solely in legitimate self-defence. It has no fighting function. Rather, through its friendly presence, it seeks to give reassurance, to relax tension, to restore calm.' These are fine words and to start with, the presence of blue helmeted troops in the big towns did give reassurance and did relax tension. However, as soon as the Congolese soldiers discovered that UN forces were not prepared to resort to force to impose their will, the latter set about discrediting the troops in question. The orders also stated, 'If a United Nations person is arrested, explain diplomatic immunity.' The Brigade Major of the Ghanaian Brigade doubted that explaining this concept in English to a Congolese who only spoke inadequate French would be much protection. He therefore rang up the UN Headquarters and asked what action a UN soldier should take if the explanation was of no avail and a UN soldier trying to effect the release of the person was threatened by a weapon. The answer given was, 'Effect a strategic withdrawal and allow the arrest to continue.' Scarcely anything could be more likely to discredit the position of UN troops than orders of this type and, in fact, that is exactly what happened. A further example of the unsatisfactory state of orders during the Congo operations was the following. The Brigade Major of the Ghanaian Brigade sought further clarification from UN Headquarters. 'U.N.O. Operation Directive No. 2 just received states that, unless members of the United Nations force are clearly guilty of some serious breach of the law, every peaceful effort must be made to prevent the arrest or effect his release. I would like to ask please what constitutes a peaceful effort since it is extremely unlikely in many cases the type of effort you have so far laid down in your directives will effect release.' The answer he received was that previous orders stood, that is, that if peaceful persuasion failed, the UN soldier should effect a strategic withdrawal.

One final story illustrated how in fact these orders worked. I had been in the Congo doing some work and was returning by air to Ghana. As there were one or two loose ends to be tied up, I left my ADC behind to do this for me. He saw me off at the airport. Having done this, he started to motor back to his hotel. It was at a time when because of interference by President Nkrumah the Ghanaian troops were very unpopular. The ADC was stopped at a Congolese road block and because he had Ghana written on his shoulder titles, he was arrested. Peaceful persuasion did not protect him from arrest or beating up by the ill-disciplined Congolese troops.

Orders must be framed to suit the task and the make-up of the soldiers involved. Loose directives may be satisfactory in cases where the troops involved are highly sophisticated but with less experienced soldiers orders need to be more precise if these troops are not to be discredited.

Having made all these critical comments on past mistakes, what precautions can be taken to make the life of the UN soldier easier in future? Firstly, it is essential to try to keep the numbers of countries contributing to a particular operation to the minimum. The more nations there are contributing troops the more complicated becomes the language problem, the administrative problem and also, of course, the political problem. Some eat yams, some eat roast beef, some are armed by the East, some are armed by the West, some speak French, some speak English and some speak neither. On balance, it seems likely that the majority of the teeth units will have to come from the smaller or neutralist countries, but such nations do not have the administrative backing to support a complicated operation. Therefore, communications for command, long-range air transport and logistic support will have to come from the major powers.

At present very little pre-planning takes place at the UN Headquarters in New York. It should not be impossible for some small planning cell to be thinking what might take place in parts of the world where trouble is brewing. An order of battle could be kept showing the contributions member nations are prepared to make to a possible UN operation, and their political acceptability for a particular operation could be studied.

In addition there is a vital need for commanders to receive some training in the peculiarities of UN operations. This can be effected by officers being attached to existing UN operations; and by courses at national staff colleges where advantage can be taken of the fund of experience gained in the past. It would be useful also if some standard staff procedures could be agreed. It is complicated enough to run a Headquarters staffed by officers from many nations without having to cope with a variety of staff procedures.

Potential commanders can be helped by understanding that there will always be a conflict of loyalties when operating under the UN. The UN solution to a particular problem may not always coincide with the interest of a soldier's parent country nor with the interests of the parties involved. Under these circumstances, a soldier, sailor or airman must accept that once he serves under UN command, he has no loyalty except to the UN. He can expect no thanks from anyone because whatever he does is bound to be criticized in some quarter.

A further aspect in which the UN operating in the field appears to be particularly lacking is in the field of public relations. Once the UN intervenes in an area, it is exposed to the full flood of criticism by the national press. It is therefore imperative that some public relations organization under an experienced public relations officer accompanies the troops into the field.

From the above one can sum up some of the common characteristics of forces seeking to contain civil conflicts.

The first characteristic is that UN forces have always in the past been called into action at short notice. This characteristic is not likely to change and clearly the present organization does not cater for short notice action.

Secondly, although UN forces are designed solely for the maintenance of peace and not to fight a war, their powers of self-defence and the degree of force they can use need very careful definition. Clear agreement between appellant and provider (UN) is needed from the very start of the operation.

Thirdly, UN forces have been, and usually will be, recruited from the smaller powers with special references to their acceptability in the area in which they are called upon to serve. Logistic support, however, will probably have to be provided by the major nations as will communications and part of the command structure.

Fourthly, UN forces have operated in the past with the express consent and 'cooperation' of the states or territories involved. I think that this must remain the rule. All have been under the direction and control of the Secretary-General on behalf of the UN. Only in this way can direct interference by interested parties be avoided or at least dampened.

I have written elsewhere of some of the military lessons to be drawn from the Congo operation. If similar operations are to be carried out by the UN in the future, a military planning cell is required in the UN Secretariat in New York, possessing knowledge of the military resources which might, in certain eventualities, be placed at the disposal of the UN by member nations. Although there have been one or two military officers on the Secretariat staff, the organization is still obviously inadequate. In addition, contingents which are flown into an area of operations must be correctly equipped for the role envisaged. Therefore instructions to cover this must be given in the move order and require forethought.

Lastly, a quotation is not out of place. In 1966 the *Economist* wrote, 'The United Nations can succeed only if those serving the Organization in the world's wilder places feel that the national speech makers in New York have not forgotten the difficulties of those far away struggling to turn fine words into deeds.'

11   THE CONTROL OF UN PEACE-KEEPING AT UN HEADQUARTERS

Major-General Indar Rikhye

In 1945, architects of the United Nations met at San Francisco to draw up the Charter to embody the peaceful aspirations of a war-weary world. Unlike the League of Nations, which ceased to function after 20 years, the UN has already established its reputation for making a useful and important contribution to maintaining world peace. Certainly the UN has successfully kept the cold war from escalating into a hot war. It has prevented innumerable international clashes and incidents from developing into major world conflict, thus helping to save the earth from the unimaginable horror of a nuclear holocaust. But there is a growing desire on the part of member states, large and small, to strengthen its peace-keeping ability. Many more, especially the small and developing nations are placing an increasing reliance on the UN for their own security.

It was inscribed in the Charter that the United Nations Organization is created to maintain international peace and security.[1] This meant the organization of machinery to preserve peace by force if necessary. The Security Council was created in order to ensure prompt and effective action by the UN,[2] and it was entrusted with the primary responsibility for the maintenance of international peace and security. Under Chapter VII of the Charter the Security Council was authorized to take suitable action when peace was threatened. To give effect to its non-military measures, the Council may include complete or partial interruption of economic relations and of all means of communications and severance of diplomatic relations. Should the Security Council consider the above measures inadequate, it may take 'such action by air, sea or land forces as may be necessary to maintain or restore international peace and security.' (Article 42).

The Charter also authorized the Council to call for contribution of troops from member nations and their employment. 'The strength and degree of readiness of their contingents and plans for their continued action shall be determined within the limits laid down by the Security Council with the assistance of the Military Staff Committee.' (Article 45).

Being a political organ, obviously some military expertise was needed. A Military Staff Committee consisting of the five permanent members was established: 'to advise and assist the Security Council on all questions relating to the Security Council's military requirements for the maintenance of international peace and security, the employment and command of forces placed at its disposal, the regulation of armaments, and possible disarmament.' (Article 47.)

It is apparent from the Charter that the whole machinery established in this basic document centred around the conviction that the great powers, the five permanent members of the Security Council, would be, if not in agreement, in possession of a similarity of views towards security problems. The political-military chain of command and control could function properly only if there were no major differences among these five permanent members. Any such difference would cause either a veto on the political level, or a deadlock in the military conduct of the operations.

Until 1948 no serious problems were encountered. When the agreements of cease-fire in Palestine and Kashmir had to be supervised, there were no UN forces involved and no enforcement action intended. Therefore, the Secretary-General, rather than the Military Staff Committee, was entrusted with the task of setting up and directing the UN Truce Supervision Organization (UNTSO) in Palestine and the UN Military Observation Group between India and Pakistan (UNMOGIP).

Korea was the first major test of the effectiveness of peace-keeping machinery as envisaged in the Charter. Faced with an emergency, the Security Council could only act because of a walkout by the Soviet delegation. When the resolution was passed authorizing an enforcement action in Korea, it was evident that, under the circumstances, control of such action could not be given to the Military Staff Committee. The method of entrusting a permanent Member (the United States) of the Security Council with the mandate was used as the solution, one which was to bring serious disunity in its wake later. It became clear that in the future if there was to be a confrontation between the two major antagonists of the cold war, peace-keeping operations would have to be controlled by an impartial chain of command, but one acceptable to both parties. The impartiality of such a chain would be the only guarantee of its acceptance.

It would be fruitless to enter into details of developments following Korea and the Suez crisis, leading to the present controversy as to the proper organ for establishing peace-keeping operations – the Security Council or the General Assembly. This is a political, highly-sensitive question which is under consideration by the General Assembly's Committee of 33 on peace-keeping and outside the scope of this presentation.

With the explosion of the Suez crisis in 1956, another deadlock in the Security Council led to the transfer under the Uniting for Peace resolution, of responsibilities to the General Assembly. Again the Secretary-General found himself with a military issue on his hands. The need for impartial military expertise was still more urgently felt. It had now become necessary to deploy a force to avoid clashes between the Israelis and Egyptians and to permit the smooth withdrawal of the British, French and Israeli forces from the Canal Zone and the Sinai Peninsula. At that time Hammarskjöld secured the services of General A. E. Martola, former Chief of Staff of the Finnish army, as his Military Adviser, established within the Secretary-General's office.

General Martola was assisted by a small group of officers. In the initial phase many of the nations contributing troops to the UNEF had sent senior military liaison officers to UN Headquarters, to determine the nature of their contingents. Once the form was established, and the force fully functional, these officers were withdrawn. But in their place a small staff of junior officers was provided at headquarters to assist General Martola. During the first years of operations, the assistance provided by the Military Adviser and his group was of great value. Later, the UNEF operation became more routine, with few serious or major military incidents and, consequently, the need for military expertise diminished. General Martola and his assistants returned to their home countries leaving behind the idea, born of experience, that in any future military operations, the Secretariat would need expert military advice.

A summary study of the experience derived from the establishment and operation of UNEF was reported by the Secretary-General to the UN General Assembly.[3] In the absence of an agreement on basic issues involving the use of military personnel by the UN, this document was to provide, in a sense, the main guide-lines for organizing future peace-keeping forces.

These main guide-lines were as follows:

(*a*) It was emphasized that there was 'no intent to influence the military balance in the present conflict and, thereby, the political balance affecting efforts to settle the conflict'.
(*b*) The force 'was *not* to be used so as to prejudice the solution of the controversial questions involved'.
(*c*) In establishing UNEF Command and in the recruitment procedures prescribed, the force was set up on the basis reflected in the Charter, i.e. the Commander would be appointed by and be responsible to the UN. The Command and recruitment was not to be from one country or a group of countries, but was to be international in character.

(*d*) As the force was raised by the General Assembly under the terms of the 'Uniting for Peace' resolution, UNEF was limited in its operations in that the consent of the parties concerned was required. It followed that the consent of the government of the country concerned was required before the force could be stationed in or operate on the territory of that country.

(*e*) The force had no rights other than those necessary for the execution of the functions assigned to it by the General Assembly, and agreed to by the country or countries concerned.

(*f*) The force was military in character, and much more than an observer corps, but it was in no sense a military force exercising, through force of arms, even temporary control over the territory in which it was stationed.

(*g*) The force was composed of national contingents accepted for service by the Secretary-General from those voluntarily offered. Military personnel belonging to any of the permanent members of the Security Council were excluded. In the selection of contingents, the UN must give most serious consideration to the views of the host government.

(*h*) A 'Status of Forces' agreement was negotiated with Egypt, so that when UNEF personnel were involved in criminal action, they remained under the jurisdiction of the law and criminal courts of their own countries.

(*i*) Another principle in the UNEF Status Agreement was that the UN activity should have freedom of movement within its area of operations.

(*j*) Stand-by arrangements, it was suggested, should be considered for military personnel and contingents for future peace-keeping operations. It was also felt that, at some stage, a standing group of military experts might be useful to keep such arrangements under review.

The critical period following the independence of the Congo brought another complicated issue to the UN. Once again the Secretary-General was entrusted to introduce a peace-keeping force into that strife-torn country. This time, in a few days, a still larger force of some 19,000 was hastily put together. The UN was engaged on a large scale in civil conflict.

The advance elements reached Leopoldville within 48 hours of the Secretary-General's request for contingents. The Commander and his staff arrived about three days later, by which time about 7,000 troops had already been deployed. I joined Mr Hammarskjöld in New York on 23 July 1960, ten days after the start of the operation.

Even though the experience of the many officers seconded from UNEF and UNTSO in the Middle East could be usefully employed by the newly created force in the Congo, the situation, the environment, the problem itself, in fact almost all the factors, were so different from those in the Gaza Strip that it was necessary to adapt, to improvise and to create as the operations progressed. The political aspects were considerably more delicate in the Congo than in the case of Gaza. Military actions were usually consequences of political decisions and were deeply entangled in the political web. Above all, this was a civil-war situation, and the political problems therefore still more delicate.

The chain of command established in UNEF (namely, Secretary-General, Under-Secretary for Special Political Affairs, Force Commander) was not enough. The distance between New York and Leopoldville, together with the urgency of the problems, did not permit the Force Commander to wait for a political decision to be taken in New York. At the same time, it would have been difficult to conduct emergency operations as they developed in the Congo relying upon exchanges of cables alone. It became necessary to have a Senior Political Officer present in the field.

This same arrangement was later also established in Cyprus, another civil-war situation. Here too, after the initial deployment of the force, the Commander became overwhelmed by political and military problems. Thus, some two months after the commencement of the Cyprus operation, a Special Representative of the Secretary-General was appointed.

Let us next examine the role of the Military Adviser.

A quick look at the chain of command will indicate that it is not possible for the Military Adviser to have any but minor executive functions. All UN operations are highly political in nature. Sometimes a small movement of a small patrol has so many political implications that it has to be decided at the highest level. In other cases, the emergency nature of the situation demands an immediate decision which has to be taken in the field by the Commander in consultation with the Officer-in-Charge. Entrusting the Military Advisory staff with any executive duties would mean a harmful duplication that could only impair the efficiency of the operation. It is above all before the force comes into being that the role of the Military Advisory staff is vital and essential.

Theoretically, the military part of a UN operation starts with the establishment of the force. However, it must be said that if the executive side starts at that time, the planning or the thinking part of it has to begin much before the first man of the force sets his foot in the operational area. The starting point of any UN operation is a resolution by either the Security Council or the General Assembly. Before any action is taken following a period of tension or an incident, the issue is debated at the Security Council.

The case of Cyprus is a clear-cut example of the way the UN's military role may develop gradually. In December 1963, when fighting broke out between the two communities in Cyprus, an emergency meeting of the Security Council was called. On 27 December 1963, the Security Council called upon the Secretary-General to observe developments in Cyprus. Early in January 1964, a former UN Commander, Lieutenant-General Prem Singh Gyani of India, was appointed UN observer. Later it became apparent that a UN peace-keeping operation might be needed in Cyprus. General Gyani was asked to assess the situation and to present his recommendations on the possible size, organization and task of a UN force to operate in Cyprus. Based on General Gyani's preliminary views and through studies carried out at Headquarters, the Military Adviser to the Secretary-General made an initial appreciation of the situation.

During the first six weeks of the new year, two sets of estimates were given to the Secretary-General. One from General Gyani, in which he recommended that should the UN be given full responsibility for restoring peace to Cyprus, a force of about 15,000 would be necessary. General Gyani was taking into consideration the events which were then taking place in Cyprus, where bitter fighting was a daily occurrence. Working in New York, I, as Military Adviser and my staff were aware that both communities in Cyprus and also other countries involved in the situation (namely Greece, Turkey and the United Kingdom) would welcome the establishment of a UN force and would work with it. With guarantees of co-operation from these countries, it was possible to present an estimate in which a force of about 10,000 would be sufficient. But, all this tentative planning would depend on the mandate entrusted to the force.

This preliminary phase of study and planning was most helpful. The result was that when the force had to be established the main lines of thought had already taken shape. In Gaza (UNEF) and the Congo (ONUC), rapid developments made it impossible to allow for detailed planning and the force had to be hastily organized. The smoothness achieved in the organization of UNFICYP proved that preliminary planning is indispensable wherever circumstances permit it. It was also based on the existing framework of the British army in Cyprus.

Once a resolution is adopted by the Security Council, the problem is in creating, organizing, assembling and establishing a force. There is no Commander in the field; there is no executive staff to carry out this task. It is up to the Military Adviser to function as the Military Executive staff of the Secretary-General during this most delicate phase. Political decisions condition the size of the force and the nationalities that will participate in it. On the other hand, once those decisions are taken, it is up to the military team, in consultation with the participating countries, to organize the force in detail, breaking down the organization into battalions, headquarters, supporting elements and other units. After all the pieces are labelled and measured for size, it becomes necessary to assemble the jigsaw puzzle in the area of operation. Units come from all over the world and have to be transported to the theatre of operations, involving large-scale land, sea or air movement.

The force will not survive without logistical support. When the units arrive in the field, they may have with them a few days of rations and other supplies. Consequently a system of logistical support must be in operation at the time of the arrival or shortly thereafter. Obtaining support units from participating countries is not enough. It becomes necessary to establish a pipeline which will start pouring *all* needed material and supplies for the incoming units the moment they become operational. Reception of troops has to be hastily arranged and their needs met. Arrangements have to cover every item from ammunition to table lamps, from spare parts to toilet paper.

Obviously, for the Military Adviser's staff to be able to do all this would demand a complex organization that could not be kept in existence permanently without great expenditure. Under the Office of General Services, a Field Operations Service within the UN was established to provide administrative support for missions abroad. They already had gained experience in support of UNTSO and UNMOGIP. Henceforth, they were entrusted with providing administrative support for peace-keeping operations. The Military Adviser's staff are only required to provide the expertise.

In the case of Cyprus, the Security Council passed a resolution creating UNFICYP on 4 March 1964. The emergency was not so acute as in the Congo, since the United Kingdom, under the Treaty of Guarantee, already had a force of 7,000 on the island, thus giving the UN force time to establish itself properly. On 6 March, the Secretary-General sent a survey team to Cyprus. This team included representatives from Field Service and from the Military Adviser's staff. At the same time, General Gyani was selected as force Commander. In Cyprus, General Gyani, the survey team and senior officers of the British force discussed the problem and presented an outline for the organization of the force, including logistical support which was to be provided, in the main, by British bases in Cyprus. This study was completed in about a week. It was agreed that the British force would gradually be replaced by the international force, with United Kingdom troops and staff providing the framework into which incoming units would fit, so creating an international force. Some of the British troops would be left as an integral part of the force.

In the meantime in New York I, the Military Adviser, and my staff, Field Service and other departments of the UN, in consultation with participating countries produced an initial organization for the force, based upon the preliminary information sent by the survey team, and started preparations for the movement of units to Cyprus. On 27 March, when the force became operational, the executive role was automatically transferred to the force HQ and the Military Adviser reverted to his advisory duties.

Summarizing, therefore, the functions of the Military Advisory staff could be listed as follows:

(1) Advise the Secretary-General, and those to whom he delegates responsibility, on military matters;

(2) Produce studies and assessments for possible and current military operations as required;

(3) Carry out the military part of the preliminary planning for establishing a UN operation.

It must be said that the Secretariat as a whole participates in every phase of this operation. When the Secretary-General becomes responsible for implementing a resolution, the entire responsibility for the conduct of the operation is vested in him. It is obvious that the Secretary-General cannot do everything himself. He has to delegate responsibility to one or more Under and Assistant Secretaries-General who will undertake the day-to-day political conduct of the operation. In the case of military operations, this is usually done by one of the Undersecretary Generals for Special Political Affairs. On the other hand, the administrative part, as I have already mentioned, becomes the responsibility of Field Operations Service which, in turn, is under an Assistant Secretary-General – the Director of General Services. Again, on the administrative side, civilian staff personnel must be shifted from New York Headquarters or from other UN Missions to the newly created force. This is done by the Office of Personnel.

Legal problems are always an important part of every UN operation. From the discussions that lead to the drafting of a Status of Forces Agreement to the most minor legal complications in which members of the force may find themselves involved, legal assistance becomes necessary. It is up to the Office of the Legal Council to take care of this aspect of the operation. Budgets, payments, reimbursements and all financial matters are the responsibility of the Controller; he has a say in every discussion that might have financial implications. Finally, public information, which must be provided daily, public relations and relations with the world press media are the responsibility of the Office of Public Information.

We have already listed the work of six Under and Assistant Secretaries-General, all working at Headquarters for the same operation. Therefore, co-ordinating action becomes imperative. If the UN had to deal with one operation at a time, it would be possible for the Secretary-General to do it himself. The multitude of problems that have to be faced by the Secretary-General, however, prevent him from undertaking personally the co-ordination in all sectors. This becomes the role of the Chef de Cabinet, or his

Deputy, who functions as a co-ordinating link between all these different departments in order to ensure that they work smoothly together.

For the force to commence operations it becomes necessary that guidance be given to the force Commander. The Secretary-General has, therefore, to issue a directive which flows from the mandate and provides the force Commander with his instructions for carrying out his tasks. At the same time, it is necessary to negotiate with the host country the Status of Forces Agreement which will enable the force to carry out its functions within the area of operations without undue interference from the host country. Based on these two documents, the force Commander issues his own operational instructions and SOPs. The ideal situation is one in which those two documents are ready the moment the force becomes operational. In Cyprus this was possible due to the circumstances I have already mentioned. This was a substantial improvement over the initial situation in ONUC where the emergency of the situation did not allow time for proper planning.

Another important agreement which has to be concluded is that between the participating governments and the UN. As a rule, the UN requires that national contingents be placed under the force Commander for operations, logistics and general demeanour. They remain under their own national command for discipline and other personnel and administrative matters. This agreement is tied in with the terms of reference which cover the broad policy of operations. Contributing countries usually insist on knowing the broad terms of the directive given by the Secretary-General to the force Commander before committing themselves to a contribution. An exchange of letters between participating governments and the Secretary-General is the normal procedure for laying down the terms under which troops are placed at the disposal of the UN.

While the terms of reference or the directive cover the operational aspects, the regulations for the force establish the administrative pattern. Since the UN will not have full administrative control of the troops comprising the force, these regulations have to be broad in nature and flexible enough to comply with national regulations. A comparison of the regulations set for UNEF, ONUC and UNFICYP, will show these similarities. Eventually it will be possible to have one standard set of regulations for all UN peace-keeping operations. Naturally, in each case, there will be a need for additional provisions applicable only to a particular operation.

In many cases, the mandate contained in the resolution is for a limited period. Naturally, this period cannot be counted from the date the resolution is passed but rather from the time the force becomes operational. This date has to be set by the Secretary-General on the recommendation of the force Commander. The resolution creating UNFICYP was passed on 4 March 1964 and the force only became operational on 27 March. In the case of the Congo, the resolution was passed on 14 July 1960 and 48 hours later the first units were arriving in Leopoldville and started operating immediately.

Once the force becomes operational, running it is a routine procedure. However, sometimes the circumstances create new problems and demand a new resolution from the Security Council, either to strengthen the mandate or to change it sufficiently to face unforeseen problems. In such cases, an additional or new directive is required from the Secretary-General. In the Congo the use of mercenaries by the secessionist government of Katanga created a situation demanding a new resolution of the Security Council which was taken on 21 February 1961. This resolution authorized the use of force by ONUC in certain circumstances to deal more effectively with the mercenary problem and with civil war.

The UN as a peace-keeping organization is still in its infancy. UNEF, established in 1956, was the first UN peace-keeping operation in which a military force was used but no enforcement action expected. Since then, the UN has felt its way in operations in Lebanon, the Congo, West New Guinea, Yemen and Cyprus. Each operation has had its own peculiarities, its own characteristics and its own problems. Some of the problems are peculiar to a single operation but others have been common to all, and it is appropriate to discuss these here.

The first major problem is the use of force – how, when and to what extent should it be used? In any army the main objective is to defeat the enemy. To achieve this purpose it is necessary to counteract him, eliminating or neutralizing his forces in order to win victory. In the UN these ideas are not usually valid. This is especially true in civil-war situations, and two of the three major UN operations have concerned civil wars. There is no enemy; there is no one to be defeated; there is no intention of eliminating and the idea of neutralizing takes on a different tone. It is not enough to neutralize one opponent; it becomes necessary to neutralize both antagonists without using force if at all possible. This conception creates three types of problems.

First, the organizational problem – how strong should the force be? It is now generally accepted that a UN peace-keeping force does not have to be stronger than any of the parties involved in the dispute. But it must be of sufficient strength to stand by itself or to defend itself effectively if attacked.

The second problem is in the field of operations – how to deploy and employ the force. In every military operation, the strategy lies in proper deployment, in placing the strength where it is needed. This is no different in UN operations. Nevertheless, it becomes important to deploy the force where it will prevent a clash : in a civil-war situation between the contending parties. This has created the misconception that interposition is the best solution for UN deployment. However, this is not always possible. In Cyprus, when fighting broke out between Greek and Turkish Cypriots in the Tylliria area during the August 1964 incident, the opposing forces were so close to each other that it was impossible for the UN force to interpose effectively. Strength was not necessary. The solution was to establish observation posts side by side with the contenders and thus be in a position to observe all activities. By doing so it became possible to approach both sides at critical moments and prevent any offensive action by negotiation before it started. In Suez, the initial deployment of the force presented a different aspect. It became necessary to bring incoming units into the Canal Zone to ensure the security of this zone and permit withdrawal of the Anglo–French forces. As a second step, the force had to be positioned in a manner that would satisfy the Israelis as to their security and, finally, it was responsible for the evacuation of all forces from the Canal Zone and the Sinai Peninsula. It was not a matter of interposition. In order to prevent a clash it was more important to secure major centres of communications than just to stand between the contenders.

West New Guinea was another case where interposition was impossible and to have attempted it would not have solved the problem. Regular Dutch forces were stationed in garrisons and had control of key centres. Indonesians were dropped by air or arrived by boat and infiltrated into the jungle. The only way of implementing the cease-fire was by relieving the Dutch garrisons with UN troops, establishing collecting points and persuading the Indonesians, scattered throughout the jungle, to turn themselves in. Radio, leaflets and other means were used to alert the Indonesian guerrillas to the fact that the fight was over and that they should report to the nearest collecting point to be repatriated. This was successfully achieved and all troops from both sides were evacuated from the area which came under temporary UN administration for a few months.

In the cases just mentioned, force was not necessary. Any use of force would have only jeopardized the operation even if the UN force had succeeded in defeating the threatening element.

The Congo operation may be taken as an example of the special problems of UN forces in a civil-war situation. The military operation in the Congo lasted for four years. The area of operations was measured in millions of square miles. The different tribes could be counted in hundreds adding up to a population of approximately thirteen million. The UN force was on the average between 10,000 and 17,000. Many different types of situations developed, each one different from the preceding one, and to be dealt with in a different way. Among its various tasks, the UN force was in the Congo to assist in 'maintaining law and order'. It therefore became necessary basically to provide security to individuals and installations. Members of the government had to be protected against their foes who, in turn, had also to be protected against the splintered security forces. Frequently, the UN was called upon to look after the security of the President or the Prime Minister or the Chief of Staff and to provide escort for Mr Tshombe, Mr Gizenga and other political leaders. Chaos and disorder reached such a pitch that only the UN was capable of protecting power plants, airports, water supplies, radio stations and other installations indispensable to normal daily living.

In civil-war situations such as this, the UN clearly cannot take sides. After the death of Prime Minister Lumumba, the Congo splintered into factions. Local leaders in Kasai, Stanleyville, Katanga and Kivu proclaimed their independence and attempted to invade their nearest enemies. Civil war erupted all over the Congo. The only possible course of action open to the UN was to secure important centres of communication, thus denying them to not one but all contenders. By securing airports, roads and key points controlling the navigation of rivers, the UN managed to confine the fighting elements to their own territories, thus preventing spread of civil war.

At the same time, internecine warfare broke out everywhere. In some places like Kasai, genocide was rife, mainly against the Balubas. Use of force by ONUC was again precluded. The Balubas had to be moved out of the threatened areas under UN escort to a safe place, thus eliminating the cause of the fighting.

In the neighbouring province of Katanga, the Balubas were strong enough to wage war against the secessionist government of Mr Tshombe. Katangese troops led by mercenaries retaliated by invading North Katanga – the Baluba territory – destroying, burning and ravaging villages. The UN had to keep them apart by preventive action. This exposed UN troops to fire from both sides. Mr Tshombe's mercenaries wanted to eliminate the UN in order to conquer North Katanga. The Balubas often mistook the UN troops for the mercenaries of Mr Tshombe and ambushed them. The UN troops had to resort to the use of force in self-defence against attacks from both sides.

After February 1961, the mandate had been strengthened, entitling ONUC to use force as a last resort to eliminate the mercenaries from Katanga. This authority was not used immediately. For two years the UN exercised the utmost restraint and endurance, while efforts were being made to reconcile Katanga to the central government. As negotiations became more protracted, the secessionist government threatened to destroy all installations and industries vital to the economy of the country and to the normal life of the population. Most members of the Security Council, the Congo Advisory Committee, and participating countries in ONUC agreed that action had to be taken immediately to protect economic installations from wanton destruction by extremists. A show of strength became necessary.

A force consisting of three infantry brigades with adequate engineer equipment, road and air transport supplies and other material, together with jet-fighter support, had been concentrated in Elisabethville. When negotiations reached a complete impasse, after all warnings were ignored, and UN troops had been under fire for four days from Katangese gendarmerie without firing back, UN troops broke out of their long encirclement by Katangese restoring their own freedom of movement and protecting economic installations in South Katanga. The operation followed conventional lines. After some resistance, the mercenaries fled and the leaderless Katanga gendarmerie collapsed. In two weeks the UN troops had secured the mining complex in South Katanga. The UN troops had resorted to the use of force only when attacked, using minimum force to achieve success. The use of force stopped the minute that success was achieved.

Another problem in such situations is a political one. Pacification in a peace-keeping operation has to be achieved by mediation while the force keeps the contenders apart. Any use of force, no matter how small, by UN troops will have political repercussions on the civil conflict in question and will impair efforts at mediation.

In brief, restraint in the use of force by UN troops is an ever-present problem. It calls for endurance, patience and restraint by the troops participating in the operation. It demands from the soldier an attitude completely contrary to the one he has been taught during his whole military career. It demands exceptional leadership and a great deal of training. Just before taking over command of the UN force in Cyprus – during his briefing period in New York – General Thimayya[4] summarized the problem by saying: 'You tie my hands behind my back and expect me to separate the fighters!'

Finally, there are some general problems affecting all peace-keeping forces, some of which are especially acute in the case of civil war conflicts. One concerns the international character that has to be given to the force. To be acceptable as an impartial third party, the UN force has to be internationalized even though the units retain their national characteristics. The force must consist of a number of acceptable nationalities, integrated through an international headquarters. Usually the problem is solved by listing a number of volunteers and possible contributors, consulting the host country as to their acceptability and only then approaching each government for concurrence. When planning the establishment of the force, possible contributors are listed. However, after clearing nationalities with the host country and ascertaining the willingness of the possible participating states, only a few acceptable nationalities remain.

Coming from different parts of the world, officers and men will have different standards of training, will be used to different staff procedures, will speak different languages, and the units will have different equipment. When organizing the headquarters, all these factors must be borne in mind. English has been selected as the working language for most of the UN operations, firstly, because it is one of the five working languages of the UN and, secondly, because it is easier to find officers and other ranks from non-English speaking countries who have English as their second language. However, difficulties are likely to arise over the language problem specially at higher levels.

Staff procedures do not create a major problem. The UN has used a combination of British or American systems and we are happy to admit that the overwhelming majority of officers and other ranks have adjusted themselves quickly in every case. The differences in equipment and scales of rations, however, make the logistical support a permanent headache. In some cases, spare parts for vehicles, aircraft and other equipment are not easily procured and occasionally it is quite impossible to obtain them. To give an example, ONUC was at one time in need of an anti-aircraft unit. One country was approached and agreed to provide such a unit. When it was in its final stages of being shipped to the Congo, its tables of organization and equipment arrived in New York and it was found that the origin of the equipment precluded the UN from obtaining spare parts and ammunition. It became necessary to cancel the request and approach another country for the unit.

Differences in types and scales of rations can usually be solved but increase greatly the cost of a UN operation. There was a time in Leopoldville when for the Headquarters personnel alone four separate messes had to be established, all with completely different types of food. Sometimes this problem is not so acute. In Cyprus all participating countries can consume practically the same rations, thus simplifying procurement and distribution.

Then there is the problem of financing. I will not debate the matter that has been of major concern for some time, namely, who should pay for UN operations. The point I wish to emphasize is that UN operations are inevitably quite expensive, even though little fighting takes place. Participating countries include many developing nations who have to be reimbursed for any additional extraordinary expenses. Pay and allowances vary from country to country. Distances involved in transporting units and supplies are measured in thousands of miles. Some countries have to call on their reserves to participate in the operation and can only do so on a contract basis for a short period. Therefore, contingents have to be rotated at more frequent intervals than in a normal national operation. All this adds substantially to the cost and keeps the UN on a tight budget. Funds are voted in advance based on estimates, or given from voluntary contributions again based on an estimated budget. Such provision as is made for contingencies cannot cover them all and the Secretary-General finds himself in great difficulty when any unexpected development takes place. If the UN peace-keeping machinery is to be maintained along the lines it has operated on during the last few years, a solid system of financing must be devised.

It is relevant to note some of the features which are peculiar to UN peace-keeping forces in general as compared with normal military operations. The essentially *ad hoc* nature of UN peace-keeping operations affects their nature and functioning from the very outset. In these operations none of the planning and preparation which are expected of normal military procedures can be counted upon. UN peace-keeping forces are called for in mid-emergency and have had to be quickly established out of nothing, without the benefit even of its anticipation. The process of organization, dispatching, concentrating and deploying the force, not to mention its logistical support, had to be telescoped into a few days. Such a procedure inevitably gives rise to all sorts of problems – organizational, administrative, and military. It particularly causes some shock at first to well-trained military men, and it requires a considerable adjustment on their part to very unfamilar ways.[5]

The UN, unlike national governments with military establishments, has no permanent logistical services or military establishment. The logistical basis of a peace-keeping operation is therefore an *ad hoc* emergency arrangement, organized by the Field Operations Service with the assistance of governments and various private concerns throughout the world. Furthermore, the budgetary scale of UN peace-keeping operations is always at the minimum level and does not allow for logistical establishments, communications, depots, etc., of the kind which normally support national armies at home or abroad. Under rigid budgetary limitations, therefore, and subject to constant pressure for new economies, the Field Operations Service has to provide logistical support for such operations as best it can. The circumstances of the setting up of such an *ad hoc* emergency operation make it inevitable that the Commander, his staff, his contingent commanders and the national contingents meet each other for the first time in the area of operations and when already fully committed to their tasks.

The *ad hoc* nature of UN peace-keeping operations has other consequences. There can be no initial standardization of stores and equipment. This leads to serious problems of administration and maintenance later on. There are no standard operating procedures to begin with, but these are soon formulated. The standard of training and method of operation of contingents vary widely. The rotation of some contingents every six months also militates against continuity and whatever common standards may be hoped for. Although there is no difficulty in obtaining infantry units, adequately trained technical support elements are far less easily available.

Again while the force Commander exercises operational command and control of the force as a whole, the national contingents exercise responsibility over their men for such matters as discipline, punishment, awards and promotions. Although this never causes any serious problem, the relationship of the force Commander with the contingents under his command is in fact quite different from, and potentially far weaker than, the relationship of the commander of a national army with the units under his command. On the other hand, the pride of national contingents and their officers and men in being part of a UN force offsets to a very large extent, the weakness in the link of command between national and international responsibilities and produces a remarkable solidarity, *esprit de corps* and high standard of discipline in these forces.

There are a number of circumstances peculiar to UN peace-keeping forces which can, and sometimes do, create considerable problems for the Commander of a force and also for the Secretary-General. In particular, they constitute potential weaknesses in the authority of the force Commander. For example, most contingents in a UN force maintain direct communications with their home countries. These are supposed to be used only for domestic and national administrative matters. When, however, as does happen, they are used for direct communication with the home government on matters which are strictly within the authority of the force Commander, or at times even on political matters, misunderstandings and confusion are very likely to arise.

Another difficulty is that, for reasons usually quite unconnected with the peace-keeping force, some contingents of a force will come to be viewed with more favour than others by the host government. This can also give rise to embarrassment and difficulty both in the relations among the contingents of the force and in the task of the Commander in maintaining its unity and morale and even in its proper use and deployment.

On the administrative side, too, there are certain potential or actual problems. The relationship of civilian and military authorities is sometimes strained even in national establishments. In all peace-keeping operations the entire financial and logistical set-up has to be under the supervision of a civilian, normally the ranking Secretariat member who usually is the chief administrative officer, and of UN Headquarters in New York. The Secretary-General has the responsibility to ensure co-ordination, sound administration, economy and accounting to the Advisory Committee on Administrative and Budgetary Questions and the Fifth Committee of the General Assembly. The disbursement of UN funds has to be kept under UN control. Inevitably this distribution of functions, administrative authority and responsibilities may lead to friction between the international Secretariat element and the Military Command and staff. In particular, the stringent economies which have to be practised in UN operations may be, and sometimes have been interpreted by the military as arbitrary and unjustified attitudes on the part of civilians which handicap the operation, while the civilians, in their turn, may feel that the military are showing little understanding for the particular administrative and other difficulties of UN operations. In only one UN operation, however, and in that only during one brief stage, has the misunderstanding between the military and civilian branches assumed an acute form. In that single instance, the relief of the Commander sooner than had been planned proved to be the necessary and adequate remedy.[6]

Another potential source of unpleasantness on the administrative side is the difference in the reimbursable allowances stipulated by governments for their contingents. This difference in the money actually paid to individual soldiers by the UN which is determined by the varying pay and allowance scales among the governments contributing the contingents, is in some cases very striking and does not fail to have an adverse effect on the relations among the contingents of the force and on its morale. All efforts to gain acceptance of an equitable scale of allowances common to all contingents have, however, so far been unsuccessful.

What conclusions can be drawn? A peace-keeping operation is not an end in itself, even in civil-war situations. It is, in fact, a practical adjunct to peace-making. It becomes necessary, when fighting is stopped, because cease-fires, truces and armistices in such situations are seldom self-enforcing or self-policing. Some third presence is required at least to verify and report the breaches. The true function of a peace-keeping effort is to create a climate of quiet which is more congenial to efforts to solve the underlying problems that lead to conflict. It may achieve this better climate in a number of ways, such as averting military confrontations by acting as a buffer through patrolling and policing activities, and through providing an added assurance by its very presence. It is not an enforcement agent. It can expect to exercise at best only a very limited degree of authority – an authority, moreover, which, unless explicitly defined in its mandate and the consequent agreements with the host country, automatically and instantly vanishes once it is challenged by the host government.

It is only realistic to accept the fact that when a UN peace-keeping operation, whether it may be an observation mission or a peace force, whether in civil war or other conflict, is no longer welcome in a country and cooperation with it is withheld, it cannot hope to continue to perform any useful function, may well soon find itself defenceless and in grave danger, and thus had best be withdrawn as amicably as the prevailing circumstances will permit. If there should be serious doubt about the wisdom of this latter course, it would be advisable to abandon altogether the notion of a voluntary peace-keeping operation, and turn to consideration of enforcement-type actions under Chapter VII of the Charter. The two cannot be mixed. It should be added, however, that it is extremely doubtful that any of the peace-keeping operations thus far mounted by the UN would have been acceptable to the governments of the countries in which they have been stationed if they had been originally envisaged in the context of Chapter VII of the Charter.

UN experience with such operations, and this was notably so in the case of UNEF, indicates that the success of a peace-keeping operation may, in itself, induce a false sense of security. The ability of the operation to re-establish and maintain quiet for an extended period may come to be mistaken for a solution of the basic problem. This can only increase the sense of shock when, ultimately and inexorably, it is demonstrated that problems of conflict may lie dormant but do not necessarily solve themselves by the passage of time, and the day may come when they will explode anew. Peace-keeping operations can serve their purpose properly only if they are accompanied by serious and persistent efforts to find solutions to the underlying problems which demanded the peace-keeping in the first place.

It merits emphasis that UN peace-keeping operations function within the wider framework of the UN as a whole. Many of the frustrations, the crosscurrents, the pressures and particularly the political stresses of the Organization inevitably have a major impact on the original setting-up of a peace-keeping operation and on its day-to-day functioning as well. The present limitations of the UN in a world still dominated by rigid concepts of national sovereignty, by power politics and by acute nationalistic sentiments are the inherent limitations of UN peace-keeping operations.

In conclusion it would not be an exaggeration to claim that the UN has already gone a long way towards establishing its ability to keep the peace, that member states are placing increasing reliance upon it to maintain world peace and show a common desire to improve its peace-keeping machinery. It is manifest from the number of public proposals made on the subject and from the offers of standby forces received by the UN from several member states.

The cold war has led to developments in peace-keeping machinery different to what was envisaged by the signatories to the Charter. As a rule, the Secretary-General is entrusted with the responsibility of their conduct. Since the original system using the Military Staff Committee cannot be used, the Secretary-General has established an impartial and parallel chain of command for the conduct of these operations. Military expertise has been established on a permanent basis. Since peace-keeping operations are highly political and sensitive in nature, they require political direction and executive action. The Military Adviser's functions are limited to minor executive functions. Experience has proved that political direction is also needed in the field. A Special Representative of the Secretary-General or an Officer-in-Charge is appointed in the field, who, together with his assistants, provides political direction to the force Commander and his subordinate commanders at all levels.

While it is possible to anticipate future peace-keeping operations, proper preparation is only feasible following authorization by the Security Council or the General Assembly. It is then important to arrange for an advance element to proceed to the area of operations as soon as possible to establish local contacts, obtain information and assist in the establishment of a force. The Secretary-General selects contingents in consultation with the host government and other interested parties. The mandate for the force flows from the Security Council or the General Assembly resolution authorizing the operation. The Secretary-General issues a broad directive covering the operation to the force Commander. Fresh directives and instructions are issued as and when necessary.

Each operation has its own peculiarities, its own characteristics and its own problems. While some of the problems are peculiar to one operation, others may be common to all. The question of the use of force in self-defence has raised many issues. Force must always be minimal and every effort should be made to avoid its use. A UN force must always aim at preventing a clash through negotiation, by its presence or by interposition. The method may vary in different situations, but the basic principle of preventing a clash is common to all.

The organizational problems are not insurmountable. With more thinking and better planning, improvements should be possible. A good deal could be done by contributing countries to prepare their troops for future operations. Troops need a sound background of the UN. Study of international affairs including settlement of disputes should be especially included in officers' training. Troops should be encouraged to learn a foreign language. Training should include mob-control, protection of vulnerable points, patrolling towns, aid to civil power, restoration and running of civil installations, sanitation and hygiene and so on. A soldier must also be competent in his professional duties before he can be an effective UN soldier, for, in addition to such skills, he needs to show self-reliance, initiative, restraint, tact and courage. Indeed, service under the UN flag demands the highest human qualities.

An attempt should be made to arrive at a standard unit establishment, and some standardization of weapons, equipment, vehicles and so on. Since, for the foreseeable future, it is not possible to have a standing UN peace-keeping force, the stand-by arrangements adopted by Scandinavian countries, Canada and some others commend themselves. Troops are earmarked or volunteer for service with the UN and are kept on an alert basis. Many other countries might do the same.

Maintenance of world peace is a most precious undertaking that is worth spending a little money on. The cost of any war would be far greater than the small amount needed for its prevention. Nations will show better judgment if they invest in peace. And if peace in the world is to be maintained, the UN is the most effective instrument for it.

TEXT REFERENCES

1. Charter of the UN, Chapter I, Article 1.
2. Charter of the UN, Chapter V.
3. UN General Assembly Document A/3943 of 9 October 1958.
4. Late General K. S. Thimayya (Chief of Staff of the Indian Army 1958–61).
5. See UNEF Report of the Secretary-General to the UN General Assembly – A/6672 of 12 July 1969 (based on a report by the author as Commander, UNEF).
6. See Reference 5 above.

12   CONCLUSIONS

Evan Luard

The preceding chapters have surveyed the principal attempts by international bodies to resolve civil conflicts in recent times, the principles laid down by international law on civil war and external intervention, and the special problems in organizing and commanding peace-keeping forces in such situations. What general conclusions can be drawn?

It may be useful to consider, first, the relative success of the various attempts by international organizations to influence civil conflicts as revealed in these studies; secondly, to examine the different *types* of role which international organizations can play in such situations; and finally, to consider in what way the performance of these organizations in dealing with such cases might be improved in the future, especially in reducing the danger that, through foreign intervention, civil wars may escalate into large-scale international war.

The record of international organizations in dealing with civil-war situations so far has been very mixed. Some would even dismiss it altogether. It could be held that, even in the two civil-war situations in which the UN played a major role, in the Congo and Cyprus, it exerted no very conspicuous influence on the outcome. In the Congo, the UN force left at a time when the civil war was still in full spate, and its result and course were not very manifestly affected by international intervention; in Cyprus, though peace has been largely maintained, the mediation mission of the UN has been wholly without success so far, and the underlying causes of the dispute quite unaffected. In the Dominican Republic a UN mediator was active in seeking to resolve the basic issues in dispute; but it was the weight of American arms rather than that of UN authority which finally determined the issue. In a few other cases observation has been attempted, with varied results. In Yemen almost nothing was achieved; in the Lebanon the UN pro-

215

vided dubious factual information, mainly after the chief danger was over, and in Laos equally dubious information about external intervention even before any significant danger had developed; in Greece the information it gathered was what most people were well aware of already. Most other civil-war situations were ignored altogether.

This is obviously a highly over-simplified judgment. The fact that peace has not been at once miraculously restored does not mean that nothing has been done at all. In the cases of observation, though the UN missions did not immediately bring the wars concerned to an end, there is scarcely a single one in which the situation was not improved through their operations. Even in Yemen, though it is difficult to dispute the generally harsh judgment passed by Mr Schmidt in his chapter, the mission was probably not quite without result. It was indeed a necessary complement and buttress to the bilateral agreement between the UAR and Saudi Arabia for a mutual withdrawal of forces. That agreement would have been even less credible and effective than it anyway was if there had been no provision at all for verification of the undertakings to withdraw. Lack of good faith in fulfilling the latter undertakings necessarily undermined the value of a mission in this case; but it does not prove that the procedure itself was at fault. This example simply shows that if one or both of the parties have no intention of fulfilling such undertakings anyway, the provision of verification facilities by international authorities will not help matters much. Even in such cases the procedure can show clearly and publicly that one side is not fulfilling its side of the bargain; and so make it politically harder for such a course to be pursued. Such a mission is not, of course, intended physically to expel foreign troops. And it is unrealistic to condemn it because it has not done so. It depends for its success, on publicity to deter external intervention. If one side is prepared to defy publicity, there is little such a procedure can achieve.

The real weakness of the UNYOM operation was different. It lay in the ambiguity of the original agreement. This did not make clear how far the withdawal provision was to be for mutual and simultaneous withdrawal by both sides; or whether a complete Saudi withdrawal was a precondition for a subsequent withdrawal by the UAR (which claimed it was only assisting the legal government). Secondly, because the mission's contacts were far more tenuous with the Royalists than with the Republicans, it was never in a position to carry out its role successfully and it was never accepted by the Royalists as being fully impartial (and General von Horn's resignation seemed to substantiate this complaint). But even during the brief period that it was in Yemen, the mission probably did marginally deter external intervention, at least on the Saudi side (as the Saudis themselves confirmed). The lesson here is that, if such a mission is to fulfil its function effectively, its terms of reference must be carefully framed, and its conduct seen to be impeccably impartial at all times.

Similarly in the Lebanon, though it may well be true, as Professor Kerr suggests, that the American intervention played a far larger role in restoring stability than the UN observer group, this does not prove that the latter did not itself play an important part. American intervention, however successful in its own declared purpose, was so only at the expense of precipitating an international crisis. That crisis the UN mission was able to assist in resolving. But more significant were the effects of the knowledge that an international body was to check the reports of external intervention. Multilateral action was substituted for unilateral intervention. Counter-action by others was discouraged. Whether or not the UN group was able to provide prompt and reliable information on the scale of infiltration (and Professor Kerr suggests it did not), it almost certainly did serve to *deter* large-scale infiltration from outside Lebanon during this period : governments such as Syria's, which had declared all reports of infiltration to be without foundation, were unlikely to permit large-scale crossings, whose discovery by the mission would prove their words to be false.[1] Furthermore, it became less possible for wild and irresponsible accusations of infiltration to continue to be widely aired (as they had been by President Chamoun and his supporters at an earlier stage) if the observer group could disprove them; in this way the mission possibly helped to convince Chamoun himself of the impossibility of pursuing his ambition to obtain a second term as President. American intervention alone, on the other hand, unaccompanied by such UN interest, might have had precisely the opposite effect, encouraged Chamoun to believe in his own strength, and so led to intensification of the civil war. Finally, the mere fact that some international body was present on the spot and sending regular reports, perhaps played some part in encouraging a more sober and moderate mood among politicians in Lebanon at this period.

Perhaps the main lesson to be learned in this case is that such an operation, to be effective, needs to be mounted early and rapidly. This is more likely to happen if UN members are at all times alert to the potentialities of UN action of this type, if they keep such situations under close observation, and if they do not allow themselves (as Western delegations did for a time during the Lebanon crisis) to be influenced by purely ideological considerations to prefer unilateral to multilateral action.

In Laos, though it may be doubted that the 1959 UN mission, or the Secretary-General's representative who followed, did much to pacify the situation, at least they provided information of a negative kind. At a time when accusations of external intervention were being freely aired, partly for political purposes, there was some value in impartial confirmation that, at that time at least, it was not on a large scale. The mistake was that neither the mission, nor the representative appointed by Mr Hammarskjöld remained present in Laos during the subsequent period in the early sixties when their services were most needed. The powers of the International Control Commission, on the other hand, were extremely limited; and since it never had any formal link with the UN, its reports never received anything like the publicity or attention which reports from a UN mission would have had. As Mr Main shows, ethnic and political divisions within Laos and the lamentable poverty of the country were quite sufficient to stimulate civil conflict, even if external intervention had been prevented altogether. So long as the outside world took little interest and made no attempt to solve these internal problems, there was no hope that measures of 'neutralization', or insulation, even if faithfully observed, could have much impact on the situation. Here the lesson seems to be that UN interest in an area needs to be consistent and sustained over a considerable period (perhaps by the establishment of a permanent sub-committee on the area concerned) rather than an occasional fitful response to immediate crisis situations, if it is to be of much effect; and that it must be accompanied by a purposeful effort to conciliate or mediate over the underlying political problems as well as the question of external intervention. Left to themselves the factions in Laos were unlikely even to reach agreement: a UN mediation might have helped them to do so.

In the case of Greece, again it can scarcely be said that UN action achieved nothing. Though the information which UNSCOB and its predecessors provided may have already been taken for granted by many, it was strenuously contested by others. Here too, therefore, the Commission probably had some deterrent effect. Unilateral accusations by the Greek government about external involvement, which were understandably not always accepted as impartial even in the West, were now replaced by the more objective evidence provided by an international body of varied membership. It was the change in the political alignment of Yugoslavia, rather than the activities of the Commission, which finally brought the revolution and its external support to an end. But it is possible that, even if that change had not occurred, the Commission's report might have been a significant factor in demonstrating that, at least in its external public relations effect (which was a significant part of its purpose), the insurrection was losing the battle. At least, as Mr Campbell points out, UN activity provided the environment within which other forms of peace-making might pursue their own course more effectively: and this is perhaps as much as UN observation in such situations can often expect to achieve.

Thus, in these cases of observation, though it cannot be said that UN action was the crucial factor in bringing the wars to an end, it is probable that in each case it marginally deterred foreign intervention (which was its main purpose) and so perhaps prevented the situation getting still worse. However, in the case of the major UN operations, over the Congo and Cyprus, a still more positive judgment may be made. In both cases, it can scarcely be doubted that the situation which resulted from UN action was substantially better than it would have been had those actions never been undertaken.

In the Congo, though the UN did not bring the war to an end, it played a substantial part in assisting in the restoration of law and order in the country as a whole. Though this task inevitably implicated the UN increasingly deeply in the internal politics of the Congo – in taking sides between Kasavubu, Lumumba and Mobutu, in supporting the central government against secession, and in containing tribal and other disturbances in Kivu, North Katanga, Stanleyville and elsewhere – this was, from the beginning, inherent in any effective peace-keeping role in an intensely disorganized state. This does not mean that the UN should never take any decision affecting the political situation in civil-war situations (where two men are both claiming to be Prime Minister, as in the Congo, a choice must be made). What is important is the establishment of effective and impartial machinery for deciding what the UN position should be on such matters, if necessary through a Security Council decision. Even in this law and order role the UN undoubtedly made a positive contribution to restoring normality in the Congo. But possibly much more important was the part it played, through administrative and technical assistance, in helping a seriously under-endowed new state to restore order to its finances, to set up an efficient police and social administration, and to train the officials who would have to take over responsibility in the future. The Congo's record of stability since that time, despite the enormous size of its territory and diversity of its people, is some tribute to the groundwork which the UN administration laid.

In Cyprus, the balance-sheet is even more obviously favourable. The UN force took over in a situation in which there had been serious fighting between the communities over several months, and in which mutual distrust was at a murderous pitch. The mere presence of the UN force did something to ease tensions. Its mediating role in various conflict situations undoubtedly saved innumerable lives. Even in the ultimate task of securing a settlement, though none of the three UN mediators has yet secured agreement, at least they have got serious talks under way between the communities; they are occasionally able to inject third-party views into the negotiations and to make suggestions to encourage progress. As Mrs Duncan-Jones points out, the ultimate success in this process of achieving a political settlement, must rest with the parties themselves. The UN will never be able to impose a settlement by force in civil-war situations. What it may be able to do is to help bring about a cessation of fighting, and to provide the conditions and facilities, even a mediator, to promote discussions among the parties and so facilitate a settlement.

Though the UN's record in dealing with civil-war situations is not impressive it has achieved something in each of these cases. By far the most serious defect in the UN's record is its failure to consider a number of civil-war situations at all. External support of rebels was present as clearly in Nigeria as it was in Lebanon, Laos or Greece, but the matter was not even discussed. In the case of Vietnam external support was far more clearly evident. Indeed, as we saw earlier, Vietnam can be regarded with equal justification as an international conflict or as a civil war; and it must remain as a standing reproach to the UN, and to its claim to be an organization to maintain world peace, that it has only once, and then only briefly and inconsequentially, discussed the Vietnam War, possibly the most bitter and enduring conflict since the Second World War. The fact that some of the major interested parties, China and North Vietnam in particular, were not represented at the UN, which is sometimes given as a reason for the lack of UN action, has never prevented continual UN discussion of Korea, which goes on to the present day.

The more important reason, in this as in other cases where the UN has done nothing, is simply that some of the parties concerned have not wished it: at certain times the United States and at almost all times the Soviet Union, North Vietnam and the Vietcong. But the opposition of North Korea has not prevented discussion of the Korean question for twenty years in the UN. The real difference between this and other cases is that no outside party has, in the case of Vietnam, been willing to defy the wishes of those mainly involved, in calling a meeting and pressing for debate. Yet it is arguable that the peace talks in Paris could well have been established under UN auspices, and that they might have started very much earlier if the UN had been willing to take a more active role in calling for such discussions. It was precisely an honest broker, a neutral itermediary, that was most needed to set the stage for these; and that is most required now to help bridge the gap during the talks. A UN mediator might have performed this role better than any other alternative, as in the Middle East. Another major lesson of UN experience so far, therefore, seems to be that members of the Security Council, and the Secretary-General himself, should not be deterred from raising in the Council major civil-war issues of this kind simply because none of the interested parties themselves take the initiative in doing this.

If this is the record of the past, let us consider, next, the range of procedures which the UN may be able to employ in civil-war situations.

Conclusions

One of the most important roles which the UN can play in such situations is that of *insulation*: seeking to prevent outside intervention and so to reduce the scale of the fighting and its international implications. This is a function that was explicitly acknowledged by most UN members in the case of the Congo operation: one of the main advantages of sending an anonymous and impartial international force, not drawn from the forces of any of the big powers, was that it might prevent a competition for influence among the great powers themselves, and the injection of cold-war politics into the area. In a sense the object of the UN operation in Lebanon was the same as that in the Congo. UN resolutions called for the withdrawal of foreign troops (meaning American troops) and the exclusion of all foreign personnel (meaning Syrian and other infiltrators); UNOGIL provided the means by which both these elements might be eased out. UNYOM, though it failed dismally, was clearly designed for a similar purpose: to bring to an end participation in the civil war by Saudi Arabia and Egypt.

Yet in other cases, where insulation was equally if not more urgently required, this role has not even been attempted. In Vietnam and Nigeria, external intervention took place on a large scale: in the form of active participation in the first case, and of large-scale arms supplies and mercenary help in the second. But here the UN made no effort at all to apply the same principles. Some form of inspection by observers, along the demilitarized zone between North and South Vietnam, and on the border between Cambodia and South Vietnam, could have done a great deal to provide hard facts on the degree of North Vietnamese infiltration, for long one of the most bitterly contested points of the war, and so probably have reduced its scale. Conversely, such observers might also have given evidence concerning the scale and type of American involvement, the consequences of American bombing, the use of chemical weapons (such as napalm), and other matters on which the United States was accused. In Nigeria they could have provided reports on a number of allegations, including the scale of assistance reaching Biafra from outside, reports of 'genocide' and ill-treatment by Federal soldiers, and so helped to create a more objective outside view of the war: the observer team that did finally operate, having been invited by the Federal government, was not everywhere regarded as impartial. In both cases, not only would hard information on bitterly contested issues have been provided, and the effect of high-powered propaganda agencies somewhat counteracted; the intervention of outside parties would have been powerfully deterred.

Usually, however, to achieve effective insulation, much more than the dispatch of observers is required. Observers may be duped, or they may be totally disregarded (as in the Yemen). Usually, therefore, there will need to be explicit agreement among the outside governments concerned. Here,

221

too, the UN may have a role to play. Often the main impetus in bringing about the involvement of external forces comes from the factions requiring assistance, not the assisting powers. This was the case in the Spanish Civil War, as Professor Hugh Thomas shows in his chapter; it has been manifestly true in Cyprus, where the Turkish and Greek communities have each sought to squeeze the maximum support from their respective patrons. To a considerable extent the same thing is true in Vietnam, in the Chinese civil war (where the Nationalists implored the United States for further assistance), in Nigeria (where both sides demanded the maximum possible outside help), in Cambodia (where the government claimed it could not obtain the arms it required from the United States) and in the civil war in Jordan in 1970, where both sides sought help from abroad. A definite commitment among the outside powers not to become involved in providing assistance can do something to strengthen their capacity and willingness to resist the demands of their clients.

It is arguable that the UN should seek more often to promote agreements of this kind among the outside powers when civil wars break out. At least the Security Council could, on appropriate occasions, pass resolutions designed to prevent assistance to one or both sides in civil conflicts. A resolution on these lines in the case of Nigeria might have had a marginal impact in deterring material assistance to Biafra by outside parties, for example. To be effective, such pressures need to be brought to bear at an early stage in each conflict. No resolution to this effect on Vietnam passed after 1961 or on Nigeria after 1968, would have had the slightest chance of being observed by outside powers. But the effect of such resolutions will be to strengthen the weak inhibitions which are placed by general rules of international conduct with the more immediate pressures of a specific and categorical injunction on a particular case.

Another important role the UN can play in civil conflicts is simply that of *verification*, or fact-finding. This has an obvious relevance to the task of insulating a conflict; a general injunction against intervention is unlikely to have much effect unless some machinery for verification is established at the same time. But it is equally important when related to mediation between the parties of a conflict. Mrs Duncan-Jones, General Rikhye and General Alexander all stress the value of objective information of this kind in some peace-keeping situations. An authoritative UN report may serve simply to remove misapprehensions and unfounded suspicions on one or both sides (as in the incident at Kophinou in Cyprus, quoted by Mrs Duncan-Jones). It may provide reliable information to the outside world, enabling accurate and reliable judgments to be formed. It may give background knowledge for UN officials without which they may not be able to pursue their peace-keeping or mediating role effectively.

Conclusions

Clearly one of the most important tasks, as we saw over Vietnam, is simply to determine how far a conflict is purely internal, and how far it has already become international.[2] Dr Higgins describes the important legal implications this can have: for the parties themselves, for outside nations, and for international organizations. The basic reason why it is essential to have impartial evidence on this point is that the parties themselves have a vested interest in asserting or denying external intervention. In almost every civil war of the post-1945 period, at least one side, and often both, have accused the other of receiving important military support from elsewhere, accusations which have in many cases been denied by the other side. In the Chinese civil war, the Nationalists, to win greater help from the American government, claimed that the Communists had received massive assistance from the Soviet Union; in Laos both sides have repeatedly made claims of a similar kind to justify external support for themselves; in Nigeria the degree of external support for the other side was one of the main propaganda issues throughout; in the Sudan today the Southern forces are said to receive help from Israel, while the government forces are claimed to have Soviet advisers. Once one accusation has become widely believed, it becomes difficult to prevent intervention on the other side to counteract it. It is thus essential that some objective information on such points should be available.

Even after the event, it may be relevant to know which external party has intervened first; judgments on the Vietnamese conflict are still confused because of uncertainty as to which forces, American or North Vietnamese, first become involved. Knowledge on this point is important in considering how some weight should be attached to a government's plea that a civil war is solely within its domestic jurisdiction and not subject to international discussions. Since today external help is easier and more common than in any earlier age, and since, in many cases, an external power helping rebel forces seeks to do it by secret and unacknowledged means (like Soviet assistance in Greece, American assistance in the Bay of Pigs operation, French assistance to Biafra, Iranian help to the Kurds, and Chinese to the Nagas), there is a vital importance in international organization, and in international opinion, having the means of verification to establish essential facts.[3]

Next, there is the more ambitious function of *peace-keeping* in civil-war situations. General Rikhye and General Alexander describe some of the difficulties inherent in this role. The most basic of these is the inevitable ambiguity of the UN force's functions no matter how it may be described in UN resolutions or in guide-lines laid down for the forces. It will always be difficult to draw a hard and fast line between 'maintaining law and order' and assisting a government against rebel factions; between 'keeping the peace' among rebel factions and intervening actively in cases of conflict. The three possible aims of the UN force in the Congo outlined by General Alexander (to maintain law and order, to support the Prime Minister against other forces there, and to end the secession of a rebel state), are activities which cannot be clearly distinguished. It could be argued that law and order could only be effectively restored in that country if the government, whether led by Lumumba, Kasavubu or Mobutu, were supported against all rivals, and if any attempt to secede, whether by whole provinces or by individual tribes, was suppressed. The difference in UN policies towards the Congo and Cyprus underlines this ambiguity of role. That difference cannot be attributed solely to the terms of the initial resolutions. The wholly different political situations in each country led UN officials and commanders to make different judgments concerning the role a UN force could usefully play. In the Congo, it was not unrealistic to conceive of order being *imposed* by the government, with UN support, on a country which was becoming increasingly disorganized. In Cyprus, any attempt by the government, or by the UN on their behalf, to *impose* a peace, or 'law and order', on the Turks by brute force, would have been the surest way of provoking further conflict perhaps for years to come.

This highlights the most profound of the difficulties the UN has in confronting civil conflicts. The UN can become involved in a full peace-keeping role in practice only at the invitation of the host government. But this in itself invites uncertainty about the task the UN force is to perform, since the inviting government may understandably feel, as the governments of the Congo and Cyprus felt, that they have the right to lay down the conditions under which the force is to operate. The fact that the UN has to reach agreement with the government on matters affecting the force, including a Status of Forces agreement, encourages the idea that the receiving government is in a position to dictate terms. But it is of crucial importance to the effective performance of its role that the UN should not concede to the host government this right. The UN could be placed in a wholly false and unacceptable situation if it can be made to appear as the agent of the existing government in putting down inconvenient rebel movements. If it is to retain any genuine peace-keeping function, the UN must retain a total freedom of action in determining how far it will, or will not, support government forces against those elements in which it is engaged in any particular situation.

The most difficult role which the UN can perform in a situation of civil conflict is the most fundamental and important, that of *mediation* between the conflicting parties. This is the only one that goes to the root of the problem by seeking to remove the underlying causes. Unfortunately, where a dispute has already become open conflict, the roots of the conflict usually go very deep, and mediation is a difficult and unrewarding task. Almost the only one of the cases since 1945 where such an effort has been made is that of Cyprus. In other cases (Yemen, Lebanon, Laos) it was assumed that the only possible UN position was one of non-involvement in the basic domestic dispute, or that the UN was fully committed on behalf of the government of the day (Greece, Congo). In Cyprus there is little doubt that the UN mediators, especially the last, Mr Gallo Plaza, have performed a valuable role, not only in bringing the sides into direct contact again, but also in occasionally proposing compromise procedures and solutions.

But it also seems likely that the UN could have performed a similar service in several other cases if given the opportunity to do so. We have already seen how, over Vietnam, the Paris peace talks might have been started far earlier and those talks might have made more rapid progress if a UN mediator, or a special representative of the Secretary-General, had been appointed in 1965 or 1966. In Nigeria, a mediator could perhaps have helped to reduce the groundless fears and misapprehensions of each side, about the intentions of the other. In Yemen, if mediation as well as observation had been attempted, the fiasco surrounding the UN mission might have been avoided. Almost all the other UN activities we have examined – the exclusion of foreign intervention, the provision of objective fact-finding, and peace-keeping on the ground – deal with symptoms rather than causes. For UN action to be brought to a successful conclusion requires some attempt to confront the fundamental issue. If it is to improve its present inadequate record, the UN will need more often to grasp this nettle too. By appointing a mediator, or a special representative, to promote agreement in such situations (as has been done over a considerable number of purely international problems) it might be possible in other cases to bring such conflicts to an end.

Finally, let us look at some of the *principles* which might have to be observed by international organizations, and by outside parties, if some of the dangers arising from civil wars, and external intervention in them, are to be reduced in the future.

We have already seen some of the uncertainties and ambiguities of international law on this question, and Dr Higgins has reviewed at length contemporary legal opinion concerning civil conflict. There is perhaps more intense discussion of this question among international lawyers in recent times than in any earlier age. The UN, too, has given considerable discussion to the question, notably in the Principles on Friendly Relations Among States, recently agreed and approved by the UN General Assembly. The principles, though by no means free of ambiguity, represent an advance on the practice, at least, of many states in the modern world. The injunction against 'organizing, instigating, assisting or participating in acts of civil strife or terrorist acts' in another state is broadly worded, and appears to apply to acts designed to assist the government as much as those to assist rebel forces. There are, however, considerable difficulties in interpretation. What represents 'assisting . . . in acts of civil strife'? How far is the supply of arms to a government trying to quell disorders within its territory, forbidden under this principle? Such matters still need clarification. But the important element in these principles is the abandonment of the confusing and uncertain distinctions between 'rebellion', 'insurgency' and 'belligerency' [4] – distinctions so imprecise that they invited subjective intepretation – and the substitution of the general term 'civil strife', which clearly covers all of these without distinction. Furthermore, there is the implication that the kind of assistance an outside state may give in a civil conflict does not depend on the stage that conflict has reached.

This points the way to a much more satisfactory set of rules concerning external intervention in civil wars. Direct assistance (that is, the training of armed forces, the dispatch of 'advisers', still more, of course, the dispatch of armed forces from abroad), whether to government or to rebel forces, would always be forbidden. So far as the supply or sale of arms is concerned, this also would not be permitted to a rebel force. The supply of arms to a legal government would obviously be permitted in normal times, or when that government was dealing only with sporadic disturbances. But it would be open to the UN, when a civil war had reached a certain point, to declare that all outside powers should maintain total neutrality; and that the supply of arms, even to the government side, should under these circumstances be forbidden. In other words, so far as this last prohibition is concerned, it would be for the international community to decide, and not for unilateral decision, that a civil war had reached a stage requiring all outside involvement to cease.

Under such circumstances there might well be accusations, by one side or another, that the prohibition was being violated. For this reason there might be need sometimes for the establishment of a fact-finding body to seek to check on the supply of arms: for example, through the inspection of captured arms.

In any case, these rules alone would scarcely be sufficient. If the crucial distinction is whether outside aid is to the recognized government or not, the rule can be simply evaded by transferring recognition to another faction. The Soviet Union was able to justify the supply of arms to Lumumba in the Congo, China to the Algerian provisional government in exile, Saudi Arabia to the Royalists in Yemen, and the United States to Laos, by claiming that they were merely assisting the government which they recognized as legitimate. Theoretically it is already illegal for a government to grant 'premature' recognition to a faction that has not acquired control of a 'substantial' proportion of the territory. But these concepts are so vague that a government can always interpret them to suit its own purposes. It would have been very difficult to say, for example, with certainty what proportion of South Vietnamese territory was controlled by the government, and how much by the Vietcong, at any particular period. Is it control by day or by night which must be measured? If a government official arrives once a week, and marauding guerrillas once a night, who is in control?

All this suggests the need for more objective criteria for determining recognition, as many international lawyers demand.[5] It would, theoretically, be possible to say that support for those rebelling against any government officially accepted as a member of the UN was not permissible. But UN membership may reflect past, rather than present, authority. Generally, members will be reluctant to expel a government once admitted, except on the grounds of total defeat (as the example of the China seat in the UN clearly shows). It might, therefore, be preferable if the UN were to make judgments in particular cases where civil wars break out. If it was felt that the representative character of the government was seriously in doubt, the supply of arms to both sides might be forbidden. This might be so, for example, in cases where a government under challenge had been imposed by an armed *coup*, or where it was not democratically elected, since here it might be thought there was some justification for rebel activity. In a sense, the precedent for this has already been set in the UN resolution on arms to South Africa (where a type of incipient civil-war situation could be held to exist) to which the supply of arms has been forbidden for essentially similar reasons.

But even if governments were to refrain from assisting the rebel faction, private nationals might do so by enlisting as mercenaries (as occurred in the Congo). Even if governments did not send arms to one side or another, private arms-dealers might do so (as occurred in Nigeria). Even if governments did not seek to promote subversion, semi-official agencies, such as the international Communist movement or the CIA, might do so (as in parts of Latin America). There is a clear means of meeting this difficulty: governments must take responsibility for the actions of their own nationals. This means that they need to prevent them from taking part in fighting in other countries, if necessary by threatening to withdraw their passports (as Britain and other countries did during the Congo war). They must control the sale of arms within their borders, so as to be able to ensure that international rules are observed (as many governments have done over South Africa, Nigeria, Vietnam and other cases). And they must take the responsibility for ensuring that semi-official organizations, such as the CIA or comparable Communist subversive organizations, do not undermine the undertakings which governments have given. To some extent, at least, international law already lays down this last obligation. Oppenheim's *International Law* states that: 'Subversive activities against foreign states . . . whether emanating directly from the government itself or indirectly from organizations receiving from it financial or other assistance . . . amount to a breach of international law.'[6]

Finally, one principle which international bodies might seek to apply more consistently in civil-war situations is respect for the wishes of the people concerned: for example, by offering to supervise elections if necessary. Civil conflicts normally concern rival claims to exercise authority in particular areas. Almost invariably in such cases each side claims to be more 'representative' of the people's wishes than the other. Even the war itself is often presented as a vindication of such claims: while the Vietcong were militarily successful in South Vietnam, this was widely presented as showing that they had greater popular support, while when the South Vietnamese government began to reassert its control from 1969, this was equally widely held to show that the Vietcong had lost support. Both claims were equally fallacious. Even in civil-war situations, military success is a poor test of popularity. Others, more objective, as well as less costly, are easily available. The only universally recognized and impartial way of deciding between such claims is by the holding of an election or a referendum. And a UN offer to undertake elections under impartial international control is one that each side will normally find it very difficult to reject without considerable loss of credibility and prestige.

Such tests of opinion have in fact been organized many times by international bodies. Plebiscites were conducted after the First World War in the Saar in 1935, to settle rival claims. The UN undertook similar plebiscites in the British Cameroons and Togoland. In the dispute between Indonesia and Malaysia over West Irian, a UN mission was sent to confirm that the people of Sabah wanted membership of Malaysia. A UN representative was sent to determine the wishes of the people of Bahrain concerning their political future. Though none of these were strictly civil conflicts, they demonstrate the role the UN can play in helping to test the wishes of the people in disputed areas. There is no way in which the UN could assist more effectively in resolving civil conflicts than in offering more frequently good offices for supervising elections in this way. It could have agreed to organize elections in the Congo while it was there; and it could still now supervise elections in Cyprus if agreement on constitutional arrangements could be reached. Finally, it may still have a role to play in organizing genuinely fair and impartial elections in South Vietnam, and perhaps in Laos and Cambodia.

Conclusions

Whether or not such procedures are more commonly used, the UN will, without doubt, continue to be confronted often with violence in internal conflicts. We saw in the first chapter how these are increasingly replacing international wars. If international peace is to be effectively secured, the UN will need to be more ready to confront such situations than in the past. Otherwise the international struggles of the past may simply be replaced by a patchwork of civil conflicts pursuing their course, undisturbed and unremarked by the UN, within national frontiers all over the world, frequently aided and abetted from without. The protracted agony of Vietnam shows that such wars can be among the most costly and cruel of our era. Unless the international community devises new and more effective procedures for confronting these situations, and the rules of conduct applicable to them, it will be turning its eyes away from the most characteristic and widespread threats to peace in our age.

TEXT REFERENCES

1. See Curtis, G. L., 'The UN Observer Group in Lebanon' in *International Organization*, Autumn 1964, p.762: 'Although there are conflicting opinions as to the degree of infiltration that took place in the period following UNOGIL's arrival, it does seem clear that the Group at least served to make infiltration more clandestine and consequently small in both quantity and type of arms.'
2. For a more extensive discussion of these issues see Luard, Evan, *Conflict and Peace in the Modern International System*, London 1970.
3. The UN still has in existence a Peace Observation Commission for this purpose, which is never used.
4. See p.19 above.
5. See Falk, R, A., 'The International Law of Internal War', in *International Aspects of Civil Strife*, ed. Rosenau, J. N., Princeton 1964.
6. Oppenheim, L., *International Law*, London 1955, vol.1, p.293.

BIOGRAPHICAL NOTES

HUGH THOMAS is professor of History at the University of Reading. His books include *The Spanish Civil War* (1961), the *Suez Affair* (1967) and *Cuba* (1971). Earlier he worked in the Foreign Office and the Royal Military Academy, Sandhurst.

JOHN KENNEDY CAMPBELL, Fellow of St Antony's College, Oxford and Lecturer in Modern Balkan History. Was a Liaison officer to a division of Greek National Guards during the rebellion of the Greek Communist Resistance Movement in December 1944. Later he returned as a social anthropologist to do fieldwork in the Pindus Mountains, and in 1961–2 was UNESCO director and Professor of Sociology at the Greek Centre of Social Sciences in Athens. He became a Fellow of St Antony's College in 1958 and is the author of *Honour, Family and Patronage*, 1964, and *Modern Greece* (with Philip Sherrard), 1968.

MALCOLM H. KERR was born in Lebanon in 1931. He has taught at the American University of Beirut and has been a fellow of the American Research Centre in Egypt. He is now Professor of Political Science at the University of California, Los Angeles. He is the author of *Islamic Reform* and *The Arab Cold War 1958–1967*.

JOHN MAIN is Senior Research Fellow in the Department of Politics, King's College, University of Aberdeen, and currently engaged in a study of the question of International Responsibility for Dependent Peoples. Between 1951 and 1969 he was in the Diplomatic Service and served in Laos from 1957 to 1961.

DANA SCHMIDT, born in 1915 and educated in America and Switzerland. Pulitzer Travelling Fellow, 1938–9. Overseas Press Club George Polk Award, 1965, for stories on the Kurdish rebellion. Author of three books: *Anatomy of a Satellite*, 1952; *Journey among Brave Men*, 1965 (about the Kurds); *Yemen The Unknown War* 1967. Two more books in preparation, on the Arabs and Israel, and on the Persian Gulf. Works now for *New York Times*.

Biographical Notes

ANNE DUNCAN-JONES was born in 1944. Educated at St Hilda's College, Oxford. After travelling in the Middle East she returned to study the situation in Cyprus in 1968. After leaving Oxford, she worked for a time as Research Assistant to David Butler, and has been responsible with him for producing the 2nd and 3rd editions of British Political Facts 1900–1967(8). Since 1967 she has been with the Current Affairs Department of BBC Radio.

ROSALYN HIGGINS, International lawyer on the staff of RIIA. Member of the Board of Review and Development of the American Society of International Law; author of The Development of International Law through the Political Organs of the UN; Conflict of Interests – International Law in a Divided World; Administration of UK Foreign Policy through the UN; United Nations Peace-keeping (3 vols.) [Vol. I and II publ., Vol. III in progress]; and author of numerous articles in learned journals.

MAJOR-GENERAL HENRY ALEXANDER, CB, CBE, DSO, was gazetted into The Cameronians (Scottish Rifles) in 1931. During the war, he served in Burma and commanded the Second Battalion The Cameronians in North West Europe. From 1950 to 1953 he commanded 26th Gurkha Infantry Brigade during the Malayan emergency. He was Chief of Defence Staff, Ghana, from 1960 to 1961 and was involved in UN operations in the Congo with the Ghanaian contingent there.

MAJOR-GENERAL INDAR RIKHYE was formerly in the Indian Army, the 6th DCO Lancers, with whom he served during the Second World War in the Middle East and Italy. Appointed Chief of Staff of the United Nations Emergency Force in Gaza early in 1958. Later was appointed Military Adviser to Dag Hammarskjöld, Secretary-General of the United Nations. Commander UNEF at the time of withdrawal of the Force in May 1967, now a consultant for international development and Chairman of the International Peace Academy Committee.

EVAN LUARD was formerly a member of the British Diplomatic Service, serving in Hong Kong, Peking and London. From 1957 has been at St Antony's College, Oxford. 1966–70 M.P. for Oxford. 1969–70 Parliamentary Under-Secretary in the Foreign and Commonwealth Office. Author of Nationality and Wealth (1964), Conflict and Peace in the Modern International System (1970) and other works.

APPENDIX

Extracts from the 'Principles of International Law Concerning Friendly Relations Among States', proclaimed by the UN General Assembly on 24 October 1970.

The principle that States shall refrain in their international relations from the threat or use of force against the territorial integrity or political independence of any State, or in any other manner inconsistent with the purposes of the United Nations

Every State has the duty to refrain in its international relations from the threat or use of force against the territorial integrity or political independence of any State, or in any other manner inconsistent with the purposes of the United Nations. Such a threat or use of force constitutes a violation of international law and the Charter of the United Nations and shall never be employed as a means of settling international issues.

.   .   .

Every State has the duty to refrain from organizing or encouraging the organization of irregular forces or armed bands, including mercenaries, for incursion into the territory of another State.

Every State has the duty to refrain from organizing, instigating, assisting or participating in acts of civil strife or terrorist acts in another State or acquiescing in organized activities within its territory directed towards the commission of such acts, when the acts referred to in the present paragraph involve a threat or use of force.

.   .   .

The principle concerning the duty not to intervene in matters within the domestic jurisdiction of any State, in accordance with the Charter

No State or group of States has the right to intervene, directly or indirectly, for any reason whatever, in the internal or external affairs of any other State. Consequently, armed intervention and all other forms of interference or attempted threats against the personality of the State or against its political, economic and cultural elements, are in violation of international law;

No State may use or encourage the use of economic, political or any other type of measures to coerce another State in order to obtain from it the subordination of the exercise of its sovereign rights and to secure from it advantages of any kind. Also, no State shall organize, assist, foment, finance, incite or tolerate subversive, terrorist or armed activities directed towards the violent overthrow of the régime of another State, or interfere in civil strife in another State;

The use of force to deprive peoples of their national identity constitutes a violation of their inalienable rights and of the principle of non-intervention;

Every State has an inalienable right to choose its political, economic, social and cultural systems, without interference in any form by another State;

Nothing in the foregoing paragraphs shall be construed as affecting the relevant provisions of the Charter relating to the maintenance of international peace and security.

INDEX

233

Index

Enosis (Union of Cyprus with Greece) 162, 163, 164
Erkwit ceasefire (in Yemen) 141–2
Essentials of Peace Resolution (UN, 1949) 21
Ethridge, Mark 54
Ethiopia 8, 13, 14, 110, 116, 131
Evatt, Dr (Pres. of UN Assembly) 58

Faisal, Crown Prince of Saudi Arabia (later King) 130, 132, 142–3, 144
Falk, Prof. Richard 170, 178, 180
Faupel, Gen. Wilhelm von 32
Feisal, King of Iraq 76
Finland 151, 153
FLN see National Liberation Front, Algeria
Force Publique, Congolese 108–9, 110, 190; see also Armée Nationale Congolaise
Foreign Legion (in Spain) 33
France 8, 53, 56, 84, 129, 173, 183, 223; role in Spanish Civil War 27, 28, 29, 30, 31, 32, 33, 34, 35; Lebanon and 66, 67, 70; – and Suez crisis 70, 197, 205; collapse of Indo-Chinese administration of 91–5; and Congo crisis 110, 122, 123; Cyprus problem and 150, 152, 161
Franco Bahamonde, Gen. Francisco 21, 27, 28, 33, 34
Franco–Laotian Convention (1949) 92
Fulbright, Senator James 78

Gaza Strip 198–9, 200
Gbenye, Christophe 119
Gemayel, Pierre 83
General Assembly (UN), peace-keeping functions of 196–7; see also United Nations
General Confederation of Labour (Greece) 52
Geneva Conference on Indo-China (1954) 94–5, 96, 97–8, 99, 100, 101, 102, 105, 106, 107; on Laos (1961–2) 102–7
Geneva Conventions (1949) 182–3
George, King of Greece 37, 40
Germany 8, 9, 11, 83; support for Nationalists in Spanish Civil War by 17, 26–36 passim; remilitarization of

Rhineland by 30, 34; occupation of Greece by 37–9, 43; see also East Germany; West Germany
Ghana, Congo crisis and 109, 110, 120, 189, 192; Yemen and 136, 140
Gibraltar 179, 180
Giral y Pereira, José 27
Gizenga, Antoine 112, 113, 117, 118, 119, 121, 206
Greece 8, 16, 17; Cyprus civil conflict and 15, 149, 154, 155, 161–2, 163, 164, 200
Greek Civil War 11, 12, 13, 15, 16, 18, 223; origins and causes of 37–43; UN and international involvement in 23, 24, 43–62, 216, 218, 220
Greek Communist Party (KKE) 17, 37–8, 39–40, 41, 42, 43, 44, 45, 46, 48, 52, 53, 57, 59
Greek-Cypriot National Guard 153, 155, 159, 162
Greek-Cypriot Police (CYPOL) 153, 154
Green Line, the (dividing Greek and Turkish sectors in Nicosia) 151, 159
Grivas, Gen. George 153–4, 155–6, 164
Gromyko, Andrey Andreyevich 47, 48, 49
Guatemala 7, 12, 13, 17, 18, 136, 183
Guinea 110, 118, 128
Gyani, Gen. Prem Singh 151, 200, 201

Hammarskjöld, Dag 100, 101, 106, 109, 113, 114, 115, 118, 121, 197, 198, 218
Haradh conference (Yemen) 142, 143–4
Harbottle, Brigadier (Chief of Staff of UNFICYP) 153–4
Ho Chi Minh 91
Honduras 7
Horn, Gen. Carl Carlson 126, 133–4, 135, 136–7, 140, 146, 216
humanitarian intervention (in civil conflicts) 175–6, 184
Hungarian Smallholders' Party 55
Hungary 7, 8, 11, 39, 176, 181
Hussein, King of Jordan 80, 81, 126, 131

Ibn Saud, King of Saudi Arabia 136

piracy, Nyon conference against
(1937) 35
Plaza, Senor Galo 159, 161, 163–4, 167,
225
Poland 8, 15, 51, 53, 55, 56, 95, 97, 99,
102
Ponte y Manso de Zuniga, Gen.
Miguel 28
Popov, Col. (head of Russian Military
Mission in Greece) 39, 40
Populist Government (in Greece) 46
Portugal, African colonies of 13, 19,
179; arms sale by 18; Spanish Civil
War and 28, 31, 32
Potsdam Conference 40–1, 45, 91, 92
Poumi Nosavan, Gen. 101
Principles Concerning Friendly
Relations Among States (UN, 1970)
22
Provisional Democratic Government
of Greece 42, 43, 57, 61

Rhineland, remilitarization of 30, 34
Rhodesia 13, 24, 179
Riad, Mahoud 138
Romania 17, 39, 40, 41, 45, 51, 57
Rosenberg, Marcel 29
Rostow, Walter W. 79
Royal Yemeni Government see Yemen
Civil War
Russian Revolution 8, 17

Es-Said, Nuri 76
Salam, Saeb 69, 70, 82
al Sallal, Brigadier Abdullah 125, 126,
129, 134, 139, 144
Saud, King of Saudi Arabia 131
Saudi Arabia 73; support for
Royalists in Yemen War by 15, 17,
19, 24, 125, 128, 129, 130, 131, 132–3,
134, 135, 138, 139, 140, 141, 142–3,
144, 145, 177, 216, 221, 226
secession right under international
law of, 174–6
Security Council (UN), peace-keeping
functions of 195–7; see also United
Nations
Sendwe, Jason 116
Slavo-Macedonian National Liberation
Front (SNOF) 42

Souphanouvong, Prince 92, 93, 94, 97,
98–9, 100, 101, 104, 105
South Africa 13, 18, 19, 179, 227
South Arabia 127
South Arabian Federation 130, 138, 139
South Vietnam see Vietnam War
South Yemen (formerly South Arabia)
17, 127; see also Yemen War
Souvanna Phouma, Prince 97, 98, 99,
104, 105
Soviet Union 21, 69; Eastern Europe
and 7, 8, 9, 10, 18, 176, 188; Chinese
Civil War and 8, 12, 223; Vietnam
and 15, 17, 18, 92; Yemen Civil War
and 15, 127, 129, 136; support for
Republicans in Spanish Civil War by
28–9, 30, 31, 32, 33, 34–5; Greek Civil
War and 17, 18, 39, 40, 41–51 passim,
54, 55, 56, 59, 60, 61–2; Middle East
policy of 72–3; Lebanon civil conflict
and 76, 78, 79, 88; as Co-Chairman
of Geneva Conferences 94–5, 97–8,
104–5; Laos and 100, 101, 102, 104;
Congo crisis and 109, 110, 111, 112,
115, 117, 120, 123, 143, 144, 189, 226;
Cyprus problem and 150, 152; Korea
and 220
Spain 8, 180
Spanish Civil War 8, 9, 11, 17, 21, 25,
26–36, 222
Spinelli, Signor Pier 140, 141
Stalin, Josef 29, 39, 40–1, 42–3, 44, 45,
55, 56, 59, 60
Stanleyville, Lumumbist rebel
government in 112, 113, 117, 118,
119, 206, 219
Status of Forces Agreement (between
UN and host country) 202, 203, 224
Sudan 13, 141
Suez crisis 7, 70, 72, 73, 80, 196, 197,
205
Es-Sulh, Sami 69, 70, 76, 82
Sweden 110, 136, 140, 151
Syria, Lebanon civil conflict and 24,
67, 74, 75, 80, 81, 85, 88, 217, 221;
union with Egypt (UAR) of 72, 73;
USA and 72, 73, 85; Palestine
guerrillas and 172

Thailand (formerly Siam) 92; civil
war in 12, 13, 18; Laos and 102, 105–6